Françoise Daucé and Elisabeth Sieca-Kozlowski, Eds.

Dedovshchina in the Post-Soviet Military

Hazing of Russian Army Conscripts in a Comparative Perspective

With a foreword by Dale Herspring

SOVIET AND POST-SOVIET POLITICS AND SOCIETY

ISSN 1614-3515

Recent volumes

20 Эльза-Баир Гучинова
   Помнить нельзя забыть
   Антропология депортационной травмы калмыков
   С предисловием Кэролайн Хамфри
   ISBN 3-89821-506-7

21 Юлия Лидерман
   Мотивы «проверки» и «испытания» в постсоветской культуре
   Советское прошлое в российском кинематографе 1990-х годов
   С предисловием Евгения Марголита
   ISBN 3-89821-511-3

22 Tanya Lokshina, Ray Thomas, Mary Mayer (Eds.)
   The Imposition of a Fake Political Settlement in the Northern Caucasus
   The 2003 Chechen Presidential Election
   ISBN 3-89821-436-2

23 Timothy McCajor Hall, Rosie Read (Eds.)
   Changes in the Heart of Europe
   Recent Ethnographies of Czechs, Slovaks, Roma, and Sorbs
   With an afterword by Zdeněk Salzmann
   ISBN 3-89821-606-3

24 Christian Autengruber
   Die politischen Parteien in Bulgarien und Rumänien
   Eine vergleichende Analyse seit Beginn der 90er Jahre
   Mit einem Vorwort von Dorothée de Nève
   ISBN 3-89821-476-1

25 Annette Freyberg-Inan with Radu Cristescu
   The Ghosts in Our Classrooms, or: John Dewey Meets Ceauşescu
   The Promise and the Failures of Civic Education in Romania
   ISBN 3-89821-416-8

26 John B. Dunlop
   The 2002 Dubrovka and 2004 Beslan Hostage Crises
   A Critique of Russian Counter-Terrorism
   With a foreword by Donald N. Jensen
   ISBN 3-89821-608-X

27 Peter Koller
   Das touristische Potenzial von Kam"janec'–Podil's'kyj
   Eine fremdenverkehrsgeographische Untersuchung der Zukunftsperspektiven und Maßnahmenplanung zur Destinationsentwicklung des „Ukrainischen Rothenburg"
   Mit einem Vorwort von Kristiane Klemm
   ISBN 3-89821-640-3

Françoise Daucé and Elisabeth Sieca-Kozlowski, Eds.

DEDOVSHCHINA IN THE POST-SOVIET MILITARY

Hazing of Russian Army Conscripts in a Comparative Perspective

With a foreword by Dale Herspring

ibidem-Verlag
Stuttgart

Bibliografische Information Der Deutschen Bibliothek

Die Deutsche Bibliothek verzeichnet diese Publikation in der Deutschen Nationalbibliografie; detaillierte bibliografische Daten sind im Internet über <http://dnb.ddb.de> abrufbar.

Cover picture: Russian soldiers having a break. © Yuri Tutov, 2005.

∞

Gedruckt auf alterungsbeständigem, säurefreien Papier
Printed on acid-free paper

ISSN: 1614-3515
ISBN: 3-89821-616-0

© *ibidem*-Verlag
Stuttgart 2006
Alle Rechte vorbehalten

Das Werk einschließlich aller seiner Teile ist urheberrechtlich geschützt. Jede Verwertung außerhalb der engen Grenzen des Urheberrechtsgesetzes ist ohne Zustimmung des Verlages unzulässig und strafbar. Dies gilt insbesondere für Vervielfältigungen, Übersetzungen, Mikroverfilmungen und elektronische Speicherformen sowie die Einspeicherung und Verarbeitung in elektronischen Systemen.

Printed in Germany

CONTENTS

Figures, Graphs and Tables	9
Contributors	11
Foreword by Dale HERSPRING	13

Introduction
Françoise DAUCÉ & Elisabeth SIECA-KOZLOWSKI 17

I   *DEDOVSHCHINA* AND SOCIAL VIOLENCE

1. Regimented Communities in a Civil Society
   Konstantin BANNIKOV 29

2. The Test of Reality. Understanding Families' Tolerance
   Faced with Mistreatment of Conscripts in the Russian Army
   Anna COLIN LEBEDEV 47

3. *Dedovshchina* as an Element of the "Small Society":
   Evidence from Russia and Other Countries
   Anton OLEYNIK 75

4. Back to the Problem
   Kirill PODRABINEK 94

5. The Reasons for *Dedovshchina* and Ways to Prevent It: A Retrospective Analysis
Igor V. OBRAZTSOV 105

II *DEDOVSHCHINA* FRAMEWORKS IN RUSSIA

6. Russian Army *Mat* as a Code System Controlling Behaviours in the Russian Army
Vadim MIKHAILIN 121

7. *Dedovshchina* and the Committee of Soldiers' Mothers under Gorbachev
Julie ELKNER 144

III *DEDOVSHCHINA* IN THE CIS

8. The Kyrgyz Republic. Is Desertion a National Tradition?
Bakit KATCHEKEYEV 175

9. Hazing in the Georgian Army: The Association "Justice and Liberty" Reports on Non-Statutory Relations
Irakli SESIASHVILI 187

IV *DEDOVSHCHINA* AND HAZING ABROAD

10. Time to Waste. Notes on the Culture of the Enlisted in the Professionalizing Czech Military
Hana CERVINKOVA 205

11. Battling Bullying in the British Army 1987-2004
James K. WITHER 221

V DEDOVSHCHINA AND RESISTANCE TO REFORM

12. The Hazing of Police Recruits: Initiation to Organization
    and Resistance to Policing Reform in Brazil
    Eduardo PAES-MACHADO &
    Carlos LINHARES DE ALBUQUERQUE   237

VI DEDOVSHCHINA AND THE ALL-VOLUNTEER FORCE

13. Is the all-Volunteer Force a Solution for Draft Problems?
    Joris VAN BLADEL   265

Figures, Graphs and Tables

Figure

1	Police recruits' socialization and ritual process phases	254

Graphs

1	Estimates of Active Duty Armed Forces Personnel	289
2	Conscription Rate over the Forces in the Soviet Union and Russia (1988-1998)	292
3	Military Participation Rate Russia-France-the Netherlands-Belgium (1988-1998)	294
4	Conscription Rate Russia-France-the Netherlands-Belgium (1988-1998)	295

Tables

1	Possible attitudes to mistreatment according to interpretations made of it	64
2	Organizations as Closed versus Open Systems	273
3	Military Organizations: Institutional versus Occupational	282
4	Manpower Development in the Armed Forces in the Soviet and Russian Experience (1988-1998)	290
5	Relative Decline of the Forces in the Soviet and Russian Manpower Development (1988-1998)	291

Contributors

Konstantin BANNIKOV, Anthropologist, Miklukho-Maklaia Institute of Ethnology and Anthropology, Russian Academy of Sciences, Moscow, Russia

Hana CERVINKOVA, Anthropologist, University of Lower Silesia AAE in Wroclaw, Poland

Anna COLIN LEBEDEV, Lecturer, Collège Universitaire Français in Moscow, Russia

Françoise DAUCE, Doctor in Political Sciences. She teaches Soviet History and Russian Politics at Blaise Pascal University in Clermont-Ferrand, France

Julie ELKNER, Doctoral Student, King's College, University of Cambridge, United Kingdom

Dale HERSPRING, Professor of political science at Kansas State University, member of the Council on Foreign Relations, and retired US diplomat and Navy Captain.

Bakit KATCHEKEYEV, free lance researcher, Kyrgyzstan

Carlos LINHARES DE ALBUQUERQUE, Professor, Department of Human Sciences, UNIFACS (Salvador University), Brazil

Vadim MIKHAILIN, Anthropologist, Saratov State University, Russia

Igor V. OBRAZTSOV, (Colonel ret.) Military sociologist, Professor of Sociology, Moscow State Linguistic University, Russia

Anton OLEYNIK, Sociologist, Assistant Professor (Memorial University of Newfoundland, St. John's, Canada), Senior Research Fellow (Institute of International Economic and Political Studies of the Russian Academy of Sciences, Moscow, Russia)

Eduardo PAES-MACHADO, Professor, Department of Sociology and Institute for Public Health, Federal University of Bahia, Brazil

Kirill PODRABINEK, Human right activist, Russia

Irakli SESIASHVILI, Former deputy Ombudsman on Military Issues, Director of the Association "Justice and Liberty", Tbilissi, Georgia

Elisabeth SIECA-KOZLOWSKI, Doctor in Sociology, Chief Editor of *The Journal of Power Institutions in Post-Soviet Societies*, France

Joris VAN BLADEL, Slavist and military sociologist, Belgium

James K. WITHER, Serving officer in the British Armed Forces, George C. Marshall European Center for Security Studies Garmisch-Partenkirchen, Germany

Foreword

If there is one thing that Western militaries have learned over the years, it is that the key to an efficient, well ordered and effective military is the Non-Commissioned Officer (NCO). It is not admirals or generals who command the armies and navies that win wars, it is the senior enlisted soldier, the NCO in the trenches with his troops who is primarily responsible for things like unit discipline, unit cohesion, and in the end unit effectiveness. Without well trained, seasoned NCOs no army will perform well on the battlefield.

Moscow has tried in the past to compensate for its refusal to delegate authority in two ways: by having political officers who interacted with the troops on a daily basis, and second, by giving junior officers the responsibility for things like morale and combat readiness. The problem is that the political officers were dropped at the end of the communist regime, and their supposed replacements have done little to deal with problems at the unit level. Meanwhile, junior officers, most of whom are working a second job to make ends meet, or just out of a civilian university, have had minimal impact on soldiers at the unit level.

For awhile the Kremlin's answer was Moscow's version of NCOs - the *serzhanty* - young recruits who were made sergeants after a few weeks course. The problem was that they had little authority at the unit level. They were assumed by other conscripts to be recruits like everyone else of their age group. Senior recruits were not only responsible for training the newcomers, they also disciplined them - a process that was abused over and over - especially as the quality of recruits declined over the years. Recruits could expect to have their belongings stolen during his two year tour of duty and to serve as a slave for more senior soldiers. In many cases the treatment handed out was much, much worse - beatings, rape, murders. While the high command talked about the problem and was fully aware of what was going on, little of substance was done to deal with it. As a result, the situation at the unit level worsened. Thus it was no surprise that many young Russian men went out of their way to avoid military service, or deserted once they put on the uniform.

The introduction of an NCO on the Western model - an enlisted person who had served 8-12 years and who had special training would go a long way toward solving the problem. But the high command resisted. Why? Because the Russian generals and admirals have not been willing to delegate authority - something that comes from Russia political culture. For example, this writer personally observed Russian admirals, who were visiting an American warship, express astonishment when they were informed that a 21 year old Petty Officer Third Class (the equivalent of an army corporal), was in charge of both firing and repairing the ship's anti-air missiles. As the Russian admiral put it, "In the Russian Navy this would be done by two officers!"

So where do we - or should I say the Russians go from here? Most of the country's officers understand the dept of the problems outlined in this book. Indeed, numerous dissertations and theses at the General Staff Academy have been written on the topic and I have spoken with many officers who have expressed their frustration and outrage over the continued existence of *dedovshchina*.

Fortunately, there is a small, *very small* light at the end of the tunnel. The Russian military is going through some major structural changes at present. For example, Putin has decided that 144,000 troops will become professional, the so-called "professional readiness units." He has also decreed that recruits will no longer serve in "hot spots" like Chechnya, and that conscription will be shortened to one year beginning 2008. In addition, he has closed down the vast majority of the country's Reserve Officers' Training Corps (ROTC) programs, limiting them now to only 35. ROTC graduates will now agree to serve three years in return for financial assistance while they attend college. Those who are not in ROTC will serve in the Army for a year once they graduate. Furthermore, there are many hints to the effect that sergeants from some of the professional units will be delegated to the conscript units.

Thus if everything works as Putin claims it will, by 2008 the quality of recruits will be considerably higher (Russian officers constantly complain about the poor quality of recruits - many of whom have been on dope or have criminal records). They believe that the better quality of recruits will lessen the tendency for recruits to resort to *dedovshchina*. In addition, junior officers will be better trained and more willing to serve. Moreover, Moscow argues that because conscripts will be serving for only one year, (and thus there will only be two - rather than four - age groups serving at any time) harassment is less likely to occur. And finally, some in the military maintain that if decent quality NCOs are seconded to training and overseeing the actions of conscripts, many of the problems associated with *dedovshchina* will disappear.

Will that happen now? It would be wonderful if the generals and admirals moved quickly to eliminate the problem. It would make the writing of a book like this one unnecessary. The biggest difficulty - as this book admirably demonstrates - is that it involves changing a fundamental component of Russian political and military culture. Not only must these *serzhanty* be given the authority they need to be effective, they will also need special training. For example, American Marine Corps Drill Instructors (DI) are chosen from the best of the best, and they go through an extended training procedure before they are let anywhere near a recruit - and God pity any Marine DI who touches a recruit in any way. The Marines believe that psychological pressure can do far more than physical brutality to build an effective combat soldier.

The approach adopted by the American Marine Corps may be an ideal, and perhaps will not work in Russia. However, the country's Military Ombudsman has made the creation of NCOs a critical part of his efforts to get the Russian military to reform. And as noted above, almost every officer I have spoken to recognizes that things must change. The real question is whether or not the officer corps will take an active part in changing the relationship between conscripts and the rest of the military or whether it will simply sit by and hope that better quality conscripts and better trained officers will solve the problem.

In the meantime, those who are concerned about the problems faced by young men being called up - and their parents - will find this collection extremely useful. There is little doubt in my mind that *dedovshchina* is the most pressing internal problem facing the Russian Army today. It would be helpful if this book were translated into Russian and made required reading for every officer. Perhaps then they would be more willing to do something to solve the problem, instead of just talking about it. Until the high commands makes the kind of changes outlined above, *dedovshchina* will continue to undermine relations between soldiers and toward their officers. As anyone who has studied military matters knows, unit cohesion is critical to combat efficiency. Without it, soldiers die and military units are ineffective.

Dale R. Herspring
Kansas State University

Introduction

*Françoise DAUCE &
Elisabeth SIECA-KOZLOWSKI*

1. Why a book on *dedovshchina*?

As specialists of post-Soviet armies for many years, we first became aware of the *dedovshchina* phenomenon in Russia in the early 90s. The term *"dedovshchina"* is common in post-Soviet Russia but difficult to convey in other languages. Indeed, simple translation does not suffice to express either its many senses or the complexity of practices it refers to. *Dedovshchina* is not only hazing, bullying or *bizutage*. Formed on the root *"ded"*, meaning "grandfather" in Russian, *dedovshchina* manifests itself as violence exerted by older conscripts on younger ones. "In the barracks, one half of the contingent terrorizes the other. This policy aims to intimidate conscripts, break their will, make them work for the soldiers in the second year of service, use the conscripts' food, clothing and money. But the brutality of terror forms and its scale are blown out of all proportion, in fact so much so that they make hardly any sense at all", underlines Kirill Podrabinek[1]. *Dedovshchina* is a military phenomenon, but influenced by Russian social, political and economic realities.

The main hypothesis of this book
Initially presented as a heritage of the Soviet Union and its totalitarian practices, it could have been expected that *dedovshchina* would disappear along with democratisation, liberalisation, and the development of civilian control over the army. However, it did not. Does this mean that these transformations had no effect on Russian society or on the army? On the contrary, we sug-

---

[1] See Kirill Podrabinek's chapter, "Going Back to the Problem".

gest that political and economic liberalisation, as conceived and carried out at the beginning of the 90s, in fact directly and indirectly reinforced tensions among soldiers, with the result that today, *dedovshchina* is all the more nurtured thanks to post-Soviet practices and new values. To test this hypothesis, we have relied on studies in various research fields dealing with Russia and other post-Soviet states, as well as with other countries.

Dedovshchina is at the crossroads of transformations which have taken place in Russia since the disappearance of the USSR. Among others, it is the consequence of historical legacy (Soviet and even tsarist), cultural tensions (inter-ethnic conflicts in the USSR), political dysfunctions (lack of democracy) and economic problems (lack of money in the army), all of which combined explain the longevity of this negative phenomenon. Although any one of these factors (military, social, cultural, political, economic) can be observed in other countries and institutions, the combination of all of them in a single institution is found only in the Russian *dedovshchina*. This is why we intend to study *dedovshchina* not only as a military phenomenon, but also to examine it in the broader context of contemporary Russian society. *Dedovshchina* is central to tensions between the conflicting trends of liberalism, communitarianism, capitalism and patriotism in today's Russia.

An in-depth study

During *perestroika* and the Gorbachev era of liberalisation, *dedovshchina* became a subject of public debate. Journalists, soldiers' mothers, veterans and military sociologists took part; stories were told, evidence produced, points of view argued. However, the publication in Russia, both in newspapers and scientific journals, of numerous articles on violence in the army was only partially satisfying: we remained unconvinced by the explanations proposed in an effort to shed light on the reality of the phenomenon. Indeed, most of these publications focused on a single aspect of *dedovshchina*, either on its military roots, its social background, or political significance. None of them studied it in its complexity. Moreover, the majority were published in the wake of the collapse of the Soviet Union, whereas today, 20 years after the beginning of *perestroika*, we have the perspective necessary to make a more complete study. The years following Vladimir Putin's election as President of the Russian Federation, the late1990s, saw considerable political and social change in Russia, making the country again very different from what it was after the first chaotic changes of the early 1990's. Yet despite political overhaul and the will to restore "dictatorship of the law" and the so-called "vertical of power", *dedovshchina* remains a grim reality. This is why it seemed necessary to put together a collective, multidisciplinary work enriched by the observations of historians, sociologists, anthropologists and political scientists[2], each of whom enlighten one aspect of *"dedovshchina"*. In this way, we hope to obtain a multidimensional, up-to-date approach to the subject. While not claiming to be exhaustive, this book aims to provoke new and broader thought on the subject of *dedovshchina* in Russia, a highly complex and disquieting reality.

2. *Dedovshchina* as a complex phenomenon

The aim of this book is to take apart the phenomenon of *dedovshchina* and to examine in detail each of the elements that make up its complexity. Contrary to widespread belief, the Russian army is not simply a hierarchical institution receiving its orders from the Ministry of Defense. Nor is it "a simple distributory system as are monasteries, asylums or kindergarten" to quote Michael Walzer[3]. Social inter-relations within the Russian army are complex.

Dedovshchina as a legacy of the Soviet era

Historically, *dedovshchina* appeared as a military problem linked to the weakness of the officers' corporation in the Soviet army and to national and interethnic tensions among soldiers from different regions of the Soviet Union. In the 1960s, violence among soldiers was commonly recognized in Soviet society, but information about it remained unofficial. It was at the end of the 1980s that *dedovshchina* came into the public sphere, presented as the leg-

---

[2] Seven contributions to this book were initially published in the first issue of *The Journal of Power Institutions in Post-Soviet Societies*, Issue 1 - 2004, "Dedovshchina: From Military to Society", www.pipss.org. One contribution initially in French has been translated into English and five original contributions have been added for the purpose of this book.

[3] M. Walzer, *Spheres of Justice. A Defense of Pluralism and Equality*, Oxford: Martin Robertson, 1983, p. 4.

acy of the Soviet authoritarian regime and considered the result of an organizational problem (power distribution in the ranks, informal versus formal hierarchies, etc.). Revelations about *dedovshchina* contributed to the discredit of the USSR. As Kirill Podrabinek wrote, "I had never been enthusiastic about Soviet government, but military service just added fuel to my anti-Soviet sentiment...". With the disappearance of the Soviet system, one of the official goals of military reform was to eradicate *dedovshchina* in the Russian armed forces. Although this gave hope to Russian society, the fact that *dedovshchina* is still alive long after the end of the USSR causes us to doubt it being solely the product of an authoritarian military system.

Dedovshchina as a cultural practice
Dedovshchina must be analysed in the framework of cultural realities in the USSR and in post-Soviet Russia. Army language, symbols, rites, army culture as a whole shows that military violence is often perceived as a "rite of passage". Despite their own previous suffering due to *dedovshchina*, older soldiers repeat violent practices against younger comrades. Such a phenomenon can thus only be analysed from an anthropological and psychological point of view. Igor V. Obraztsov suggests that apart from the formal, institutional structure, there are always informal attitudes and relations between servicemen. In Russia, this phenomenon is by nature chronic due to its long standing existence. In addition, other examples of hazing can be found in closed institutions in Russia such as prisons, orphanages, schools, asylums, hospitals, mafia-type organizations, etc. In a political system based on formal equality, informal differentiations were introduced through *dedovshchina*.

Dedovshchina as a market practice
Political and economic liberalization did not eradicate hazing in the Russian army, on the contrary. Along with post-Soviet economic liberalisation, market practices invaded the military sphere. The lack of state resources led to financial penury in the army and to the growth of informal economic networks involving officers and soldiers. Hence, one aim of this book is to shed light on how *dedovshchina* was reinforced by economic liberalisation inside the army due to the lack of state resources: first, because young conscripts were used as a free labour force, some officers imposing tasks on them for their own

benefit and older soldiers exploiting younger ones for economic purposes; and secondly, because economic liberalisation gave rise to social differentiations among citizens. Today, rich and well-educated young people living in the city are more able to escape military service than poor people people with a low level of education living in the country. The former are involved in a new, anti-military market, created for the purpose of avoiding military service and on which can be purchased false medical certificates, bribes and so on.

Dedovshchina as a civic cause
It was *dedovshchina* that caused society to become mobilised in post-Soviet Russia. The Committees of Soldiers' Mothers, founded at the end of the 1980's, have often been considered the *avant-garde* of contemporary Russia's civil society. And indeed, it was thanks to the support of the media and foreign NGOs that these Committees first managed to introduce the issue into the public sphere and question the State as to its responsibility. Initially moved by their own problems with *dedovshchina* (the hazing of their sons), they transformed their personal grievances into general public mobilisation. Today, the Committees of Soldiers' Mothers advocate for the professionalization of the army and the end of the war in Chechnya. Yet once again, despite these mobilisations, *dedovshchina* remains a widespread phenomenon in the Russian military. Fifteen years after their creation, the Soldiers' Mothers' Committees are still busy helping out young conscripts and are still involved in the denouncing of *dedovshchina*, but the political result of their action is limited.

Dedovshchina as a domestic reality
Despite the existence of the Committees of Soldiers' Mothers, little open protest against *dedovshchina* has been voiced in post-communist Russia. Why have civil associations been unable to mobilise larger groups of the population? Probably because individuals manage the problem on their own, each young person fighting *dedovshchina* individually (*dedovshchina* is one of the main causes of draft evasion). In the large Russian cities, most Russian young men of conscription age elaborate personal strategies in order to avoid military service. They thus learn to escape state obligations using informal

links and resources. In this singular attitude towards politics, people prefer "exit" to "voice".

3. Contributions to this study

This book, "*Dedovshchina* in the Post-Soviet Military: Hazing of Russian Army Conscripts in a Comparative Perspective", focuses on the Russian case because of the very nature and weight of the Soviet heritage. However, in order to gain a fuller understanding of *dedovshchina* in the Russian army, a comparative approach is needed, since comparison as a scientific tool makes it possible to deconstruct the complexity of the phenomenon. Comparison will be used here to give perspective on three points. The first is institutional: social practices in the Russian army must be compared to those in other closed institutions - prisons, detention centres for juvenile delinquents, etc. The second is chronological: *dedovshchina* in the Russian army is best studied in comparison with Soviet and pre-revolutionary practices. The third is geographical and cultural. In order to gain insight into Russian *dedovshchina*, we propose comparisons with other CIS countries (Community of Independent States), as well as Brazil, the Czech Republic and even Western countries, such as Great Britain. These comparisons show that in contemporary armies, violence among soldiers seems to be a universal phenomenon found in both professional and drafted armies. However, the comparison of violent practices in various armies around the world allows us to identify specific features linked to those countries' sociological, political or anthropological contexts. Hazing, for example, seems to be more violent in the armies of transitional societies (Latin America, East-European countries), where social tensions encountered by citizens in their daily lives are carried over to and sometimes intensified in the military institution. The comparison of what goes on in Russia with the situation in other countries makes it possible to identify universal, transitional and national characteristics of military violence.

Dedovchshina and social violence

The first part of the book, "*Dedovshchina* and Social Violence", is devoted to the sociological dimension of *dedovshchina*. In "Regimented Communities in a Civil Society" (the last chapter of *The Anthropology of Regimented Society. Relations of Dominance in Social Interactions among Russian Soldiers*, published in Moscow in 2002), Konstantin Bannikov explains that in the Russian army, commanders refer to the lawlessness and violence "reigning in civvy street as a strong argument in replying to society's claims on bullying". Officially, they try to convert a man into a perfect soldier. However, the experience of systematic violence acquired by young men during 2-3 years of service, first as objects and later as subjects of hazing, is transferred into civil life, - a process which is equally damaging to both society and the army. Bannikov analyzes the consequences of the spread throughout society of the archaic violence produced by the Russian army. In response, in "The test of Reality. Understanding Families' Tolerance Faced with Mistreatment of Conscripts in the Russian Army", Anna Lebedev studies family letters to the Moscow-based Committee of Soldiers' Mothers in the aim of understanding the perception of military violence in Russian society. She deals with the ambiguities of Russian society, where *dedovshchina* is considered the main reason for draft evasion, but accepted as a social necessity. This chapter shows this lack of opposition as originating in the image of the army in Russian society: national service and the abuse associated with it are seen as an essential initiation for an all too often socially disadvantaged population.

In his chapter "*Dedovshchina* as an Element of the 'Small Society': Evidence from Russia and Other Countries", Anton Oleynik, one of the best specialists of Russian prisons, offers a comparison of informal relationships among prisoners and among conscripts. His "small society" concept is useful to describe what Bannikov calls "archaic rituals" in the army. As Oleynik explains, the "small" society is characterised by a non differentiation of the spheres of everyday life, personalized relationships, imperfect control of violence, duality of norms and an imposed authority. Wherever it exists, in Russia as well as in the West, the "small" society produces phenomena similar to *dedovshchina*. Kirill Podrabinek, a human rights activist in Moscow gets "Back to the topic". Indeed, he was demobilized from the Soviet army in 1976. One of the first Soviet citizens to describe *dedovshchina* in the Soviet army, his testimony was circulated in dissident milieus. Today, he tries to understand the reasons why *dedovshchina* continues to be prevalent in the post-Soviet context. In "The Reasons for *Dedovshchina* and Ways to Prevent it: A Retrospective Analysis", the military sociologist Igor V. Obraztsov explains that the historical roots of *dedovshchina* are not only Soviet, but go back to the period of demolition of the Russian Imperial army and the construction of an "army of a new type " - Red, then - Soviet (1918 - beginning of 1920). At this time, the existing values systems for army life and the traditional character of mutual relations between servicemen were rejected.

Dedovshchina and its "support system"
The second part of the book is devoted to factors that underlie the continuing existence of *dedovshchina* in Russia. Indeed, this can only be understood in the more global context of Russian history and culture. In "Russian Army *Mat* as a Means of Code Speaking", anthropologist Vadim Mikhailin shows that language plays a specific role in the creation of a man's identity as a "military", i.e. a member of the armed forces. The military milieu has always been ideal for "*mat* speaking" (slang), the use of which offers various and sometimes the only possible means of impact on one's equals, subordinates, or even superiors. In "*Dedovshchina* and the Committee of Soldiers' Mothers under Gorbachev", Julie Elkner provides an historical account of the Committee of Soldiers' Mothers' role in breaking the taboo on *dedovshchina* in the Soviet military in the late 1980s. The Committee's activism played a crucial role in opening up the military to public scrutiny and in influencing public perceptions of military service. The article also traces the military's unsuccessful attempts to counteract the soldiers' mothers' exposure of barracks violence and to reinstate the old boundaries of acceptable public debates on military issues.

Dedovshchina in the CIS
The third part of the book is devoted to military violence among soldiers in other post-Soviet states. Indeed, since *dedovshchina* was an all-Soviet phenomenon, all post-Soviet republics now have to deal with it. Comparison allows us to define the similarities and differences in today's post-Soviet armies. In "The Kyrgyz Republic. Is Desertion a National Tradition?" Bakit

Katchekeyev, a free-lance researcher from Kyrgyzstan discusses how tyranny and extortion on the part of senior soldiers and commanders produce *dedovshchina* and make way for the gradual rule of the arbitrary. The ongoing reform of the armed forces - including the President's decision to reduce the service term from 18 months to 12 as of 2006, the transition to a contract army, plus Western training and equipment assistance - seems to have little impact on the hazing issue: indeed, AWOL statistics have not dramatically changed in recent years.

Quite the contrary, in *"Dedovshchina in the Georgian Army"*, Irakli Sesiashvili, director of the Georgian Association "Justice and Liberty" shows the link between the political context and the situation in the army: according to his analysis, since the Georgian Rose Revolution of 2003, soldiers' conditions have progressively improved.

Dedovshchina and hazing abroad

In order to pinpoint the specificity of *dedovshchina* in Russia, two chapters are devoted to cases in other countries. The first concerns a former Sovietised army, that of the Czech Republic and the second a Western European army, that of the United Kingdom. In her chapter on Czech conscripts, "Time to Waste. Notes on the Culture of Enlisted in the Professionalizing Czech Military", Hana Cervinkova, anthropologist from the University of Lower Silesia, explains that the culture of enlisted men is based on opposition to the military, and by extension, to the Czech state, which defines the enlisted as neophytes - mutually equal and indistinguishable entities in transition to being full male citizens of the Czech state, as well as transitory entities before the military is professionalized in 2006. The article analyses the various material and ritual elements of the conscripts' culture by means of which they resist official efforts of equalization. She describes social phenomena close to those in Russia: army service is informally divided into four separate parts and one's place in the hierarchy is determined solely by the time he has spent in the military. This reality clearly echoes that of the Russian army. However, military service in the Czech army appears to be a wasted period of time for young people and will soon be abandoned in the framework of NATO. Will professionalization of the army resolve hazing problems? In his article on the British army, "Battling Bullying in the British Army 1987 - 2004", James Wither, serving officer in the British armed forces in the George C. Marshall European Center for Security Studies (Garmisch-Partenkirchen Germany), suggests that recruits in professional armies can be as vulnerable to mistreatment as those in conscript militaries. As he puts it: "Because basic training deliberately isolates soldiers from wider society and necessarily stresses physical toughness, it intrinsically creates an environment in which bullying can occur". Although British recruits are not confronted with mistreatment comparable to *dedovshchina,* the Army has struggled to eliminate incidents of bullying from the ranks, which have tarnished the British Army's image. The article seeks to provide instructive insights for those militaries of the successor states of the Soviet Union that are currently blighted by *dedovshchina.*

Dedovshchina and resistance to reform
Eduardo Paes-Machado, from the Department of Sociology and Institute for Public Health, Federal University of Bahia and Carlos Linhares de Albuquerque, from the Department of Human Sciences, UNIFACS (Salvador University) in Brazil present an interesting point of view on hazing and resistance to reform. In their article "The Hazing of Police Recruits: Initiation to Organization and Resistance to Policing Reform in Brazil", they deal with the implications of hazing for police identity and education. Hazing is analyzed as a component of an informal, alternative, academic curriculum that undermines the new, official teaching curriculum. It is seen as an example of dualistic logic in new police training, pointing to prospects of democratization while maintaining authoritarian methods of socialization. This case study is quite pertinent in the framework of a comparison with Russia. Indeed, Brazil dealt with a democratization process which, at the beginning of the 1990s, seemed similar to the Russian "democratic transition". Fifteen years later, the Brazilian experience is still quite useful in trying to understand the failure of democratization processes in Russia.

Dedovshchina and the all-volunteer-force
In the final chapter of the book, Joris Van Bladel, slavist and military sociologist, Belgium, proposes a reflection on the theme: "Is the all-Volunteer force a solution for draft problems?". This question is important for the future of the Russian armed forces. Indeed, in discussions about *dedovshchina* and other

major problems concerning the recruitment of Russian soldiers, the professionalization of the armed forces is often given as a solution. According to Van Bladel, this may be so if we understand professionalization in the Huntington sense of its having a subjective and an objective component: subjectively, the military corps has the professional and democratic ethos and, objectively, the law is subscribed to by the officers' corps. However, the claim that professionalization is a solution to the draft does not hold true if paid soldiers simply replace drafted ones and no structural changes are made. In such a case, professionalization will only add to the chaos now existing in the Russian armed forces.

I *Dedovchshina* and Social Violence

1 Regimented Communities in a Civil Society[1]

Konstantin BANNIKOV

Commanders are quite right to refer to lawlessness, violence, xenophobia, etc. reigning in civvy street as a strong argument in replying to the society's claims on bullying. "Look at yourselves," they say. Indeed, people joining up the army come from socium, not from cosmos, and they are people, not angels, with all human vices and virtues, merits and shortcomings. Being guided by higher officers, service regulations or military idealism, commanders try to convert a man into a perfect soldier, to say an angel.

This comparison is arch-typical rather than metaphoric as the image of a perfect soldier reminds you of an angel, if anything, or at least a saint rather than an ordinary man. Judge for yourself: like an angel (saint), a good soldier is not an initiator, but an executor and transmitter of the will of God; like an angel (saint), he is devoid of vices; like an angel (saint), he is devoid of individual distinctions, up to sexual. According to the medieval Christian scholasticism, those who live in Heaven are all sexless, equally dressed and of equal height. That's why Heaven is free of conflicts. Heaven is like a model army unit.

The mission to transfigure "sinners" into "saints" in the army is assigned to commanders. The service regulations entrust the commander with responsibility for the soldier's morale, expecting telepathic abilities from the former. "They came from civvy street, they are all different, some of them cannot speak Russian, so why should I be responsible for what is on their minds? There is a safe in my office, with a stamp on it - this is what I may be respon-

---

[1] Translated from the Russian by Yelena Golovkina. This article is an edited chapter of K. Bannikov's book, *Antropologiia ekstremal'nikh grupp. Dominanthye otnoshenie sredi voennosluzhashchikh srocnoi sluzhby Rossiiskoi Armii*, RAN, Moskva, 2002.

sible for," says an indignant officer, a friend of mine. Both the Church and psychoanalysts have failed to serialize the transformation of sinners into saints. That depends on a person.

Because of specific peculiarities of ideological work with troops in the Russian army, a moral and psychological aspect substitutes for the fundamental base of material incentives any professional army rests upon. The absence of real stimuli reduces the entire service motivation to "honorary duty", "civil responsibility", "patriotism" and other witch-words. Even the highest categories of civil consciousness require material and legal support. *Dukhi* (ghosts)[2] experience mixed patriotic feelings when the state anthem, no matter how solemn the tune, catches them in a "crocodile pose" or scrubbing toilets for a twenty-fifth hour a day.

It is common pleasures of life - neither rank-and-file soldiers, nor officers seem to be averse to - that really stimulate service. You will find proof of that in any demob's[3] album[4]. But these pleasures are prohibited by service regulations and therefore unlawful. Allowed only to civilians, they are deathlike to soldiers. Service in general and its separate elements such as a "holiday cross-country race" or an "army song drill" are supposed to be the source of pleasure for model soldiers. But their real pleasures are on "that" side of the fence through which they go AWOL since on "this" side they are not supposed to be satisfied and there is no way to satisfy them. Can we really expect normal soldiers to satisfy their urge for alcoholic drinks with military training and their sexual instinct by putting a gas mask on? And as human wishes aren't limited to that, deprivation strain is fairly high and leads to violations of service regulations.

We agree that the pleasures of civil life are to blame for the deviant behavior of servicemen. But disciplinary standards set by service regulations can hardly be accepted as a norm, something officers working with troops actually mean when they say: "If you don't want to live like normal people, let's

---

[2] *Dukhi*: new recruits that have just been conscripted (literally "ghosts", "souls") [Editors' note].

[3] Demob for demobees, in Russian *dembelia* (from *demobilizatsiia*): conscripts nearing the end of their two years' service and already included in the demobilisation order [Editors' note].

[4] Demob's album, in Russian *dembel'skii al'bom*: a self-made album, a chronicle illustrated with comics and photographs [Editors' note].

live according to regulations", assuming that life according to regulations is incompatible with normal human life.

The experience of systematic violence young men acquire during 2-3 years of service, first as objects and later as subjects of hazing, is transferred to civil life, which is equally damaging both to society and the army. Hazing-related morals can be observed almost anywhere nowadays - at school, at work and inside one's family, and we shall take a close look at it below. Despite the death-inflicting function of a serviceman, it's not in the army that violence is born. Violence is inherent in human nature. But whereas in an open society aggression is rarefied, the army, by virtue of its isolation, accumulates psychophysical energy and eventually becomes a collector and transmitter of a social conflict. The army condenses rather than generates violence.

Considering the educational and socialization functions assigned to the army, the general conflictogenic situation constitutes itself as a norm and participates in the building of life scenarios.

The utopian nature of official law leads to dual-law mentality, which is on the whole a landmark situation for Russia when traditional Russian law consciousness is seen through a conflict between official truth and people's truth. Steven Frank, who analyzed this phenomenon in his brilliant research of law foundations of a Russian commune of the second half of the 19th century[5], explains the all-too-familiar Russian "mess" in the context of legal anthropology and attributes its phenomenology to dual-law mentality blaming the latter on a gap between official state laws and people's law. But now let's consider the political and public image of the Russian army and what happens when it is discredited.

---

[5] S. Frank, "Popular Justice, Community and Culture Among the Russian Peasantry 1870-1890", in *The World of the Russian Peasant: Post-Emancipation Culture and Society*, Boston: Boston University Press, 1990.

1. Channels transporting dominant army relations to civil society

Imagine that you are 19-20 years old but already wield unlimited power in your mini-society. Your word sets the surrounding human mass in motion. You inspire fear and awe. Nobody dares to say "no" to you, least of all offer resistance. And then you, great and almighty, are demobilized and find yourself in a new social environment where, the moment you enter it, you are nothing, and which is governed by other principles of winning authority, long-forgotten by you, so you have to start it all over again. You have to drop those simple and clear methods of self-assertion that enabled you to savor the sweet taste of power over people. And as you don't feel like dropping them, you start thinking how to use them. There are three ways:

1. A civil society is miscellaneous, so you are looking for a suitable niche where your dominant ways would fit in. First, this is militia or police where military service is compulsory for getting a job; second, these are private security firms, lots and lots of them, for the transitional period can be interpreted as disintegration of the totalitarian model, in the course of which violence stops being an exclusive prerogative of the state but remains a significant social factor. Demand for people with experience of violence is fairly high in transitional societies.
2. A civil society is labile, so you can transform some of its structures and instill the principles of organized violence acquired in the army. They will strike root there where people like you get together or in newly-formed closed sociums where time is a factor in social self-fulfillment as in hostels for students of higher schools oriented predominantly at young men with considerable enrollment privileges for demobs, for example, traditionally "male" departments of pedagogical institutes (departments training labor instructors for secondary schools) or the Moscow-based Mining Institute, etc.
3. Society reproduces itself in you, so you can build a new "cell" by creating a family of your own based on hazing-style relationship.

By its attitude to forcible conscription as a principle of manning the army, society is divided into two parts with largely homogeneous sex and age structures. "For" are predominantly people of older generations with a patriarchal way of thinking, who perceive dominant army relationship as a useful necessity. Their logic rests on the following arguments: "he who hasn't served is not a real man", "I served, so let others serve", "I suffered, so let them suffer too". The acceptance of violence as a life principle distorts the notion of normal social relations and spreads a belief that being fit for violence is a criterion of social success, while being a former victim justifies the violator in his own eyes, hence the brutal ambitions of all those "real" men living according to "real" concepts based on their knowledge of life they "spooned up" while "smelling powder" or "doing porridge".

The majority of middle-aged and older men wish all young people to go through the army. Personal compensatory motives of their "well-wishing" clearly prevail over the idea of young men's duty to defend their homeland. This idea appears only slightly or is totally absent. Social opinion polls conducted by VTsIOM[6] in 1999 show that the majority of men of middle age and older support conscription, while the majority of women (except those who automatically share their husbands' opinions) as well as draftees, first-year soldiers, junior officers inclined to retire from service, and especially students, who are given a deferment for a period of study, oppose compulsory recruitment.

This divergence of views has nothing to do with widespread beliefs that young people are afraid of difficulties or that women are the "weak" sex. On the contrary, here women emerge as the "strong" sex capable of consolidating against the state machinery and protect the rights of their men, often risking their own career, health and even life. As for the youth and students, they are driven by aversion to irrational actions that military service de facto consists of rather than by fear of problems. In civil life most young men have far more problems and responsibilities than compulsory service soldiers exempted, at least for two years, from the main problem - making responsible decisions.

Young people are a social category whose energy and life position are crucial to society as a whole and their energy finds other applications, no less worthy than performing an "honorary duty". They hate going to the army, not because they fear the "hardships and privations of military service", but be-

---

[6] VTsIOM, Vserossiikii Tsentr Izucheniia Obshchestvennogo Mneniia, www.wcioma.ru [Editors' note].

cause irrationalized activity and interpersonal relations humiliate human dignity. Many young men challenge the recruiting machine by defending their right to alternative service despite the risk of being persecuted by the state, which signals a mature personality factor, a very important social indicator.

The sex and age distinctions inside the two groups - supporters and opponents of a voluntary army - stem from different vectors of life force expansion. A total rejection of compulsory military service in the female and youth strata shows that women attempt to preserve life forces in the biological taxon and young men seek to achieve maximum self-realization in the social-information taxon.

Demobs' jargon abounds in associative parallels between hazing and patriarchal family relations and echoes the objectives of educational work in society and the army. "Regulations will stand you in good stead in civvy life! Think of how you will bring up your own children!" some officer admonished his subordinates. Back in civvy street demobs successfully practice hazing in their families.

Of course, none of them creates a disciplinary cell at home. The majority of demobs consciously try to drop barracks-style ways, seeing that they evoke a negative response in a civil society.

A large percentage of young men marry in the first few months after being demobilized, while still having to re-adapt themselves to civil life, create a proper material base and acquire a profession that would enable them to occupy their place in society. Early post-demobilisation marriages are motivated by an urge to set up a family as a means of self-preservation and of asserting one's authority over this world, which semiotically corresponds to fatherhood, a role 20-year-old *"dedy"*[7] take too literally. That's the morals reigning in the so-called "difficult families" fall within extreme group psychology.

Every 6 months demobs with hazing-affected consciousness pour into civil institutions. Thanks to its powerful adaptive mechanism based on jargon and elements of collective subconsciousness, *dedovshchina* (hazing) successfully introduces itself into a civil society and imposes its own principles - systemic violence and aggression. Through diachronic transmission channels *dedovshchina* finds its way into teen-ager socializing. These channels are

---

[7] *"Dedy"* (seniors, grandfathers): soldiers of the "fourth period of service" (from the 18th to the 24th months), enjoying all possible privileges [Editors' note].

unlocked by many demob-oriented civil institutions as, for example, pedagogical schools offering enrollment privileges for demobs, especially in the 1980s. As a result, *dedovshchina* struck deep root at certain departments: future labor and sports training instructors reproduced the habitual hierarchy. Another example is police. You can't get a job there unless you served in the army. The conduct of rank-and-file "cops", even barely analyzed, shows how the force of law transforms into the law of force. In post-Soviet times legitimized aggression in mass consciousness became self-accomplished and malignant in character when the "law of force" equalized law-enforcement bodies and the criminal world in a perverted system of values, in which they equally control all spheres of social, economic and political life.

2. Extreme group values and big politics

The "law of force" successfully exploited by politicians and intriguers at all levels became a measure of social prestige and social values. Once on the political orbit, having passed through all stages in its climb from micro to macro levels, it ends the institualization of violence on a nationwide scale. National consolidation around the Chechen problem is not creative but destructive consolidation operated by the same mechanisms that guide a crowd consolidating around the abuse of an outcast. When recruitment of volunteers for the Chechen front was announced, hosts of marginals flooded army registration and enlistment offices, a fact that is both indicative and symptomatic: when a regular army resorts to help from marginals, it's time to change the army.

The Chechen problem highlighted the state of consciousness and the system of values in the army. From a conversation at a remote frontier post on the Russian-Mongolian border at the beginning of the second Chechen war:

- What do your guys think about it?
- Many say they would like to go to Chechnya.
- Why?
- Because there is a war there and we are who, we are soldiers. Look, I've been here for two years and not a single

incident has occurred... I fired 9 cartridges before the oath, - that's all. And there it's different, there you can shoot to your heart's content...
- Shoot? You mean at people?
- Sure, not at jars. But are Chechens people? They are bandits!
- How do you know? Have you been there?
- They say so on TV.
- You won't shoot at everyone they point at on TV, will you?
- You know we are soldiers. If we came to the army, let's serve and not paint that fence over there for the fifth time. Let commanders above decide who are people and who bandits. And we must defend Russia!
- At first you said you just wanted to shoot.
- And that too.
- Will your family be upset if you are killed?
- Well, most likely they will.

The dialogue reveals destructive energy seeking an outlet and eventually finding it. The soldier started with verbalizing his psychological discomfort (boring routine, inconsistency between reality and status). Hoping that war will bring relief, he finds arguments to substantiate his destructive wishes but totally disregards the key factor of possible psychological discomfort - responsibility for killing other humans, leaving that to commanders. The dialogue with power embodying law and truth takes place in the soldier's head. The moment he relieves himself of responsibility, official ideology fills a lacuna in his consciousness with quasi-patriotic ideas. The discomforting thought "to kill people" is replaced by a comforting slogan, "to defend Russia!".

Patriotic ideas in diffused consciousness are stimulated by the expectation of an arch-foe as a negative factor of consolidation. As a result, aggression erupts through unlocked frustration channels into one's perception of foreign ethnicity.

The above episode would seem unimportant, had we not observed similar trends elsewhere before when young people volunteered to fight in Afghanistan and other "hot points" just to show off their courage rather than out of patriotism. The analysis of some youth groupings shows how patriotic moods transform into extremism[8]. The political elite is trying to exploit the passionate energy of the youth in its own interests, and very seldom - in the interests of the youth. Reading materials from the State Duma with its powerful military lobby, one begins to doubt that the law on a professional army will ever get passed. Members of the Duma Committee on Defense believe that "a professional army is an anti-state affair"[9].

Judging by the lawmaking activity of Duma "defense hawks", chances of anti-militarist organizations' initiatives winning approval are bleak. Commander of the North-Eastern military force, State Duma deputy Vice Admiral V.F. Dorogin drafted a "code of deputy's honor" he thinks all deputies should comply with. "My code is based on Disciplinary Regulations of the Russian armed forces, which sounds logical as the majority of our deputies are servicemen, yes, they wear civil clothes but they are reservist officers and therefore must follow disciplinary rules", he said in an interview published in the 30 May, 2000 issue of the *Komsomolskaia pravda* by Olga Gerasimenko[10]. Incidentally, military units in the force he commands are notorious for exceptionally brutal hazing with a high percentage of death cases. These facts were reported by the press and are cited in the present research[11]. It's hard to expect deputy Dorogin to back any lawmaking initiatives clashing with Civil Service Regulations into which he put his whole heart.

"It's been already the third consecutive State Duma trying unsuccessfully to change the commander's "investigative" status because the army brass apparently hates to let go of its "legal sovereignty," argues *Novaia gazeta* observer Anna Politkovskaia[12]. Unit commanders see this "legal sovereignty" as a guarantor of their independence from prosecutors when investi-

---

[8] A. Korzlov (ed.), *Molodezhnyi ekstremizm*, Sankt-Petersburg 1996, p. 112.
[9] *Inostranets*, no. 44(304), 10 November 1999, p. 5.
[10] O. Gerasimenko, "Gosduma ukhodit v zaviazku", *Komsomol'skaia pravda*, 30 May 2000, p. 7.
[11] V. Iakovlev, "Komandir skazal 'net' ", *Novaia kamchatskaia pravda*, no. 19(183), 27 May 1999, pp. 1 & 4; V. Iakovlev, "Na kontrakt cherez kontakt" Rassledovanie NKP, *Novaia kamchatskaia pravda*, no. 23(187), 24 June 1999, pp. 1 & 3; V. Iakovlev, "Tikhaia obitel' dedovshchiny", *Novaia kamchatskaia pravda*, no. 37, 7 October 1999; V. Iakovlev, "Na myse Zheltyi ochen' skuchno...", *Novaia kamchatskaia pravda*, no. 42, 11 November 1999; I. Sergeiev, "Oruzhie na zakusku...Kazarmy tankogo batal'ona mogli stat' kamchatskoi 'goriachei tochkoi'", *Novaia kamchatskaia pravda*, no. 5, 10 February 2000.
[12] A. Politkovskaia, "Dedskie igry", *Novaia gazeta*, no. 23, 15-18 June 2000, p.3.

gating crimes committed by their subordinates. Prosecutors play more of an advisory role here[13]. "This partially answers the question the soldiers' mothers keep asking all the time, that is when all this hazing is going to stop. Well, as long as the unit commander retains his role of a "body of investigation" ... this sadistic practice will continue unabated! ... *Dedovshchina* is a powerful tool for keeping people under control and no one wants to let go of this tool. No one, except the privates"[14].

This organized violence as a "management tool" is finding its way from the army into big politics simply because there are people who want this happening. Marginalized political parties like, for example, the Liberal Democrats, are seeking freedom for military criminals such as Colonel Budanov who raped and killed a young Chechen woman. We can hear noisy demands coming from just about everywhere to let the Colonel go or else...
Barkashov's neo-Nazis[15] have formally applied to supply the Russian armed forces with a well-trained cadre of their own. Add to this a wealth of similar developments and you will see how attractive the system of organized violence is to marginalized groups and how much support they are getting in the upper echelons of Russian power.

Petty officers often fall victim to this systemic irrational violence too. All this, plus the disproportionate and ineffective use of force in Chechnya, experts say, is changing the "cultural genotype" of the previously "people's" Russian military that is now quickly turning into a "Czar's" own army. As a result, many opposition-minded officers are now being phased out and the armed forces are gradually turning into a police force meant to stamp out internal dissent. Another possibility is the army quickly morphing into a third political force poised to join in the political power struggle.[16]

---

[13] *Ibid.*
[14] *Ibid.*
[15] A. Barkashov is the leader of the extreme nationalist Russian Nationalist Union (RNE) movement [Editors' note].
[16] V. Serebriannikov & Iu. Deriugin, *Sotsiologiia armii*, Moskva, 1996, p. 204.

3. The ethnic aspect

There is every reason to see the ethnic side of violence that has gripped the Russian armed forces as stemming from domestic aggression being taken out on people of different ethnicity. The Russian society that, throughout the 20th century, went through a spate of ethnic and social metamorphoses in search for identity and unity, regularly seeks all sorts of metaphysical antipodes represented by a socio-ethnic cross section, from "enemies of the people" to the "enemies of the human race". No other socio-professional group has so painstakingly been divided into *"churbany"*, *"uryuki"*, *"khokhly"*, *"zhidy"*, *"ary"*, *"dagi"*[17], *"katsapy"*[18] and other *"talabaitsy"*[19] than the army however. Even convicts appear to be totally "ethnic-blind"[20]. Outbursts of social frustrations within one ethnic group degenerating into chauvinistic outrages normally peak out at the start of military campaigns sparked by ethnic conflicts.

In a peacetime conflict-ridden society the lack of an unconditional external enemy encourages the search for a conditional internal one and multiple ethnicity and the quick personnel rotation is the only thing that prevents a steady domination by members of a certain nationality. The principle of social supremacy is even more important here. Therefore, even in the case of ethnic hierarchies (the so-called *"zemliachestvo"*[21]), it is still reproducing the existing social structure. Each time you have a numerically prevailing and closely knit ethnic group they will invariably be the bosses and all others - the underdogs. Not all nationalities have such ethnic mafias though. East Europeans, unlike Caucasians and Central Asians, rarely form such "mafias". Dagestanis or "dags", as they are normally called in the army, are particularly consolidated and aggressive[22].

---

[17] Derogatives for Asians and Caucasians, Central Asians, Ukrainians, Jews, Azeris and Dagestanis [translator's note].
[18] Ukrainian derogative for Russians [translator's note].
[19] Derogatory ethnic nickname for non-Europeans [translator's note].
[20] L. Klein, "Etnografiia lageria", *Etnograficheskoe obozrenie*, no. 1, 1990; V. Kabo, "Struktura lageriia I arkhetipy soznaniia", *Sovetskaia etnografiia*, no. 1, 1990.
[21] *Zemliachestvo*: groups formed on loyalties derived from common regional origins [Editors' note].
[22] See I. Sergeiev, "Oruzhie na zakusku...Kazarmy tankogo batal'ona mogli stat' kamchatskoi 'goriachei tochkoi'", *Novaia kamchatskaia pravda*, no. 5, 10 February 2000.

This phenomenon speaks of certain peculiarities of a national temperament, outlook etc. One should also bear in mind that the originally compensatory functions of both these *zemliachestva* and *dedovshchina* in a vastly exaggerated form reflect the innate problems dogging the Soviet society. In many mono-ethnic units, for example, there is an a priori feeling of animosity towards Muscovites that eventually degenerates into a strong desire to humiliate one by hazing him. "*CHMO*"[23] for example, may stand for "*Chelovek Moskovskoi Oblasti*" (Moscow Region resident). This does not mean a certain trait of a Muscovite's character, of course, but rather the socio-psychological imbalance resulting from Moscow's traditional political, economic and informational preponderance in a multicultural Russia, let alone the USSR.

The very same compensatory mechanism is at work within an ethnic community, but it works more on the socio-regional plane than along purely ethnic lines. Ethnic groups, which have actually suffered from metropolitan oppression, are particularly aware of their ethnic identity. Domestic xenophobia on the part of the Russian majority is perceived equally acutely as deportations and other acts of political repression. We know many cases of the so-called "reverse" racism. During my army days I served with a multiethnic unit and was occasionally derided as "*churka*" (Asian mug) by my non-Slavic colleagues. "*Churka*" in the army means a member of any ethnic minority. If, for example, your company is largely made up of ethnic Russians, all non-Russians will be called "*churkas*", if, say, Dagestanis are in a majority, then the term will apply to all non-Dagestanis, above all Slavs, etc.

Here is an example of such harassment as taken from letters sent home by members of an ethnic majority.

> ...Today we helped a "*churka*" clean up the quarters. We poured some water, then grabbed him by his arms and hands and used him as a mop. We then took him into the office. The whole idea belonged to our company commander. It was the first such experiment...

---

[23] *Chmo*: army pariah belonging to the lowest stratum in the army hierarchy [Editors' note].

And so on and so forth... I personally know the authors of such racist slur and you may rest assured that in their own cultural milieu they are nice and well-educated people all. Moreover, some of their close friends belong to the very same ethnic groups they so viciously derided in their letters. A real paradox, isn't it?

To my mind, this paradox stems from the classless environment the military system is holding out for in its eternal quest for faceless uniformity. The human mind, however, rejects everything that is nondescript, just like Order rejects Chaos.

The factor of different ethnicity is meant to concretize the chaos of alienation, to personify the sense of uncomfortably by defining the habitat as the immediate surroundings, which is off limits to aliens. The ego is placed inside a circle which boundaries are equally blurred and depend only on one's ability to more or less clearly define his ethnic origin.

Ethnic negativism is the product of the collective subliminal that is not affected by positive personal relations. The negative is the opposite of the positive construed in the field of the unknown through negative presentation of one's own image. Therefore positive and negative ethnic identities form different mindsets. That's why a decent Russian who has Chechen, Jewish and Kazakh friends, may, in a situation of an ethnic identity crisis, easily start using all sorts of racial slurs irrespective of his personal friendships. Similarly, any Russian serviceman who finds himself within, say, a Caucasian environment, may suffer for his "Big Brother" status. In a different situation, say, during a vacation trip to the Caucasus, he would be welcomed by the very same people who once abused him in the army. This meaning that even though ethnicity may be of little relevance in personal relationships, it may come to the fore within the cultural vacuum of extreme group acquiring the features of a metaphysical archetype of "friend" and "foe" which might even lose it cultural properties.

4. Public perception of the military and the problem of a transition to a professional army

The mere fact that most of the men who have served in the army have been talking about this all their life reflects the effect the so-called "dominance relationship" may have on the human mind. The more so since this experience represents a phase of socialization and is extrapolated to other areas of human activity.

In socially controlled societies (totalitarian and certain traditionalist societies too) people take a generally favorable view of the armed forces. Just like a marginalized mind regards military service as a good thing because it gives a marginalized person a much-wanted chance to integrate into the rest of the society.

The militarization of the Soviet society started at an early age with the social and educational systems preparing the growing generations for war. Therefore, military service was seen as the culmination of the socialization process, a sort of an initiation and access to the world of "real", adult men. This continued until clashes of the real and ideal eventually transformed the system of public values in the late 1960s which has since been drifting away from the "state-always-comes-first" priority towards the preponderance of the individual over the state.

While in the West the need for a switch to a new-type armed force was realized in the early 1970s, the Russians' perception of the draft army started changing in the early 1990s. The reasons for this change of wind are as follows:

- publication of systemic abuses and crimes against humanity in the military;
- the democratic process changed the individual's role in the society and with regard to the state. It was probably the first time in Russian history that society realized that the state owes as much to the individual as the individual owes the state, and that if the state fails to meet its obligations to the individual, the latter has every right to respond in kind;

- the wars in the Caucasus laid bare the inefficiency of the "cheap", non-professional army;
- the human rights groups were instilling in people the all importance of human right and liberties;
- that one's right to alternative military service is guaranteed by the Constitution.

The high degree of psychological and institutional openness in Russia, the people's increasing involvement in the global educational and productive process and the liberalization of the mobile and global telecommunications system ushered in a wealth of new social values. While in the 1950s and 60s military service was a matter of prestige, draft dodging in the 1970s and 80s was increasingly loosing its immoral connotation while in the 1990s draft evasion was overwhelmingly seen as a matter of prestige (especially in the cities), a chance to challenge the society which is so characteristic of the young people's mentality as a whole. It's not because young people are so bad these days, it is because youngsters are now taking a very different look at the society they live in and have to adjust to the modern lifestyles which are so different from what existed back in the 1950s and 80s.

These days Success and Prestige depend more on one's education and personal initiative, one's openness to the outside world. Therefore, two years of forced exclusion from normal life are hard to make up for. Each new generation is more integrated into the global process of information integration than the previous one, and is less constrained by all kinds of social clichés and biases.

Hence the changing emphasis from fulfilling one's duty to society to the prestige of choosing one's own priorities. A person with a competitive educational background is thus creating his or her own system of "unsinkability" irrespective of how "unsinkable" or "sinkable" the surrounding society may be.

The armed forces provide a tale-telling picture of the growing social stratification of the Russian society where rural dwellers with secondary education account for the lion's share of those being drafted.

Whereas in a militarized society the armed forces are a centerpiece of the public attention, in an open, democratic society, the army is just one of many channels of social fulfillment. The continuously encouraged pragmatism of the young people's mentality, along with a raft of socio-psychological changes happening in post-industrial societies have created new principles of building modern-day armed forces[24]. In Russia the past decade also witnessed a whole range of socio-psychological factors causing and resulting from the general downfall in both the role and prestige of the military. "The hushing up of the causes behind the mass-scale loss of military and civilian life, a desire not to look for the culprits purportedly not to traumatize the society may only heighten the temperature of public wrath and indignation which, in turn, could trigger powerful social upheavals."[25].

Such obvious problems eventually changed the public's perception of the military as a whole. According to a February 2001 survey conducted by the VTsIOM pollsters, 69% of Russians would hate to have their close relatives drafted into the army, including due to the high death and injury rate in Chechnya - 38%, hazing and violence - 30%, poor living conditions, inadequate food and health hazards - 18%, moral degradation, alcoholism and drug use - 10%, useless loss of time - 6%, crime enhancing environment - 5%, etc...[26] Considering the fact the Russian military's traditional image of a people's army, it is clear that such dramatic changes would be impossible without a fundamental transformation of the public mindset in favor of a leaner but meaner professional army. The need is dictated by a change in the very idea of war and peace, which originated with the start of the global spread of weapons of mass destruction.

The public mind responds to reality faster than the political mind does with the society pressing the government to speed up the switch to a voluntary, professional army. According to a February 2001 VTsIOM poll, 84 percent of respondents opted for a professional, volunteer-based armed force.

This pressing need for an effective military, however, goes ignored by the powers that be and openly rejected by the powerful military lobby. Even competent analysts like V. Serebriannikov and Iu. Deriugin, who fully realizes the objective need for a professional army, admit this may not sit very well

---

[24] Serebriannikov & Deriugin, 1996, *op. cit.*, p. 207.
[25] *Ibid.*, p. 204.
[26] The sum of the answers exceeds 100% as respondents were allowed to give more than one answer. (see www.polit.ru)

with certain moral principles of the so-called "enigmatic Russian soul." These questionable argumentation calls for a more detailed comment.

"Unlike the Western armies where military service is based on the liberal idea, legal norms and a clear-cut "patron-client" contract," V. Serebriannikov and Iu. Deriugin write, "the Russian army has traditionally hinged on moral principles and collective psychology." Add to this the so-called "patriarchal" tradition and you will get a complete list of principles that govern the Soviet/Russian army, a list that boils down to just one word - *dedovshchina*.
The history of the Russian army so idealized by our respected analysts is replete with cases where the "conciliarism and collectivism, these two cornerstones of the old Russian army[27], did not prevent it from "firing at its fellow citizens fighting for their rights"[28]. Neither conciliarism nor collectivism or any other pillars constituting the "moral basis" of the Old Russian army ever prevent it from effectively crushing the sprouts of separatism across the Russian Empire. Furthermore, was it not the Red Army whose high morals the authors are so sure of, that the Soviet government leaned on purging its own people? And can we call any army (except a people's militia) an army of the people, especially one that is run by a political party?

The authors believe that *dedovshchina* is actually a thing of the past decade and resulting from a clash between "the alien idea of individualism and the inherently collectivist nature of the Russian military community"[29]. Right? Wrong! The first official acknowledgement of "barracks-floor hooliganism" came from the Soviet Defense Minister way back in 1962. But even before that, in the late 1950s, there already were witness accounts of old timers taking the newcomers' uniforms and things like that. The closed systems of total control are bound to destroy themselves by their own energy, which has no other way of releasing itself. Therefore, it was Mikhail Gorbachev's *perestroika* that precipitated the end of this system but just the other way round: *peterstroika* was an attempt to hoist the armed forces and the whole society out of the systemic crisis that was fraught with irreversible consequences. The problem is that reforms started when these consequences were already very much visible.

---

27 Serebriannikov & Deriugin, 1996, *op. cit.*, p. 226.
28 *Ibid.*, p. 222.
29 *Ibid.*, p. 211 & p. 226.

The above inconsistencies are enough to question the expediency of appealing to speculative layers of ethnic morality when analyzing the prospects of a transition to a professional army. In politics, the fine moral categories are better suited for making camouflage, rather than load-carrying structures.

2 The Test of Reality: Understanding Families' Tolerance Regarding Mistreatment of Conscripts in the Russian Army[1]

Anna COLIN LEBEDEV

Hello to all who work at the committee of soldiers' mothers. We are mothers of unfortunate soldiers and we're writing to you. We live in a small town and we more or less all know each other. There has been the autumn call-up, the children have been taken into the army. After their incorporation, you take the bus, you wait at the stop, at the hospital, at work, everyone asks you where your child is doing his service. Our son was taken, he's not far away, three hours from home. We got the first letter two weeks later, we were really happy, but we were soon saddened by what we read. We gave our son everything a soldier needed, but when he got to Orenburg, the sergeants took what they wanted of it. The rest was taken when he got to his unit. I found a lot of parents whose children left at the same time as ours. They all write the same thing: the sergeants took everything, there's a terrible *dedovshchina*. We got our last pennies together, bought what a soldier needs and went to the army unit. Certain children, after two weeks' service, ended up in hospital with pneumonia. The weather's bad, their boots are soaked, they're not allowed to dry them out. Is this human? Having done six months or a year, the sergeants wake the children up at night demanding money and filter-tipped cigarettes. Where are the commanders? They get beaten up in a way that leaves no bruises. That's why children run away from the army or commit suicide. Two women were talking next to me on the bus. The son of one of them was beaten up, she couldn't even recognise him. The second woman's son was in a construction battalion; the children are beaten up and he began wetting the bed.
The children are weak and ill now. Most of them are ill there. Because if you can buy you child out, if you've got

---

[1] Translated from the French by Kevin Balston.

money or you know any doctors, your child doesn't go into the army. You can't get anywhere with the '*dedovshchina*'. Once upon a time, they wanted to restore order but they've quickly let it all drop and forgotten our children. It's awful how their health declines in two years and the state they come back from the army in. What can parents do, how many tears must they cry? In fact, they train our children for the hot spots[2]. How will they get on [with one another] when they're holding real weapons? We wanted to go and complain to the commander, but our children begged us [not to] with tears in their eyes, because they'd get killed. So, what can we do, how can we carry on? We're afraid even to tell you the number of their unit. If we're found out, God forbid, our children will go to their graves. Please don't mention our names or addresses. We are in P.... military district, S.... *oblast*, K.... village, military unit number..... There's also a *dedovshchina* in T..... We're looking forward to your answer. Goodbye. Once again, please don't give our names and addresses. Goodbye. We're waiting for your answer. [2000]

Tens of thousands of letters like this have arrived at the Committee of Soldiers' Mothers in Moscow since 1989. A poignant account of the mistreatment endured by soldiers during their national service, but also a gripping illustration of mothers' attitudes when faced with the situations experienced by their sons. The mother's initial trust soon gives way to disappointment and worry when her son tells her about the conditions he is doing his service under. "A terrible *dedovshchina*," concludes the mother, thereby qualifying events. "Is this human?" she wonders. "Where are the commanders?" she asks, blaming the disastrous situation in the barracks on a leadership problem. National service is spoken of as injustice undergone by the poor, because the rich have found corrupt schemes for getting their children out of it. If a mother's first reaction is to approach the military hierarchical superiors, her indignation quickly changes to fear. The soldier demonstrates that a complaint from her could be dangerous for him. In such a situation, where all exits seem barred because the commanders appear to be a party to the mistreatment, a mother

---

[2] This expression refers to zones of armed conflict or potential danger.

is disorientated and afraid to denounce any mistreatment. She calls on the Committee of Soldiers' Mothers to take action, but is incapable of taking any herself.

Neither acceptance, overt opposition nor collective action: this attitude sheds particular light on the question of mistreatment in the Russian army. The persistence of mistreatment in the Russian army can not be explained merely from the soldiers' point of view. Because this army only functions through its interaction with society, which supplies the conscripts, its raw material, the relative tolerance of Russian citizens regarding mistreatment is one of the elements leading to their perpetuation. Due to the existence of possible action, as taken by the Committee of Soldiers' Mothers, the lack of action from society is all the more significant and raises certain questions.

At this point, it is necessary to specify the terms used so as to give assistance in reading. As far as possible, I would prefer to avoid using the term of "*dedovshchina*", heavy as it is with connotations linked to the phenomenon, its origins and those taking part in it. Grouping the taunts, harassments, hierarchical acts and conflicts between generations under the term "*dedovshchina*" blurs our vision of the facts as they really are and smoothes reality over to the point of rendering all analysis impracticable. Rather than using the term "*dedovshchina*", we will prefer to consider the reasons why the people involved use this word and the references underpinning its use.

In this context, we do not wish to find a new, more exact word, better adapted to the phenomenon, but to view mistreatment in the army in its diversity and complexity as seen by those undergoing it and those around them. The aim of this work is not to emphasise a fact of national service but an experience, inasmuch as it conditions behaviour and positions. The key to the reading, which will show mistreatment in the army up is, thus, to be found somewhere between the facts and their interpretation, on the level of imagination, values and clichés which incorporate the basic facts into a coherent picture and give them substance.

Discourse on national service in post-Soviet Russia seems, at first, to boil down to two completely opposing positions. The first consists of stressing dysfunctioning in the army and favorising reform and suppression, or reduction, of compulsory conscription. Such is the position held by human rights organisations, as well as certain journalists and politicians. The second, on the contrary, glorifies national service as the duty of all citizens and salutes the values of courage, endurance and honesty bestowed by the army. This polarisation of opinion, which gives visibility to the debate on national service in Russia, is obviously less apposite when reflecting on individual, and much more complex, positions. Here, we are not attempting to separate the 'pros' and 'cons' of national service, nor to identify any position between the two, but to understand the variables which play a part in the formation of a vision of national service. The latter will give keys for reading in order to better comprehend attitudes to mistreatment in the army.

This analysis will rely on two main sources: on the one hand, the letters of complaint sent to the Union of Committees of Soldiers' Mothers of Russia[3] by soldiers' families and, on the other hand, the texts from round tables on the perception of the army and national service organised by the FOM[4] in 2002. Among the letters written between 1991 and 2002, we have essentially selected those where mistreatment or poor conditions during national service were the object of the complaint. Most were sent by soldiers' mothers who contacted the Committee of Soldiers' Mothers when their child's situation seemed intolerable. In this critical situation, the mother gives her interpretation of the mistreatment undergone by her child and names those she holds responsible. She also writes retrospectively on the way she imagined national service would be, before being personally confronted with it and having her hopes dashed. Even if these letters provide extremely rich material on the perception of national service in Russia, the round tables are an indispensable complement to them. In effect, the retrospective vision of national service to be perceived in the letters is necessarily reconstructed and remodelled by the traumas inciting the mother to put pen to paper. Round tables, however, where participants are not directly engaged in national service issues, shed a more general light on the imaginary vision of national service in Russian society.

To account for the persistence and relative acceptance of mistreatment, we shall first identify the social group confronted with national service and its hazards. It will be seen that, far from being representative of the population

---

[3] For practical reasons, we shall call the addressee of these letters "Committee of Soldiers' Mothers". The organisation is often spoken of using this name.
[4] Public Opinion Foundation, an organisation for opinion polls and surveys.

as a whole, recruitment for national service only concerns certain fringes of the population, those most fragile and least able to defend their rights, which is not without consequences on their attitude when faced with mistreatment. Secondly, we shall examine conscripts' families' perception of national service. The notion of masculinity will be essential in understanding what is still, for many families, a primordially character-forming moment in the life of a man. In this vision, where national service is glorified, what reading of mistreatment is to be made by families? Thirdly, we shall attempt to show the palette of attitudes adopted by individuals in the face of mistreatment and which varies according to their interpretation of the events endured by their child. In other words, we shall be considering the moment when the ideal vision is put to the test of reality.

1. An army of workers and farmers

The description 'army of workers and farmers' was that given to the Red Army by the Soviet authorities, to underline its closeness to the people. Today, the expression has been reborn, but with a very different connotation. "We have an army of workers and farmers," affirms one man questioned at a round table, "those who don't earn much and can't afford a bribe have to serve"[5]. The evolution of the socio-professional background in the recruitment of conscripts, and the problem this poses regarding the nature of the army thus made up, are mentioned by the soldiers themselves. Without giving precise figures, the authorities regularly affirm that the majority of conscripts come from poorer families[6].

This situation is illustrated by letters sent to the Committee of Soldiers' Mothers, mostly written by women living in great financial precariousness[7].

---

[5] FOM, Voronezh, 13th February 2002.
[6] See, for example, the interview given to *Krasnaia zvezda*, the army's official newspaper, by O. Teslenko, on 13th July 2002 http://www.redstar.ru/2002/07/13_07/1_02.html.
[7] Thus, half the letters, sent from all over the country, come from villages, 28% from small towns and only 12% from cities. The writers' financial precariousness often comes through very precisely in the letters. "On my breadline pay, 550 roubles, I could not go even though, in the depths of my soul, I wanted to, and I wasn't able to borrow the money," writes a mother who regrets not being able to go and see her

They relate, often bitterly, ever-growing bartering in national service, when a bribe opens the way to exemption or a delay in starting.

> Frankly, there's never been any justice in our country and there never will be, because the rich control everything now. Their children with their military papers bought back live lives of luxury and those like my poor, only son have to tempt fate." [1997]

> The fact is that anyone who has been able to pay [*otkupitsa*] doesn't go into the army. I've got nothing to pay with, so they want to take Guena. When I asked I. why some boys of my son's age were exempted from national service, he said, "We're moving towards capitalism. You can get more information from the store. [1994]

There is, in fact, a real exemption market, notably studied by Igor Kliamkin and Lev Timofeiev in a work dedicated to the economy in the shadows[8]. On this barely legal market, families wishing to spare their child from national service can obtain exemption through corruption, especially of civil servants or army doctors. Although widely known about, the system is, however, relatively hard to gain access to, linked as it is to heavy risks for both the supplier and the asker. Moreover, the cost of this corruption is rather high and varies between 500 and 2000 dollars, depending on the complexity of the conscript's case. What is more, alternatives to corruption of civil servants are available on this market: a certain number of private entrepreneurs[9] offer to free national service conscripts for and by varying prices and means. Thus, according to a 2002 enquiry carried out by a journalist in Moscow, the conscript can be fictitiously enrolled for university for 550 dollars, leading to a delay in starting one's service. Inaptitude for medical reasons may be obtained

---

son. "I am a second-degree invalid. Now, after the rises, my pension is 730 roubles. I have no husband." "After demobbing, my son wanted to go to the police school [...] but we have not even enough money to pay for his journey there. Also, when my son came back from the army, I had nothing but potatoes to put in front of him. My irregular income is barely enough to support the family and there is no one to help us. I am unemployed."

[8] I. Kliamkin, L. Timofeiev, *Tenevaia Rossiia*, Moskva: RGGU, 2000.
[9] Of which we can imagine the highly variable juridical status, ranging from complete illegality to perfectly recognised, legal activity.

from 30 dollars upwards. Complex medical conditions with legal aid cost up to 1500 dollars[10].

Corruption is not the only way for a young man of an age to serve of escaping the army. A certain number of medical conditions, as well as the status of student or his family situation influence delays in beginning national service, or partial or total inaptitude.

Between corruption and the use of legal means, the percentage of an age group accomplishing its national service is constantly diminishing. According to official figures, only 10% of young men in any particular age group are actually serving, compared to 27% in 1994[11]. The result of this situation, pointed out by the military authorities themselves, is the modification in the social background of conscripts, coming as they do from ever poorer and more fragile classes. In spring 2004, according to the Ministry of Defence, 40% of incorporated soldiers had, when called up, no professional or academic activity; 21% were from one-parent families and 5% had been in trouble with the police[12].

This state of affairs, perfectly illustrated by complaints to the Committee of Soldiers' Mothers, is not without consequence on the perception of national service by those whose children are enrolled. Service becomes an injustice inflicted on the poor, an extra burden of suffering that families in difficulty have to bear.

> Why should our children have to suffer for little rich boys and members of the government? Of course, no one looks out for anyone else. These days, you really can't get through to anybody, especially if you've got no money. [1997]
>
> They not only took him into the army and sent him so far away, but now he's been stationed in Daghestan, so his mate told me in a letter. Is it fair? If we're second-class citi-

---

[10] M. Chizhov, "Prizyv v armiu: chernyi rynok belykh biletov", *Argumenty i fakty*, no. 50(1155), December 2002.
[11] Cf. the press conference of 30th March 2004, held by General-Colonel Vassili Smirnov, available on the Ministry of Defence of the Russian Federation website, http://www.mil.ru/articles/article5380.shmtl
[12] *Ibid.*

zens, then they can do what they like with us and the New Russians and all those up above [*verkhuchka*] live off us. How can it be so? [1999]

One of the reasons for the persistence of mistreatment affecting soldiers is to be found in this transformation of the socio-professional make-up of the generations of conscripts[13].

Families whose children are enrolled in the army and whose situation is ever-more precarious, have no means of fighting mistreatment. The absence of financial resources has already been mentioned, but conscripts and their parents also lack social resources.

Thus, soldiers' parents who decide to contact the Committee of Soldiers' Mothers frequently speak of extreme distance, both geographical and symbolic, between them and sources of information or the authorities:

> We are in a village and we don't know the rules or our rights. [2001]
>
> We are far from Moscow. We can't get to an appointment with the people responsible for our son's fate. [2001]

The wealthier and better educated classes of the population, those liable to resist by pulling on their resources, overwhelmingly choose to get their children out of national service through corruption, or the delay in entering the army granted to young people in higher education. Between defection and speaking out, to use Albert Hirschman's terminology[14], they choose defection. If this strategy saves a considerable number of young men from mistreatment, it also indirectly contributes to the perpetuation of the latter. The "gaps" in the enrolment system mentioned earlier maintain a paradoxical balance, since they save individuals and, at the same time, keep the system of mistreatment going. To support this hypothesis, let us recall the moment when the movement of soldiers' mothers came into being. It was a very precise

---

[13] On the subject of the socio-professional background of conscripts and draft dodgers, see also: F. Daucé, "Les paradoxes de l'insoumission en Russie", *Courrier des Pays de l'Est*, La documentation française, no. 1022, February 2002, pp. 36-43.

[14] A. Hirschman, *Exit, Voice and Loyalty: Responses to decline in firms, organizations and states*, Cambridge, MA: Harvard University Press, 1970.

moment in 1989, when a political decision suppressed a delay in national service for students. At that moment, the most active and educated fringes of the population were confronted with the problem of the mistreatment experienced by their children. This head-on collision, along with new avenues offered by the liberalisation and opening-up of Soviet society, was at the origin of the first collective action by soldiers' mothers against mistreatment. It is, moreover, interesting to note that, although bills have been regularly submitted on the subject, the delay in national service for students has never since been called into question. Should we perceive here the authorities' awareness of a precarious balance not to be upset, in order to preserve national service as it is?

2. "I thought the army would be my second home"

It is, then, a fact that only a minority of families are concerned by the problem of mistreatment in the army. Still, as a potential threat hovering over any family having raised a boy, national service is a real social problem on which no one can fail to take a position. It is tempting, on realising the massive scale of avoidance, to postulate a negative attitude from the public to the military institution. The high visibility of the army's problems could, also, give credence to the idea of citizens' loss of affection for the army and national service. This would be too simplistic a description of an ambivalent reality.

68% of the Russian population have had experience of the military, either directly or via a close family member who has served or worked in the armed forces[15]. When asked, "Do you see more negative or positive elements in today's situation in the Russian army?" 72% of Russians answer, "More negative elements"[16]. Nonetheless, among those who have been involved with the military institution, half consider that the army did them more good than harm[17].

---

[15] FOM survey of 1500 people, 7th/8th Sept. 2002 http://bd.fom.ru/report/map/d023608
[16] FOM survey of 1500 people, 15th/16th Feb. 2003 http://bd.fom.ru/report/map/d030711
[17] FOM survey of 1500 people, 7th/8th Sept. 2002 http://bd.fom.ru/report/map/d023608.

A bad image of the army in general does not seem, then, to compromise the importance with which the military institution is bestowed. On the contrary, the harshness of military life counts among the army's qualities. Only 1% of people questioned stressed poor material conditions as something negative experienced in the army, and a mere 5% consider that "extra-reglementary relations"[18], meaning mistreatment, are to be counted on the downside of their experience with the military. Inversely, for 16% of those questioned, the endurance acquired during national service constitutes one of the positive points of going into the army[19].

These results alone give a glimpse of the acceptance of poor conditions during national service. However, they are largely insufficient in understanding the nature of this adhesion. In this aim, the values and attitudes associated with the military institution should be examined more deeply, so as to comprehend the role attributed to national service. National service takes root in the heart of families' functioning as an indispensable, formative time, a symbolic test in the acquisition of virility and, finally, as a reason for pride in the family.

3. A formative time

The conscript's family and, more exactly, his mother, play a key role in the individual's interaction with national service. This is manifested doubly: the mother is at once the one against whom national service is carried out, in an opposition of the domestic and outside worlds; she is equally the one with a right to stand up for her child and watch out for his well-being.

As guardian of the childhood world, it is the mother who gives her son over the military institution[20] to make an adult of him, in what appears to be an essential initiation rite. The young man should, then, return from the army transfigured, mature and detached from his mother.

---

[18] Official name for mistreatment.
[19] FOM survey of 1500 people, 7th/8th Sept. 2002 http://bd.fom.ru/report/map/d023608.
[20] "I gave [*otdala*] my son to the army" is one of the most frequent expressions encountered in letters to the Committee of Soldiers' Mothers.

> Someone coming back from the army has changed into a man, while someone who hasn't been in is different, all the same. [FOM 2002][21]

> I think [national service is useful] for adapting a bit to life, you see. Here, we mums take care of them. In the army, they have to look after themselves. What do we teach them: goodness, lad, be good and kind. [FOM 2002][22]

Awareness for the need for this break from the mother and the accompanying anguish are very strong with soldiers' mothers. The maternal relationship with national service is built up around this anguish.

An expression stigmatises a boy who refuses to break away from his mother, "*mamen'kin synok*", "mummy's boy". As the threat of this accusation seems to hang over conscripts' mothers, the latter make a show of their goodwill when faced with national service.

> I didn't try, unlike some, to buy his exemption or to get him into a psychiatric hospital. On the contrary, I always told my sons they had to do their duty to their country, that they're men, the army gives a lot of good things and that they'd come back strong and healthy. [1999]

> As a mother, my heart was torn when the call-up came, when our children were dying in Chechnya. But my son wasn't afraid and didn't try to get out of doing his national service. He understood he could end up in the butchery of the war. My worries as a mother were limitless faced with the approaching 'misfortune'. No, I didn't swear by or curse fate and maybe that's why no death certificate came to my *isba*. [1997]

A mother's acceptance of the very principle of national service as a formative time arises from two values linked to quite different logics: masculinity and patriotism.

---

[21] FOM, Moscow, 24th September 2002
[22] FOM, Moscow, 24th September 2002, 62-year-old woman

4. A masculinity rite

The virility that only the army seems able to confer on a young conscript is an element inevitably associated with the idea of national service.

To the question "what positive things did the army bring you or your friends and relatives?", endurance, education and the accession to masculinity come first on the list with 16% of total answers[23]."'The army made a man of him"; "a man must be a man - there's no masculine endurance if you don't go in the army"; "he matured, his view on life changed"; "he left as a snotty kid and came back as a man": the upside of national service is judged in these terms.

This vision of national service is largely inspired by the memory of the Soviet era:

> I'd like to remind you of how it used to be. When a boy's at school, he's told: you'll go into the army, you'll come back, you'll get married, you'll find a job. Meaning that someone back from the army is already considered as an adult. And someone who hasn't been in the army is still seen as a child at 18. [...] It was the main thing the army used to give, the feeling of becoming an adult, becoming a man. [FOM 2002][24]

The other positive points of national service put forward are equally revealing: they tend to be traditionally male qualities. Thus come, in the following order: physical strength (8%); discipline (7%); autonomy, responsibility (6%); bravery, willpower (6%). According to 5% of the population, the army gave their friends or relatives the chance to learn a trade.

It would, however, be restrictive or erroneous to speak for a uniform version of warring masculinity imposed on all. Mistrust of the army, as revealed by opinion polls, and evidence of dysfunctioning in the military system have considerably tarnished the uniform's prestige. It is not uncommon to hear criticism of the army's function of making boys into men from the men themselves.

---

[23] FOM, survey of 1500 people 12th September 2002. Open question.
[24] FOM, Voronezh, 15th October 2002

> It makes no difference whether you've been in the army or not. I know a lot of people who haven't been in the army, who studied at university, and they live and work very well. It all depends on the man himself, if he's sociable and open. [FOM 2002][25]

> There never used to be any rush to join the army, there still isn't, and I wasn't dying to do my service either. In those days, anyone could hide themselves away in the universities. [FOM 2002][26]

Paradoxically, women more strongly emphasise the importance of national service in acquiring the masculinity that they themselves feel incapable of giving their child:

> My son didn't go into the army. He's 29 today and I really regret it. [...] Because he can't find his feet in life. Someone who has had a character-building experience, whatever it is, you understand, can do things, but he still needs his mum at 30. [...] I don't consider he's managed to become a man. It would have been better if he'd been killed there [in the army], God forgive me for saying so. At least I'd have known he was a man. When he was 16 or 17, my boy used to say, "I'll go into the army, absolutely. But I'll go to Chechnya, that's where I want to go." You understand, he was a fighter. I stamped that out in him, not only me but also the television and all those who were coming home from there. All those programmes quite simply scared him. He said, "Mum, do whatever you can, as long as I don't have to go." Mum did what she had to, although I should have kicked him in the backside and pushed him into it. [FOM 2002][27]

A considerable number of mothers who send requests to the Committee of Soldiers' Mothers bring their children up alone and make implicit refer-

---

[25] FOM, Voronezh, 15th October 2002
[26] FOM, Moscow, 15th October 2002
[27] FOM, Saint Petersburg, 15th October 2002

ences to the army's educational function. In the letters, as well as at the round tables, a vision transpires of the army as the only masculine element in a world where masculinity is defective.

> I'm bringing my son up on my own because there aren't many men in our little town. On the other hand, there are plenty of alcoholics, so it's better to live alone with your son. [2001]

> I consider that the army trains men, even so. What's more, there are practically none left in our generation. [FOM 2002][28]

The men, absent or indifferent, are not judged capable of carrying their task out: preparing boys for national service and, more generally, "making men of them". The mother becomes the person facing the army in a direct relationship which is no longer merely between the private world of the family and the military institution, but also between the feminine and the masculine. In this perspective, the officers become parental and, more precisely, paternal substitutes for the child confided by the mother. The expression 'officer fathers', in common use in Russia, indicates this extremely particular relationship with the officer figure. This being so, the mother expects the officer to behave like a father, as is shown by the incomprehension and disarray expressed by the mother when this expectation is flouted.

> I brought Evgueni up alone, the State didn't help me. When I sent him into the army, I thought that there were the commanders, that everything would work out. Where were they looking? I think there's a lot of them and that's why they couldn't keep their eye on him. How can we confide our children to them? Why did I manage to keep watch over him and bring him up for 18 years? [2000]

The relationship with the army is built up in this permanent tension between maternal values and the vision of national service. For the mother, this

---

[28] FOM, Samara, 24th September 2002. The person making this remark was a 24-year-old woman.

relationship supposes an effort in reconciling military and civil logic, the demands of military sacrifice and humanistic values.

5. Patriotic references

In the letters written by mothers to the Committee of Soldiers' Mothers, patriotic references have a double function. In the first place, one hopes the use of references imagined as those of the person one is writing to will convince him or her, encourage recognition and put forward an argument that will be appreciated. In fact, the Committee of Soldiers' Mothers is often perceived by those sending letters as an organ of the military, sometimes even political, authorities[29]. Thus, when the imagined addressee as an institution associated with the army or the authorities, the patriotic register conjures up common ground providing a link between the writer and the addressee. All the same, it would be wrong to limit patriotic references to this function of arguing one's point and to infer, by so doing, any artificial character on them. Something more profound and essential is to be uncovered in the attachment to patriotism, recurrent in the letters and the round tables.

When the individual goes beyond his or her personal situation and sees themselves in relation to the authorities, the patriotic argument shores up a symbolic indication of their place in this relationship. A show of patriotism is not only an argument for being "well thought of", but also a sign of individual's will to adhere to a system of socially recognised values, so as to appear among society's better elements and not on its sidelines.

---

[29] The perception of the Committee of Soldiers' Mothers as an institution at the heart of power is very clear from the way the addressee's identity is written on the envelopes. A large number of letters are sent quite simply to: "The Committee of Soldiers' Mothers, Moscow". Sometimes, however, the address mentioned is even more revealing than no address at all: "The Committee of Soldiers' Mothers, Moscow, White House". It is interesting to note that the Russian Ministry of Defence itself maintains the confusion by setting up parents' associations linked to it (what are sometimes known as GONGOS - "Governmental Non-Governmental Organisations"). In 1996-1997, the Council of Soldiers' Parents of Russia, founded by the Ministry of Defence, was located at 2, Il'Inka Street, an address to be read some years later on one of the letters received at the Committee of Soldiers' Mothers: "Moscow, Red Square, 12 Il'inka Street, Committee of Soldiers' Mothers". On this subject, see also F. Daucé, "'Soldiers' Mothers' search for a place in Russian society", *Revue d'Etudes Comparatives Est-Ouest*, no. 2, June 1997, pp. 121-153.

If mothers whose children are doing their national service feel this need to resort to patriotic values in order to maintain a dignified position in society, it is because of another value whose omnipresence they note: money.

National service, which parents were unable to spare their children, then becomes a motive for pride. Upholding the patriotic act of defending one's country in a society judged as being dominated by money, conscripts' families feel they are confided with a role, that of the last moral bastion in a henceforth mercenary society.

> We're a family of eight brothers and everyone has conscientiously carried out their duty in the armed forces of the Russian Federation. [2001]

> He made his own decision to join the army straight after leaving school. When it became necessary to serve, not in the Moscow suburbs but in Chechnya, M. wasn't a coward and didn't refuse, even if family reasons and his mother's poor health would have justified him in doing so. [...] He fulfilled his military duty to the country with dignity, he took part in armed combat, in intelligence and in cleaning [zachistki] [...] He didn't hide behind anybody else. [2001]

It must be remembered that, in the Soviet era, national service was a real opportunity for geographical mobility in a system where any movement of the population was very strictly controlled. To this was added a possibility for social mobility, as soldiers had the chance of learning a trade during their service.

National service is still seen today as a way of social advancement, especially among the poorer classes and in rural areas. Such is the case of these grandparents who see their grandchildren's stationing in Moscow as a chance:

> Our grandsons are coming to the end of their service. Their two years will be up on 10th December and they'll come home to the sovkhoze, which is as dilapidated as after the war. There's no work and for those with a job, no pay. The youngsters have got nothing to do. Stealing, boozing,

> scraping, selling hooch, it's frightening to live with. We're afraid that our grandsons will go off the rails as well. What can they do without work? Get up no good at night and sleep during the day? [...] We ask you to find somewhere for them after their service, so they can stay in Moscow. [1998]

To understand families' reactions to mistreatment endured by their children, we must bear in mind one vision of national service evoked above, to see what place this mistreatment, known to all, occupies in this image of national service. How can one accept the unacceptable, stand hunger, punches and humiliation in the vision of the national service one has chosen to accept and see in a favourable light?

In the process of reading and interpreting events, and in the game of transformations which goes with this reading, one can find some of the reading keys which enable us to account for the relative acceptance by society of mistreatment in the army.

"It doesn't seem to me that the army is an army"[30]

Despite the theoretical knowledge an individual may have of the way national service works, the army remains an opaque universe for parents. The rules on how it functions are not always evident.

> I can't work out what my son's doctors and commander want from me and my son [...] Maybe you'll get a clearer and more sensible answer [...] I've tried, several times, to speak to the unit commander myself. But I couldn't get anywhere with them. Until folks help me and make a request through the military enlistment office. [2001];

> I don't even know what it's called, the staff headquarters or something, the place where they give out exemptions. [1994].

---

[30] Letter from 1993.

The very existence of a right that soldiers and their families could get is often doubted:

> Please tell me if I'm allowed to fight so he doesn't have to go in the army, or if I have no rights. [1996]

In this context of uncertainty over the military institution people are faced with, interpretation plays a large role. When confronted with the problem of the mistreatment endured by her child in the army, the mother interprets what is happening to her son in order to make sense of events and bring her own vision of national service into line with the new experience.

Attitudes encountered in letters written to the Committee of Soldiers' Mothers seldom totally accept mistreatment or denounce a system of mistreatment. In their majority, they lie between these two points; they complement and are superimposed on one another. Thus, the interest in categorising will be to account for different logic in reasoning and to give a hint of the wide range of attitudes adopted by individuals faced with mistreatment (see Table 1).

Degree of acceptance	Reading of mistreatment	Action
+	Teaching method	None
	Excessive teaching method	Denunciation and search for individual responsible
-	Accidental anomaly	Denunciation and search for individual responsible
	Anomaly	Opposition, denunciation, search for individual or collective responsible.
	System	Opposition, denunciation, organised action

Table 1 – Possible attitudes to mistreatment according to interpretations made of it.

The extreme case, where mistreatment is unreservedly accepted as an inherent part of one's experience in the army, is seldom met in letters written to the Committee of Soldiers' Mothers. Indeed, complaining in writing supposes a certain dissatisfaction with the way national service is going. On the other hand, this attitude does not seem exceptional at round tables:

> I don't approve of [certain people's attempts to avoid national service]. My son did his three years ago. I sent him personally, off my own back. I brought him up alone [...] They should all go in. It makes men of them. Who will defend us if they stay tied to mother's apron strings? Mine did his service and came home. I'm not saying it was easy. There must have been all sorts in there. He didn't complain and I didn't go to see him. [FOM 2002][31]

Mistreatment is sometimes seen as a problem for weaklings; a phase which hardens the soldier up, teaches him to stand up for himself and fight.

> Who means about *dedovshchina?* Those who can't do anything, who can't wash the floor, sew [their collar] on, nothing. They get clouted, they're taught a lesson and they come running straight back: "Mum, *dedovshchina!*" They run away. And parents take part in that. They start getting their last pennies together, as long as their boy doesn't have to go into the army. And the lout lives at their expense. [FOM 2002][32]

In a certain number of cases, the families, while accepting the principle of harshness in the army, denounce excessive humiliation and abuse, seemingly out of proportion with the objective of the fault committed. Thus a mother, worried about the state her ill son is in, is anxious that he is being badly cared for and that he has lost a lot of weight during his service. She more or less begs pardon for interfering in her child's national service:

> We understand a soldier must be a soldier. But the medical attitude towards patients must be normal and humane. These are children, not animals. And they must be fed normally. [1998]

---

[31] FOM, Novossibirsk, 24th September 2002.
[32] FOM, Novosibirsk, 24th September 2002.

It is sometimes difficult to draw a lie between acceptance of mistreatment and refusal to take action, linked to parents' conviction that action is useless.

> Witnesses who saw him unconscious with pain got on to me, asking why I wasn't doing anything about it. What could I do? Today, they often take ill boys into the army. Healthy ones buy their way out of it [...] I resigned myself to it and said to my son: seeing as you're apt, you'll serve with God's help. Of course, as a mother, I really pity my son, because I know what's waiting for him in the army. Who else can he defend if he can't even defend himself? But I can't do anything about it because I haven't got any money. [1998]

Most often, however, mistreatment is actually perceived as an anomaly in national service. In the letters received by the Committee of Soldiers' Mother, the anomaly is judged sufficiently serious to call for action.

Making sense of mistreatment means tracking down those responsible for it. When mistreatment is seen as a routine accident or a one-off event, responsibility is always attributed to an individual. Such is the case of this mother who targets the commander of her son's military unit with the accusation of being behind the problem:

> There's no control over the soldiers in this garrison, they're left ton their own devices. No one really cared before, but now it's even worse. The unit commander doesn't give a damn about the fate of my son or any of his soldiers. Why then do we mothers have to entrust our sons to such weak, cold-hearted people as Major N.? [1994]

> Neither the president, nor the division or unit commanders are guilty, but the deputy commander of the enrolment office of Narofominsk and Colonel B. Them and them alone, for whom everything humane has become foreign and indifferent! [1997]

In other cases, those held responsible can be ethnic communities, overrepresented in certain regions and accused of having it in for Russians. "Caucasians" but also, more surprisingly, Buryats or Kazakhs are described in detail as henchmen towards young soldiers.

> After sending a few days in this military unit and speaking with soldiers in the barracks, [my husband] found confirmation of his idea that cruel extra-regulation[33] relation are still carrying on. People of Caucasian nationality are especially ruthless. They are well-built and strong, 24-25 years old, measuring 180-190 cm, tough with huge fists. They drink for days on end. They're fed separately from the other soldiers an get big meals. These drunken Caucasian beat up young recruits from other nationalities. [1997]

> He said that, during the day's work it's OK, you work as you want, but that all hell breaks loose when you get back to the barracks in the evening. There are only Kazakhs and Kazakh officers in the place, and they pitch in. I don't know what goes on, he won't talk about it. [1992]

> I went to see him [...] and I got a shock. He was there, thin, with spots all over his face and pockmarks like after smallpox. There were unhealed wounds up his arms. I told him to tell me, not to cover up, where he was, how his service was going, why he hadn't written. In B., it turned out that they were mainly locals [Buryats]. Their regiment is the biggest, 1500 of them for only 90 Russians. Also, most of them are about to be demobbed, they're finishing their service. The officers are also from the area. So there was no point asking him questions. It was clear they were beaten up and that letters from home were torn up in front of them, they weren't allowed to read them. [1999]

Identifying a guilty individual is also a way of asking for atonement.

> I want strict measures to be taken against the guilty parties, so that those who inflicted torture [*istiazaniia*] on my son do not go unpunished. [1993]

---

[33] See above for the explanation of this term.

By individualising responsibility and analysing mistreatment as something dysfunctional connected to particular circumstances, one is able to reconcile the theoretical vision of the virtues of the army and national service with the discordant reality. By means of this adjustment, soldiers' families, in a certain manner, cross out the phenomenon of mistreatment by removing any idea of generality from it. From then on, families wish to "put things in order' and return to a kind of military "state of nature", thereby breaching the gap between the real and the imaginary.

An unsigned letter, written by a group of soldiers' mothers, illustrates this type of attitude very well: "We ask you to check and to restore order in the military unit..." So write these mothers in their letter. The injunction to "restore order" gives their request its fullest sense. "We, parents from the Rostov *oblast* and the Krasnodar region, have sent our children to serve in the army. It works out that we haven't sent them into the Russian Army, as we would have liked, but to a disciplinary camp." For parents, the mistreating army becomes a non-army, somewhere that does not call their vision of national service into question. "No, this isn't the army! We haven't prepared our children to serve in an army like that!" Parents describe the problems encountered by their children during their service in detail:

> The youngsters are beaten up to the point of needing to have their wounds treated in the Stavropol military hospital. [...] Those who can still stand look like victims of malnutrition in wartime. And no hygiene! To start with, they aren't taken to the baths for months on end. They're covered with lice, their clothes and ears are crawling with lice. Of course, their bedding isn't changed either. There isn't one gram of fat in the porridge they're given. The soup they get at lunchtime is so thin they don't eat it with a spoon - they just drink it like tea. They can't even remember what meat smells like.

Other problems are enumerated: the lack of toilets; washing all together in the river; the "consumptive" coughing or diarrhoea certain soldiers suffer from; no medication in the infirmary. The military unit is called a "disciplinary camp" or even a "concentration camp".

The garrison commanders are very clearly held responsible for this situation by the letter-writers. "The commanders turn a blind eye to everything and don't even want to see what's going on right under their noses. It's all down to vodka. The commanders drink and all the others join in with them. They leave the brigade in the hands of the sergeants, who find this total arbitrariness [*bespredel*] suits them."

Since, for the letter-writers, responsibilities are clearly defined, poor functioning in the military unit does not call the principle of national service itself into question: "they left to serve with pleasure, it's a shame they landed up in a disciplinary camp"; "we leased them to you [*otdali v arendu*] to defend the Motherland. So give them the [necessary] conditions."

The anonymity of the letter reveals the writer's fear of rebelling against the military institution[34]. "We parents beg you to set up a commission and check for yourselves": rather than acting independently, the writers prefer to contact an organisation they imagine as being more powerful. Even if, in these cases, parents threaten to encourage their children to revolt, or to come and abduct them from barracks, these are only extreme solutions that they would rather not put into practice. It is not the families' job to right dysfunctioning but, as this letter would suggest, that of a public watchdog. This considerably limits citizens' possibilities for action against poor national service conditions.

It is no surprise that the writers of this letter do not consider the principle of mistreatment itself on use the term "*dedovshchina*". Speaking of "*dedovshchina*" means accepting the more general and systematic nature of mistreatment and seeing something else in this phenomenon than a one-off anomaly.

> There's no order in the army nowadays, only lawlessness [*bespravie*] and *dedovshchina*, it's worse than being in prison. [The officers] turn a blind eye to it all. How many destinies have been fractured, all this goes on unpunished - will there ever be an end to it all? Someone must put a

---

[34] It is interesting to compare this kind of attitude, when the letter-writer anonymously points out an individual as being responsible, and the tradition of informing used in the Soviet Union, which did not call the functioning of the system generally into question. On this point, see: F.-X. Nérard, *5% de vérité. La dénonciation dans l'URSS de Staline*, Paris: Tallandier, 2004.

> stop to the arbitrariness [*bespredel*] and crudeness [*khamstvo*] which are reigning in the army. [1998]
>
> There's awful *dedovshchina* everywhere, soulnessness [*bezdushnost'*] and crudeness [*khamstvo*]. [2001]

The reference to *dedovshchina* that the writers accuse of being the root of the mistreatment endured by their children, raises more questions than it gives answers. The parents may believe they know the principle of this phenomenon but they do not understand the logic behind it.

> Their father and I are categorically opposed to my sons being mutilated by the "*dedy*"[35] as well. And where are the commanders? Why is there such arbitrariness [*bespredel*] in the army? [1999]
>
> Why is there such lawlessness [*bezzakonie*] here? Why are the "*dedy*" so cruel, they're only a year older? They've got their mothers waiting at home for them, too. OK, so he was disobedient or he didn't do what they wanted, we're all characters, but he didn't deserve to get killed for that. I sent my son into the army healthy and I got him back in a coffin. [1995]

Two terms are characteristic and recurrent when evoking the situation in the army and when systematic mistreatment is brought up: lawlessness (*bezzakonie*), sometimes referred to as "lawfulness" (*bespravie*) and total arbitrariness (*bespredel*). The absence of laws of lawfulness comes under relatively precise accusation. The notion of arbitrariness, on the other hand, is less exact; it englobes a group of things held as unjust. The term *bespredel*, like *dedovshchina*, camouflages more than it enlightens. It pins a name on the phenomenon rather than clarifying it. They are both used for describing a disparate reality, a bundle of different events. Thus, the term *bespredel* refers to the poor situation of the army in general as well as each particular manifestation of this situation: mistreatment; lack of money; material conditions; attitude of the commanders... This term, originally from criminals' slang, indi-

---

[35] "*Dedy*" (grandfathers): the term applied to second-year national service recruits, who are most frequently accused of mistreatment the younger ones.

cates more especially total opacity in the military world, violence founded on exorbitant common-law rules and, therefore, the individual's impossibility for anticipation or action[36]. Once again, the only action seen as possible is individual - protect one's own boy and punish those directly guilty. More general change is mere pie in the sky, just as one hopes for sunshine after the rain without having any influence over climatic conditions.

> Can't anything be done about *dedovshchina*? They wanted to restore order in the past but they quickly forgot about it and forgot about our children. [2000]

The "they" referred to by the writer is the authorities, in the widest sense of the term. They alone can take action, whereas individuals can only endure. People contact the Committee of Soldiers' Mothers as if writing to an organ of power. They ask the Committee both to solve individual problems on behalf of those concerned and to take on the army's problems in general.

> Your organisation has influence and well-deserved authority. I think I could obtain justice with your help. [2000]

> Your committee has access to the State Duma and he beg you to carry our voices and fears for our sons to them. At present, your committee is the only ray of hope for a better future for our children. [1998]

Moreover, faced with a closed world, whose rules escape them, soldiers' families are often afraid of taking action, anxious that this would only worsen the soldier's situation:

> I can not put my name, as I am afraid this could come to bear on the commanders' attitude towards my son. [1999]

---

[36] On the term *"bespredel"*, its usage and history, see S. Krylossova, "Les particularités d'emploi des mots argotiques en russe contemporain", University of Nancy http://www.univ-nancy2.fr/DepRusse/docs_lies/argot.doc

> We beg you not to mention our son's name so that it doesn't come back on him. Things are already difficult enough for us. [1998]

Tones should, however, be added to this picture. Active opposition to mistreatment in the army, and organised and collective action, play a part in the interaction between the army and the rest of society. The Committees of Soldiers' Mothers, initially set up by mothers whose children were faced with the problem of mistreatment, give the most striking example of this? Since 1989, Committees have sprung up all across the country. There are more than 300 organisations of soldiers' mothers today in Russia[37]. The conditions in which this type of movement emerges are particularly interesting when trying to understand the Russian population attitude to mistreatment in the army. Collective commitment originates in a personal background which pushes the individual to take action. In the case of movements opposing poor conditions during national service, mothers traditionally choose to defend others' rights after defending those of their own sons.

A letter written in 1992, three years after the appearance of the first movements of soldiers' mothers, furnishes an interesting example of this wowering between inaction and organised action.

A woman, introducing herself as the chairwoman of a local Committee of Soldiers' Mothers, informs the Moscow Committee of problems encountered by soldiers' parents in her region:

> The concrete facts pertaining to violations of the military legislation in application, the disorder and poor daily conditions in national service, have been explained in my letter to the Perm *oblast* commission for social defence of soldiers and to the Committee of Soldiers' Mothers of the *oblast* [...] Moreover, I have underlined the fact of physical violence perpetrated on national serviceman ... who served in the ... unit [circumstances]. This being so, kindly search for ... [circumstances: mother without news]."

---

[37] Figures from the Union of Committees of Soldiers' Mothers of Russia.

She then goes over the setting-up of her Committee: "Our Committee, in the town of D., was organised fairly recently. I took the organisation of the Committee into my own hands upon learning that my son had also been sent to Northern Ossetia without full military training or his parents' written consent." The mother's worries, backed with her awareness of action needed, sparked off her commitment: "we mothers understand that no one, but ourselves, will defend our sons. This is why we must get together, hold meetings and make demands without fail! For the moment, we have done very little." Still, the decision to take action is limited by fear: the mother asks the Moscow Committee to take care of the problems met in her son's military unit on her behalf: "It is understandable that I have not been able to contact the division commander direct, in order to carry out the necessary checks. Also, so as to protect my son, please do not mention my name."

Beyond fear, without resorting to collective action, which conditions allow for acts of opposition? As we have seen, families' reactions to mistreatment relies on their vision of national service and the fashion in which facts fit in with this vision. Action can be but limited when the ideal image of national service resists facts contradicting it and when it is strong enough for the individual to reinterpret mistreatment as a mere mishap to be got round. Inversely, action becomes possible only when enchantment collapses and the vision of the army incorporates the facts of mistreatment for what they are.

Like this mother who "'stole" her child from the barracks, following mistreatment and the army's refusal to take care of his health problems. Neither financial resources, nor social connections gave rise to her act. At the end of her letter, the mother leaves a clue as to her social standing: "Excuse me if I've made any spelling mistakes. I am an ordinary worker, I have written things down as they were and my sight is none too good." "I do not know," she writes, "if you will blame me, but I could not sit at home twiddling my thumbs waiting for my son to be killed or for him to do something stupid to himself, so I went back to the garrison." Wishing to avoid her son being accused of desertion, she adds, "My son did not run away: I kidnapped him. I saved him as I could, please understand." This action brought the mother to change her standpoint on national service: "I also have a twelve-year-old boy. I will not put him in the army and make the same mistake again. Until order is restored in the army, no one will serve, no one needs an army like that. They run away and will continue doing so. No one would run away if it was any good. They would have done their service properly, then come home." Such was also the case of this other mother who, not wishing her son to serve in the army, forbade him to attend his appointment at the enrolment office. "Please help me keep my only child out of this hell they call the Russian Army," she asks the Committee of Soldiers' Mothers. "Please tell me exactly what to do now. "Please send me the texts of the laws which can help protect my son. Please tell me how to resist in my struggle against this system, which has made our sons into small change in its political games; they are nothing more than objects to be bought and sold and abused inhumanely, cannon fodder in fact. No one bears any responsibility for this." However, even if this mother's step was active, in that she felt able to oppose the military institutions, it was still an individual act tending, once more, towards avoidance, as is the case with the majority of the Russian population.

Conclusion

This reflection on the acceptance of mistreatment has been based on the power of the imaginary in relation to national service. The attachment to a vision of the army still largely shored up by references to the Soviet army has, in effect, a real influence on the role attributed to national service, as an initiation rite and a source of pride. The specificity of the population group concerned by national service - often one-parent and rather impoverished families - adds to this phenomenon. For the mother, the army becomes, then, a masculine and paternal substitute, a source of pride and a way of regaining honour in a society where she feels somewhat degraded. In this context, the individual adapts their perception of mistreatment to the ideal vision of the army they wish to keep, sometimes at any cost. In this case, the real gives way to the ideal. The military world becomes magical, all the more so because the magic is carefully maintained by the military itself. The conclusion is, nevertheless, not fatalistic: it is possible to take action.

3 *Dedovshchina* as an Element of the "Small Society": Evidence from Russia and Other Countries

Anton OLEYNIK

In modern western writings on the post-Soviet Russia the idea that market and political reforms have not led yet to the expected results, i.e. the emergence of democracy and free market, is not welcome. Few are those western scientists who admit the unintended or undesigned results of intentional human actions in the context of former socialist countries[1]. They expect there the emergence of a "corrupted and partly mafia-type economic system"[2] instead of cherishing the illusions about perfect competition and open economy.

The refusal to accept the post-Soviet reality can be explained in different manners. Western advisors played during the 1990s an active role in blueprinting the programs of reforms for Russia as well as for most other former socialist countries. These programs have been based on the know-how accumulated in the West; they reflected an ideal type of the western political and economic systems. According to B. Badie's term, reforms in post-Soviet countries have got many features of the importation of western models. The act of importation is the "transfer to a given society of a model or a political, economic and social practice invented in the other historical context; this model or practice derives from a completely different social order"[3]. The longer the distance between the current and the original institutional contexts, the more there are chances that the importation will lead to unexpected results. A model, that has proved its efficiency in one society, can create a dis-

---
[1] J. Stiglitz, *Globalization and Its Discontents*, New York: W. W. Norton, 2002; W. Andreff, *La mutation des economies postsocialistes. Une analyse économique alternative*, Paris: L'Harmattan, 2003,
[2] *Ibid.*, p. 348.
[3] B. Badie, *L'Etat importé. Essai sur l'occidentalisation de l'ordre politique*, Paris: Fayard, 1992, p. 126.

order in the other society[4]. The institutions promoting the exportation of western models (like the IMF or the World Bank) and their advisors are partly responsible for not taking seriously into consideration the limits and the possible perverse effects of such transfers.

Another explanation of the prolonged silence in respect of post-Soviet transformations consists in economic considerations. Russia is one of the largest producers of oil and gas in the world, and the leading industrialized countries, especially its neighbor the European Union, must take this fact into consideration while evaluating the current situation in this country. The price of telling the truth might be too high: the exclusion from taking opportunities on the emerged market, whatever corrupted and imperfect it is.

The next consideration concerns methodological issues. One can wonder whether the analytical tools available to western scholars fit well the problems observed in post-Soviet countries. The history of social sciences in Russia has been characterized by a long debate between the two camps: the «westernizers», those who believe in applicability of western theories in the Russian context, and the "slavophiles" (or the "romanticists" called by analogy with the romantic school in Germany) arguing that western theories are of no help in understanding the Russian history[5]. The controversy between the advocates of the two camps is still going on. The "romanticists" argue that the Russian culture have a number of particular features which makes standard western theories irrelevant. For example, they emphasize that the assumption of the utility maximization does not correctly depict the sense of economic activity in the Russian culture. In Russian, the "*khozaistvo*" (a special term for business) "includes not only a business side, i.e. the search for profit; it has a social, public dimension as well. The economic activity has to satisfy public demands and social needs"[6]. Consequently, according to the "romanticists", the model of rational choice tells us very little about the Russian economy.

---

[4] *Ibid.*; A. Oleinik, "The Costs and Prospects of Reforms in Russia: An Institutional Approach", *Theme* (University of Niš, Serbia), vol. 26, no. 4, 2002 (http://facta.junis.ni.ac.yu/teme/teme4-2002/teme4-2002-01.pdf).

[5] See, for example, J. Zweinert, "Shared Mental Models, Catch-up Development and Economic Policy-Making", unpublished manuscript, Hamburg: Institute of Economic Systems, Economic History and the History of Economic Thought, 2004.

[6] M. Voeykov, "Eurasian 'Theory of Economy Management' as an Organic Part of the Russian Economic School", *Voprosy ekonomiki*, no. 12, p. 103 (in Russian).

The opposition between universalistic and particularistic points of view prevents social scientists from speaking about the particular problems of post-Soviet transformations in a language comprehensible for both Russians and Westerners. There exist two extreme cases: either one applies a standard model and, consequently, misses particular aspects in understanding the current situation, or the researcher puts a too heavy emphasis on particular features and, as a result, his or her voice is not heard by fellow colleagues in the West. The last case occurs even if the researcher speaks English or another western language: it is necessary but yet insufficient condition for being heard and correctly understood. Without finding a compromise between universalistic and particularistic models (formulated in whatever language) the correct comprehension of the problems arising in the post-Soviet Russia seems to be very problematic indeed.

One of the possible ways for searching the compromise implies that one perceives the particularities of the Russian (or any other) culture through the lens of the institutional analysis. Culture is then thought as a particular configuration of the institutions, both formal and informal, that can be found everywhere. The list of such omnipresent institutions includes family, the State, trust in different forms (generalized, personalized and institutional), authority relationships (including property rights as power over material objects), contracts, and so on.

Two approaches within the institutional theory should be particularly emphasized. The first is called "old institutional economics". All models and categories of the old institutional economics derive from the process of grounded theorizing, i.e. they are empirically constructed. "Direct application of the grounded theory methodology to economic realities produces context embedded theories"[7]. Otherwise stated, the old institutionalism allows rewording the arguments of the "romanticists" in the terms of the institutional analysis. The second approach, the new institutional economics[8] lies more

---

[7] Ye. Vladimir, "On Pragmatic Institutional Economics", paper presented at a conference of the European Association for Evolutionary Political Economy, Maastricht, November 2003; see also Ye. Vladimir, *Economie institutionnelle des transformations agraires en Russie*, Paris: L'Harmattan, 2003, pp.18-30.

[8] For an overview, see Th. Eggertsson Thráinn, *Economic Behavior and Institutions*, Cambridge: Cambridge University Press, 1990.

closely to the universalistic way of thinking. With the help of the new institutionalism the "westernizers" give an institutional meaning to their ideas.

Once the common language is found, there is a need for fining a solution of the following problem: how to put universal institutional categories (family, the State, and others) into a particular, country-specific context? The methodology of "descending" from the abstract (universal models) to the concrete (particular phenomena), that has been developed in the Marxist philosophy, seems very promising in this respect[9]. The researcher takes a general category or model and then puts it in a context. To fit well the new context, the category needs modifying. For example, instead of studying the role of trust in structuring everyday interactions in general, one can compare a particular configuration of the trust in the different forms in Russia with that in a western country.

Let us consider a particular configuration of the universal institutions called "small" society[10]. It fits well the case of post-Soviet transformations and, more surprisingly, the situation in some spheres of everyday life in the West. In what follows we will briefly discuss the notion of "small" society (Part 1). Then it will be shown how the «small» society produces the phenomenon of *"dedovshchina"* (Part 2). Finally, we will discuss empirical evidence from Russia and other countries. Everywhere where the "small" society exists, it gives rise to *dedovshchina*: in Russian army, in prison, even in western universities (Part 3).

1. "Small" society as an institutional construction

Constructing an ideal type of society that is characterized by the lack of differentiation of spheres, the personalization of relations, the imperfect mastery of violence, the duality of norms and the domination of imposed authority serves to qualify the situation in which the "small" society is found as a result of incomplete modernization. In other words, the transformation of the "small" society, which is both localized and personalized, into a "large" society, has

---

[9] A. Oleinik, "A 'Small' Society: Theoretical Framework and Empirical Evidence", *Universe of Russia*, vol. 13, no. 1, 2004 (in Russian).

[10] A. Oleinik, *Organized Crime, Prison and Post-Soviet Societies*, Aldershot: Ashgate, 2003, with a foreword by Alain Touraine.

not been completed. This observation bears no value judgement; it merely reflects a particular structural and functional organization of society. As a result, we need to avoid using adjectives such as primitive or less civilized to describe it.

Non differentiation of spheres
The structural definition of modernization implies the transformation of the simple society, without means for separating the various spheres of daily activity, into a complex society, including several normative sub-systems. Each sub-system has a degree of autonomy that is not negligible with respect to the others, and interference is reduced to nothing within the framework of the ideal type of modernization. "The functional differentiation of sub-systems, particularly the separation of politics and religion or economics and politics, the formation of a universe devoted to science, art, private life, are all conditions of modernization"[11]. The theory of conventions speaks of the following spheres of activity (*les cités*): merchant, industrial, civic, domestic, opinion, inspiration. The ecological city and the city by projects were added to this list more recently[12]. In a similar manner, M. Walzer constructs seven spheres of justice (each of them has its own criteria of justice and "rules of the game"): money, kinship and love, political power, security and welfare, office, recognition, divine grace and education[13].

Personalized relationships
One of the aspects of the interpenetration of fields of activity lies in the fact that the choice of a partner during the course of social interaction is not free. This choice depends on the membership of the potential partner in a chain of personal relationships. All interactions take place within this chain and it is not possible to have one partner for commercial activity, another for civic activity and so on. The need to have a personal knowledge in order to organize any social activity makes each member in a local community the universal part-

---

[11] A. Touraine, *Critique de la modernité*, Paris: Fayard, 1992, p. 237.
[12] L. Boltanski, L. Thévenot, *De la justification. Les économies de la grandeur*, Paris: Gallimard, 1991; L. Boltanski, E. Chiapello, *Le nouvel esprit du capitalisme*, Paris: Gallimard, 1999.
[13] M. Walzer, *Spheres of Justice. A Defense of Pluralism and Equality*, Oxford: Martin Robertson, 1983.

ner. As a result, the local community, regardless of its form - family, traditional community, friendships, "friends of friends", the Mafia - closes in on itself. The family represents the ideal type of personalized relationships that are closed with respect to the outside world. The analysis of the domestic city described by the advocates of the theory of conventions illustrates the manner in which a "large" society is built without taking leave of the "small" society. In the domestic city, all social relations reproduce domestic relations. In this case, "the greatness of individuals depends on their hierarchical position in a chain of personal dependencies"[14].

The domestic order allows for relationships of a different nature (merchant, civic, industrial, etc.) as long as they fit in with the logic of personalized relationships. Let us take a close look at the construction of merchant relationships within the domestic city. There are several examples of this anchoring in societies that are in the process of modernizing as well as in certain segments of modernized societies. An American anthropologist, Jane Ensminger, studied how the Orma, an African tribe, organized economic activity. It appeared that "The Orma still place an exceedingly high premium on having at least one close relative of the family in the cattle camp", making it easier to control the conditions for handling herds and reducing the opportunism of shepherds[15]. Also, the development of commerce in the regions in which the trader has no family or relatives often involves the marriage of his daughter with someone residing in the region in question. Domestic rooting also serves as a trade device in certain Latin-American countries where "the 'extended family' has been transformed into a network of commercial or productive relationships"[16]. As in the case of the Orma, domestic anchoring helps to reduce transaction costs within a local community. In particular, the involvement of relatives in commercial activities reduces the costs incurred by the businessman to control and prevent the opportunistic behaviour of his agents. Personal dependence transforms into a guarantee that the contract will be fulfilled[17]. This same logic accounts for the willingness of bankers,

---

[14] Boltanski, Thévenot, 1991, op.cit., p. 116.
[15] J. Ensminger, Making a Market. The Institutional Transformation of an African Society, Cambridge: Cambridge University Press, 1992, p. 116.
[16] H. de Soto, L'autre sentier. La révolution informelle dans le tiers monde, Paris: La Découverte, 1994, p. 13.
[17] Ibid., p. 131.

diamond brokers and stock brokers to form relatively closed societies that support them in their commercial activities. The New York Stock Exchange, the London bankers, the international network of diamond merchants can all be considered as examples of business that is built on the basis of personalized relationships[18].

Imperfect control of violence

The third marker on the path to modernization concerns the manner in which violence is controlled on a daily basis. There are several ways in which to manage the conflicts that arise in daily life. Institutionalized violence, which implies a State monopoly of violence, is only one method among others. Moreover, institutionalized violence is the only means for managing conflicts that is accepted in a modernized society. In order to provide a brief overview of the entire range of means, we will refer to an anthropological study made by René Girard. He looked at the steps involved in controlling violence that preceded the institutionalization of violence. According to Girard, the first step involves the search for a replacement victim. "Unappeased violence strives and always manages to find a spare victim. In place of the creature that excited its fury, it will suddenly substitute another that has no specific reason for attracting the lightning of violence, other than the fact that it is both vulnerable and within reach"[19].

It should be noted that, as a general rule, the replacement victim does not belong to the local community within which the violence was born. It is individuals from outside the domestic world who are transformed into the targets of violent acts - strangers as well as the King - if their actions do not fit in with the logic of the other members of the community. As the border between the "small" and the "large" societies starts to erode, the nature of violence changes. If there is no longer any difference between those who are in and those who are out (crisis of differences), such differences must be recreated through the mythic development of a scapegoat victim. "In place of widespread reciprocal violence, myth substitutes the formidable transgression of a

---

[18] J. Coleman, *Foundations of Social Theory*, Cambridge, MA: The Belknap Press of Harvard University Press, 1990, pp. 109-110.
[19] R. Girard, *La violence et le sacré*, Paris: Bernard Grasset, 1972, p. 15.

unique individual"[20]. According to Girard, the Oedipus myth can be explained by the logic of creating a scapegoat victim rather than through psychoanalytical reasoning. The third step that precedes the institutionalization of violence supposes the construction of a victim that can be sacrifice. Unlike the scapegoat victim, whose strangeness was artificially constructed, the sacrificial victim is not found either inside or outside the community. The sacrificial victim takes the form of monstrous doubles that are potentially incarnate in each member of the "small" society. "The [monstrous] doubles provide, between difference and identity, the equivocal median that is essential for sacrificial substitution, for the polarization of violence focussed on a unique victim"[21]. The community no longer needs to search for an external enemy or expel "scapegoats" in order to channel violence, they simply need to progressively unveil the doubles hidden behind the appearances of people who are personally well-known.

Duality of norms

The opposite behaviour, on the one hand, with respect to the members of the community who really are in and with those, on the other hand, who are others, strangers who are really out, raises the idea of the duality of standards as criteria that encompass incomplete modernization. This duality of standards goes against the movement modernization and the major consequence of modernization is to erase the differences between individuals belonging to various communities. "A certain dynamism draws first the West and then all of humanity towards a state of relative lack of differentiation never encountered previously"[22]. In other words, the degree of the duality of norms can serve to measure the progress made by a given society towards modernization. The greater the duality, the greater the distance from modernization and vice versa. The idea of degree is important to us since it helps to avoid simplistic, black and white judgements as to the nature of the society in question. Instead of qualifying a society as modern or not modern, it would be preferable to evaluate the degree of its proximity to the ideal type of modern society.

---

[20] *Ibid.*, p. 115.
[21] *Ibid.*, p. 224.
[22] *Ibid.*, p. 261.

We would like to stress the fact that the situation of dependence, the imposition of norms on a society, creates conditions that are particularly favourable to the duality of norms. The norms imposed are associated with an external enemy that provokes hostility, hate, violence whereas the native norms are associated with the community itself and promote voluntary submission, solidarity and non-violence. "This is especially clear in the case of Goffman's 'total institutions'. These organizations manifest the principle of in-group solidarity and out-group hostility [as a consequence of generated ambivalence]"[23]. As the dependence becomes increasingly obvious, the norms are increasingly dual in nature.

When speaking about the duality of norms, there is no term that is unequivocally imposed. The list of alternatives includes such couples of terms as us/them, actor/adversary, friend/enemy, insider/outsider. The constitutive principle of the Mafia, the opposition of "one's own people" to all the others merits being discussed in more details. The Mafia fits in with the logic of the network, with the exception of its openness to the outside world. The Mafia structure, as a symbiosis of the clan, a traditional structure, and the network found in modern society, highlights the elements that constitute the ideal type of a «small» society valid for our study: the non-differentiation of fields of activity, personalized relationships, non-institutionalized violence and the duality of norms. In practice, each operating principle of the Mafia has a double nature: traditional and modern at the same time. For example, relationships of friendship are given a new meaning in the Mafia organization. "The friendship of the Mafioso is virtually deprived of the qualities usually associated with that term. It places a veil over what was simply a prosaic exchange"[24]. It is not possible to either reduce the Mafia to the traditional society or associate it with modernization since it provides us with an image of incomplete modernization. Therefore, the qualification of Mafia proposed by Pino Arlacchi appears to be the most pertinent to us: it is "strange mixture of the traditional and the modern"[25].

---

[23] N. Smeilser, "The Rational and the Ambivalent in the Social Sciences", *American Sociological Review*, vol. 63, no. 1, February 1998, pp. 8-9.

[24] D. Gambetta, *The Sicilian Mafia. The Business of Private Protection*, Cambridge, MA: Harvard University Press, 1993, p. 201.

[25] P. Arlacchi, *Mafia et compagnies. L'éthique mafiosa et l'esprit du capitalisme*, Grenoble: Presses Universitaires de Grenoble, 1986, p. 225.

In order to reduce the cultural connotations of the Mafia for the time being, we will attempt to expose its structure using the grammar of the institutional economics. From this point of view, the mafia organization presupposes an amalgamation between the domestic city and the city by projects. On the one hand, it is a world marked by a profound division between the interior and the exterior. "Composed of a series of personal dependencies, the world is ordered by the opposition of the interior and the exterior between which passages are either arranged or closed"[26]. On the other hand, personalized relationships are mobilized to attain a goal, a project chosen to bypass a traditional constraint. Mobilisation by projects is positioned in the heart of the city by projects. "The project temporarily brings very disparate individuals together and is presented as a very active segment of the network for a relatively short period of time, enabling the individuals to develop more lasting relationships that are then put on hold while remaining available"[27]. In both cases, relationships are founded on a personal knowledge. In both cases, social interactions take place primarily within the chain of personal acquaintances. The only pertinent difference concerns the dynamic aspect of the personalized relationships. In the first case, the relationships are established in advance and not likely to change over time; in the second, they are "elective" and likely to take on a new structure as often as necessary in order to attain an objective. The relative homology of these two cities lead Luc Boltanski and Eve Chiapello to develop "the hypothesis of a substitution or rather an absorption of the domestic logic by the connectionist logic" in order to trace the main lines of the evolution of western societies[28]. As for the "small" society, we would prefer to speak of an amalgamation of two cities: neither domestic logic nor logic «by projects» enjoys absolute domination over the other. Furthermore, there is no compromise, no reconciliation of the two logics: each action excludes neither the domestic interpretation nor its interpretation "by projects".

Imposed authority
There is a misleading similarity between the "small" society and the traditional society. The last one is usually described with the help of very similar terms:

---
[26] Boltanski, Thévenot, 1991, *op. cit.*, p. 218.
[27] *Ibid.*, p. 157.
[28] *Ibid.*, p. 205.

little, small, local, and so on. For example, the little community of the Mexican village Chan Kom has four distinctive qualities: distinctiveness (where the community begins and where it ends is apparent), smallness, homogeneousness and self-sufficiency[29]. However, traditional societies exist without any reference to the State. Even if the State's institutions like a school function within the traditional society, they play a marginal role. A theory of the traditional society can be developed without any special emphasis on the relations with the State and its representatives. By contrast, the study of the «small» society necessitates comprehension of the nature of authority relationships, both formal and informal. The "small" society derives from a particular type of the formal authority, i.e. the imposed authority.

In keeping with the usual definition, the authority of an individual (or an institution) over others translates into the possession of the right to control their actions. The concept of authority does not inevitably evoke the imposition of the will or the arbitrary power of the holder. Authority has a voluntary character "only if the individual holds the right of control over a particular class of his own actions and holds the right to transfer that right to another"[30]. In other words, the individual voluntarily submits to the authority as long as he is not able to fulfil his interests better by maintaining control of that authority and as long as the scope of the authority is limited. James Coleman refers to this type of authority as conjoined, as opposed to disjoined for which the sole purpose is the compensation that the individual receives for transferring the right to control his actions[31]. To this latter, we can add the authority that is imposed through coercion that denies the individual compensation. Imposed authority does not necessarily appear illegitimate. However, its legitimacy may be based on grounds other than rational considerations.

---

[29] R. Redfield, *The Little Community. Viewpoints for the Study of a Human Whole*, Uppsala and Stockholm: Almqvist & Wicksells Boktryckeri AB, 1955, p. 4.
[30] Coleman, 1990, *op. cit.*, pp. 69-70.
[31] *Ibid.*, p. 72.

2. *Dedovshchina* as a by-product of the "small" society

Let us turn now to the phenomenon of *dedovshchina* and its assumed connection with the "small" society. According to our hypothesis, the institutional structure of the "small" society creates favorable conditions for social practices called by the Russian term non translatable into Western languages, *dedovshchina*. *Dedovshchina* consists in harassing young soldiers by the elders. Military service in Russia takes two years (in the Navy - three years). This two-year term is divided in four six-month periods. A soldier who just starts his military service (during first six months) is called "spirit" (*dukh*), or "young" (*molodoi*). The reference to a ghost is not accidental: the beginners have the minimal rights in a military city; they must simply obey to all others. The hardest and the least pleasant work (like cleaning public toilets) are in reserve for them. An initiation rite marks the passage from the lowest rank to the next, the status of "pheasant" (*fasan, sekach*). It usually consists in an act of symbolic and/or physical violence (like beating the rear as much times as the number of months that the soldier has spent in the army). Like the "spirits", the "pheasants" hardly have any rights; however they must fulfill many obligations. The principal one concerns learning obedience. The next informal rank, that of "*salabon*", or «scoop» (*cherpak*), for the first time gives an opportunity to direct youngest soldiers. The terminal rank, the status of "old" (*starik*), or "grandfather" (*ded*) allows the soldier to enjoy full rights in the military city. All others are compelled to respect and even serve them. The "olds" have disproportionately more rights than obligations. They are free to do virtually everything what they want.

First argument for looking at the military in Russian society from a perspective of the "small" society consists in a very particular type of authority relationships. The army lies very close to E. Goffman's ideal type of total institution. "A total institution - a link between residence and work, where a large number of individuals, placed in the same situation, cut off from the outside world for a relatively lengthy period of time, lead a cloistered life, for which the terms are explicitly and painstakingly regulated"[32]. The last part of the sentence merits being particularly emphasized. The formal authority tends to

---

[32] E. Goffman, *Asiles. Etudes sur la condition sociale des maladies mentaux et autres reclus*, Paris: Ed. de Minuit, 1968, p. 41.

regulate all aspects of everyday life, despite the eventual resistance from the part of rank-an-file members. The army teaches to obey even if the individual does not see any rational reason for the transfer of rights to control his actions: sanctions against non obedient behavior might be very severe and sometimes even humiliating.

Compulsory character of the military service in Russia allows finding additional arguments about the imposed nature of authority. The projects of substituting the voluntary service for the compulsory service, actively debated in the end of the 1990s[33], have recently been abandoned. The idea that every young man, including students at the universities, must get military experience becomes dominating in the political discourse. Probably the underlying argument is that the individual must learn obedience in everyday life (i.e. in the army) before accepting obedience as a key feature of the political system. Otherwise stated, the logic of a democratic system based on everyday democratic practices appears reversed: "the common individual must have experience of democratic self-government in his everyday life if he is to learn to participate meaningfully in the democratic governance of civil society"[34].

The army, like any other total institutions, excludes differentiation of the spheres of everyday life. The omnipresent control is one of the facets of this non differentiation: the superior has a legitimate right to control every aspect of the everyday life of his subordinates, by day and at night. Instead of a plurality of rules of the game, there is only one coordination mechanism, - through fiats[35]. The other aspect of non differentiation of the spheres of everyday life concerns the conditions of permanent co-presence: life in casernes and the exercises promoting team-spirit erase the border between the privacy and the public life. Soldiers live and do exercises together; they have no

---

[33] 84% of Russians were in favor of the professional army in 2001. See L. Gudkov, "Mass Identity and Institutional Violence". Article Two. "Particularism and the 'Enemy' factor: the Army and the Post-Soviet Russia", p. 44, *The Russian Public Opinion Herald*: Data, Analysis, Discussions, no. 2 (68), 2003, pp. 35-51 (in Russian) p. 49.

[34] L. Putterman, "The Firm as Association versus the Firm as Commodity. Efficiency, Rights and Ownership", *Economics and Philosophy*, vol. 4, no. 2, 1988, p. 260.

[35] For a brief overview of bureaucratic coordination, see J. Kornai, *The Socialist System. The Political Economy of Communism*, Princeton, NJ: Princeton University Press, 1992.

chance of getting separate partners for professional activities, leisure, intimate connections and so on.

The mixture of norms resulting from, on the one hand, the compulsory submission to the formal authority, and, on the other hand, non differentiation of the rules of the game corresponding to different spheres of everyday life varies from one local context to another. Its parameters depend on the particular persons, officers, sergeants and soldiers, involved in interactions. There are no universal and context-free norms structuring everyday life in the army. For example, the system of informal grades (ghosts, pheasants, grandfathers and others) is not the same in different regions and forces, the ranks and the initiation rites can take various forms. This fact confirms the thesis about the importance of personalized relationships in the military city. The lack of common normative frameworks becomes especially evident when one compares the Russian army with the other total institution, the post-Soviet prison. The people, who got experience of life in both total institutions, argue that informal norms in the army, if they do exist at all, are more contextual and personalized. A young man convicted of a crime shortly after his military service in the elite paratroops witnesses: "Everything is based on physical force. I was at Kursk, Briansk, Tver. It's easier to live here [in prison, - A.O.]. There, there was *dedovshchina*... Pure physical force, humiliation... physical and moral pressure"[36].

Localized and personified relationships within the "small" society produce violence on everyday basis. Due to the lack of clear borders between different spheres of everyday life, conflicts arisen in one of them spread quickly to all the others. A quarrel among two mates damages their co-operation required in the course of exercises and, vice versa, a professional conflict inevitably acquires a personal dimension[37].[38] It is important to note that the imposed character of authority relationships makes undesirable and even impossible the resolution of everyday conflicts through addressing to the

---

[36] Quoted in Oleinik, 2003, *op. cit.*, p. 104.
[37] Andreff, 2003, *op. cit.*, p. 348.
[38] This problem exists as long as the army remains the total institution. A solution found and applied in the Antique Greece can be emphasized: promotion of emotional, affective and even sexual bounds between soldiers was seen as a guarantee against spreading personal conflicts to the battlefield (see M. Foucault, *Histoire de la sexualité*, Paris: Gallimard, 1984).

superior. Whatever are the intentions of officers and other members of the formal hierarchy, the institutionalization of violence progresses very slowly in the context of the imposed authority.

In the "small" society control of violence implies other mechanisms than its institutionalization. In R. Girard's terms, the military city produces replacement victims: negative emotions and violence are channeled toward first-year soldiers (the "spirits" and the "pheasants") holding the lowest ranks in the informal hierarchy. Violence generated in everyday conflicts makes its path toward young soldiers: in the quality of replacement victims, they play an important role in ensuring a relative stability of the military city. The "roosters", these pariahs of the prisoners' community, perform a very similar role of "lighting-rod" for the violence generated in prison on a daily basis[39]. The only difference consists in the fact that the "roosters" have no chance of changing their status: they were converted by force into passive homosexuals for major crimes against the prisoners' community, whereas first-year soldiers can hope to get a more respectable and safe rank. However, their promotion does not automatically depend on the length of the military service. The respect of the dual norms counts much more: one must agree that he, as a first-year soldier, has no rights but manifold duties, although his older fellows enjoy full rights without being bounded by any obligation.

Taking into consideration the functional role of *dedovshchina*, the fight against it has a very small chance of success without reforming the institutional organization of the army as a whole. As long as the "small" society continues to exist in the armed forced, the practices of *dedovshchina* will remain one of its inner vices.

3. Phenomena similar to *dedovshchina* in other contexts

The "small" society gives rise to the phenomena similar to *dedovshchina* not only in the army, but everywhere. One can postulate the following heuristic regularity: the more similar an institutional context to the "small" society, the higher the probability that there exist practices of harassment comparable

---

[39] Oleinik, 2003, *op. cit.*, pp. 96-101.

with *dedovshchina*. Generally speaking, these practices of social harassment have in common several elements: sharp discrimination of newcomers and outsiders (*dedovshchina* itself implies age discrimination); channeling violence towards newcomers and outsiders; initiation through transforming the newcomer into an object of violence.

According to Iuri Levada and his fellow colleagues from the VTsIOM, the army has become one the basic mechanisms of socialization during the Soviet rule. At that time the absolute majority (45-60%) of young Russians passed through casernes. There young men get accustomed to the rules of the "small" society that they start to reproduce once the military service has finished. For young men, "*dedovshchina* is a system for re-socializing, transforming the individual. [...] The soldier, who has finished his military service, leaves the caserne with a double moral [one, universal, was learned at school, the second, 'virile', in the army, - A.O]. Physical violence and a hierarchical perception of the society are mixed up with the institutionalized violence of the army"[40]. Due to the fact that girls are usually socialized by the young men that accomplished military service, *dedovshchina*, as Levada claims, became for the Soviets a kind of initiation rite. Thanks to *dedovshchina*, they learned the principle of "unconditional submission to an eldest person"[41]. More recent studies show that the post-Soviet army continues to be the major institute of socialization. "The army and the police remain central institutions symbolically representing the terminal values of the 'collective whole' and the priority of common interests over private ones"[42].

The explanatory model developed by Levada and his fellow colleagues has been criticized for reducing all problems of the "small" society in the (post-)Soviet Russia only to *dedovshchina*, i.e. socialization through the army[43]. However, it helps to shed light on two very important aspects: first, the congruency, or the "selective affinity", between the military city and the Russian society; second, the construction of an enemy as a result of the *dedovshchina*-type socialization. As far as the first aspect is concerned, the "selective affinity" can be explained by supposing that both societies, the military

---

[40] You. Levada, *Entre passé et l'avenir. L'homme soviétique ordinaire*. Enquête, Paris: Presses de la Fondation Nationale des Sciences Politiques, 1993, pp. 144, 146.
[41] *Ibid.*, p. 144
[42] Gudkov, 2003, *op. cit.*, pp. 35-51.
[43] Oleinik, 2003, *op. cit.*, pp. 28-32.

city and the post-Soviet Russia, lie more or less closely to the ideal type of the "small" society. *Dedovshchina* constitutes a "natural" link between these societies because imposed authority, non differentiation of spheres, personalized relationships, imperfect control of violence and duality of norms exist in both of them, although in a varying degree.

Who are the homologues of the newcomers and the olds in the framework of the post-Soviet Russia? Violence generated on an everyday basis is channeled towards strangers (newcomers in the Russian culture) who transforms into enemies. Russia has a long history of constructing enemies in the popular mentality, i.e. searching for replacement victims and victims that can be sacrificed. Now Chechens in particular and the natives of Caucasus in general take the place of the "internal" enemies[44]. It seems that Chechens have much less rights than the "native" Russians even from an official point of view: at least, the selective checks of papers performed by the police (only the people who look like Chechens, the natives of Caucasus or Asiatics are checked) became a common practice. As far as the "external" enemies are concerned, the public hostility to the NATO (40% of Russians think that the recent enlargement of this organization represents a credible threat for Russia[45]) proves that such category has not disappeared from the Russian mentality.

In order to verify whether the model of the "small" society can pass the test of universality, we need to apply it to some similar to *dedovshchina* phenomena that exist in the western context. In his analysis of the ambulance service at a hospital located in the Southern France, Jean Peneff argues that there is a "relative exploitation of the beginners (interns); the hospital and the medical staff as a whole profit from delegating the least prestigious tasks to the neophytes"[46]. Some elements of the "small" society are easily recognizable in the everyday life of the hospital described on the basis of a participant observation. For example, the privacy can be hardly respected in the hospital, this concerns not only the patients[47], but the medical staff too[48]. The profes-

---

[44] *Ibid.*, pp. 185-187.
[45] See Gudkov, 2003, *op. cit.*, p. 49.
[46] J. Peneff, *L'Hôpital en urgence. Etude par observation participante*, Paris: Métailié, 1992, p. 156.
[47] As E. Goffman mentioned it in the above quoted study.
[48] *Ibid.*, p. 77.

sional efficiency in a non negligible degree depends on the personalized relationships maintained within a team. There is an "obligation to cultivate intensive interpersonal relationships within a team because its members spent a great deal of time together"[49]. One can wonder whether the type of authority relationships structuring the everyday life in hospital lies close to the imposed authority. Due to the asymmetry of information, the physician sometimes acquire power over the patient (i.e. he or she loses the right to revoke the authority once voluntary transferred to the physician). However, the disjoint or even conjoint authority usually structures the relationships between the physicians. So, the "selective affinity" between hospital and the "small" society is far from being perfect, consequently, the local analog of "*dedovshchina*" (at least in the form observed by J. Peneff) seems much less violent and oriented to learning obedience.

The same considerations can be applied to the case of the French *bizutage* or the American ragging (the jokes addressed to the newcomers at the school and the series of initiation rites through which the newcomers receive citizenship in the city). Non differentiation of spheres and personalized relationships do exist at school. Nevertheless, the issue of the authority relationships at school merits being predominantly discussed. According to the advocates of the critical sociology, school has always been a place of symbolic violence. Symbolic violence means substitution of more subtle methods of imposition for brutal and explicit methods[50]. The teacher has in this context power over the pupil, i.e. the imposed, although in a subtle manner, authority structures the relationships between them. School, like the army, teaches obedience. The imposed authority as a centerpiece of the «small» society produces *dedovshchina* in a form adapted to the context of school. It should be noted that the organization of science in schools of thought give rise to the elements of the imposed authority too. Consequently, violence in the university and academic milieu (sometimes it takes the most explicit forms) can be interpreted as a by-product of the "small" scientific society[51]. It is the price to

---

[49] *Ibid.*, p. 105.
[50] P. Bourdieu, J.-C. Passeron, *La reproduction. Eléments pour une théorie du système d'enseignement*, Paris: Ed. de Minuit, 1970.
[51] A.Oleinik, "Banished to Solitary Confinement in a Tower...? On the Institutional Organization of Science", *Social Sciences*, vol. 34, no. 3, 2003, pp. 44-51 (Russian journal printed in English).

pay for incapacity of scientists to modernize their milieu, to transform the "small" society into a modern one.

Probably here one should find an explanation of the prolonged silence in respect of the post-Soviet transformations mentioned in the Introduction. The "smaller" the scientific community, both in the West and in Russia, the less chances of getting a critical assessment of post-Soviet transformations we have. So, the only way to go out of this situation consists in modernizing science as a source of the advices related to policy-making and, after this, in modernizing the post-Soviet Russia. Such reforms will lead to the disappearance of *dedovshchina*, whatever form it takes.

4 Going Back to the Problem[1]

Kirill PODRABINEK

In 1976 I was back home after doing a two-year compulsory military service. All I saw and experienced in the Soviet Armed forces wouldn't fit into a normal civilized narration pattern. Whenever I thought of what I had been through there, I started seething with rage and nearly lost self-control. Actually, I had never been enthusiastic about Soviet government, but the military service just added fuel to my anti-Soviet sentiment... When I realized that I would never know rest until I wrote a story about military hazing, I produced a feature story I called "The Poor Devils", which was published by the *"Samizdat*[2]*"* underground publishers in 1977. It was that same year that I found myself behind bars. Later on my story was read out in "The Voice of America" and other "voices", broadcasting from beyond the "Iron Curtain", found its ways into foreign magazines and *"Poisk"*, (The Searches), a legal *Samizdat* edition of the *perestroika* period. Actually, my feature story was the first to raise the problem of military hazing in the Soviet Union. All I did was to describe the phenomenon, not even discover it... Millions of people had been through the humiliation and violence of the Soviet Army barracks, millions of young men tormented and maimed, so many just killed or brought to suicide. But he who publicly raised the issue was to be ready to serve a term.

In 2003 I was over 50 and taken off the books as a reservist. The country that made me take the oath as a young man is no more. Neither the USSR, nor the Soviet Communist Party exists any longer. Today we are said to be living under a different political regime, in a multi-party democracy. Today Russia is said to have been following a path of civilized development. But

---

[1] Translated from the Russian by Eugene B. Prytov. This article was first published in Russian in the Moscow journal *Index* (chief editor: Naum Nim), no. 19, 2003, available at http://index.org.ru/ under the title "Vozvrashchaias' k teme".

[2] *Samizdat* [Russian: *sam*, self + *izdatel'stvo*, publishing house, from *izdat'*, to publish]: the secret publication and distribution of government-banned literature in the former Soviet Union; the literature produced by this system [Editors' note].

is that so? Today Russian Presidents indeed hug their counterparts from civilized western nations when meeting them for talks. Russia is a member of the Council of Europe, where a member-nation is supposed to adhere to the ideals of humanism and democracy. Today in Russia we seem to be enjoying the freedom of speech, we can speak of or write anything we like (although, of course, having this piece of writing published in a newspaper or magazine is a totally different matter)... Let's cast a glance then at what newspapers and magazines write about military hazing in today's Russia. I've got to admit they do brief Russian society on the Army-related problems. But as a man who follows comment on this subject-matter, and who sometimes even offers his own comment on it, I am not quite content with the way the problem is dealt with in these publications. It is true that the stuff published features numerous instances of conscripts' humiliation and torturing. They are tortured, starved and killed by their own fellow-servicemen, - soldiers and officers. Periodicals depict hazing vividly and in every detail. In fact, the evil is so widespread that I myself know a person, the son of a friend of mine, who was sent back home just three months after the call-up. The beating he took was so savage that he became crippled for life. My other friend's son was killed in barracks. Several times I myself offered assistance to deserters who fled from army despotism. Everybody in Russia knows that military hazing is thriving in this country. Now and again the press and even TV channels come up with comments on hazing. But, strangely, answers to the two main questions have invariably been hushed up. Why does hazing exist at all? Who must be held responsible for it?

As for the reasons... Well, I suggest we shouldn't rashly plunge into the depth of time and ontology. Of course, humans are sinful and nothing human is alien to them. Of course, we have the damned legacy of Soviet government, as we had the legacy of Tsarist Russia ways before, and so on down the line into remote antiquity. But some former Soviet republics boast no military hazing whatsoever. And the people called up to serve in their armed forces also represent the same species of homo sapiens, if only in part. True, in terms of democracy the former Soviet Baltic republics are closer to the West than Russia. But is it democracy that the problem is about?

Actually Tsarist Russia was by no means a developed democracy. Alexander Kuprin[3] depicts scenes in his novel "Military Cadets" involving senior cadets attempting to boss around their junior mates. This prototype of hazing, brought to the military school by accident, was soon banished from there with the approval of all cadets. But if we leaf through a newspaper in today's Russia we invariably come across reports about hazing at the Suvorov and Nakhimov military cadet schools[4] in St. Petersburg! It is impossible not to draw comparisons. Alexander Kuprin points out in the same novel that it was shameful for an officer to overlook his soldiers' getting their feet frost-bitten in a drill or at a military parade. By tradition, privates and sergeants were warmly clad, while the officer who commanded them wore boots of thin shoe-leather. When I was in the army, in the Soviet Army that is, we, the ranks, were sent to a snow-covered steppe for a military exercise and almost froze to death there, while our commander got into a specially set-up booth every now and then, to warm up. The soldier in the Tsarist Russian Army was never hungry. Hungry ranks were a disgrace to their officers. By comparison, in this day and age we read about the underfed Russian soldiers on Russkii (or Russian) Island (a symbolical name, isn't it?). All right, let's assume that the commanders' brutal treatment of the ranks, deprived of civil rights, did or does exist in different armies. I can't think of hazing elsewhere but the Russian Army. Perhaps, historians will be able to help me out.

Let's take the Spartan Mora (or regiment)[5], or the Roman Legion during the Republic. These were known for strict discipline, with every serviceman being certain that he serves his Fatherland whether conquering other countries or defending his own one. Of course, Spartans did retreat on their commanders' orders. But those who shrank in the face of danger and fled the battlefield were dishonoured as civilians, - a severe punishment to both these men and a deep shame for their next of kin. The Roman Legions boasted a system of numerous spurs and penalties, the Legions that conquered half the world largely thanks to their unparalleled discipline. Could the armies, inspired with patriotic spirit and discipline-welded, cultivate hazing? It is ridicu-

---

[3] Alexander Kuprin is a Russian writer (1870-1938) [Editors' note].
[4] Military (Souvorov) and naval (Nakhimov) cadet schools for the Russian elite [Editors' note].
[5] The largest unit in the Spartan army was the *mora* [Editors' note].

lous to even ask the question. So, is it patriotic spirit and discipline that are needed to eradicate hazing? How about the Barbarians that attacked Rome and that, even if patriotically motivated, had a very vague idea of discipline? What historical source has made even if a casual mention of unmotivated and systematic violence that some ancient warriors would commit against others? Whether Gauls, Teutons or Parthians? ... Now let's take the case of foray-making nomads. Those had no patriotic spirit, but were firmly disciplined. Sometimes discipline was extremely strict, like in the Golden Horde tumens. A Mongol warrior was in for harsh punishment for breaking any of numerous rules, like a ban on urinating at the camping-ground or killing their horse the wrong way... He would have his back spine broken and be left to die. No chronicle has ever reported about hazing with the Tartar-Mongols. Now, let's take armies that had neither patriotic sentiment, nor discipline. For instance, lance knights or Cossacks, runaway serfs with their free for all. Obviously, it was often that they argued, fought and killed each other because of the loot or mischief-making... But even those people would not think of practising hazing.

Let us now move to a closer historical period when the forcibly recruited young men came to be confined to barracks. They certainly failed to get on, but can you think of Royal Prussian officers tolerating, encouraging or organizing hazing? Thereby incapacitating the Army and creating a threat to their status and eventually, perhaps, even life? No, Sir!

True, one can come across some hints at hazing in modern literature, for instance "The Adventures of Werner Holt"[6]. But these are occasional, rather than systematic outbursts of hazing. Hazing in the form of a general, commander-encouraged system of military "organization" is a purely domestic invention. An invention that is actually approved of by the authorities. For this is the only way to qualify the connivance at hazing by the President, the Executive, the Legislature and the Judiciary. It strikes the eye that in the armies that know of no hazing the servicemen are united around some core idea, whether patriotic sentiment, civic-mindedness, duty, honour, discipline, profit, the expectation of gain, whatever. Hence the conclusion: the Russian Army lacks such unifying factors. Of course, the Russian Army boasts decent offi-

---

6   Dieter Noll's novel [Editors' note].

cers, conscientious commanders, honest soldiers, people who defend self-respect and their mates' dignity. On their own initiative. But what would be the right word to describe an army that is generally struck by the leprosy of hazing? The most precise definition is certainly riff-raff. Now, how would you call a Government and society that choose to have this kind of army?

One can understand anything (not accept, but understand): whether organized coercion of a totalitarian system, a break-up of society, a period of trouble, war-time atrocities, man growing disastrously wild. But it's impossible to comprehend hazing. Possibly, hazing can be traced back to the biosocial background, it has signs of hierarchical coercion, typical of some animal and human communities (especially if these are forced to coexist within a limited area). Normally this kind of coercion is evolutionary in character and socially justified. Or, at least, is rationally motivated. Or it may be irrationally motivated but taken as rational by the subjects of coercion (one can see this at detention centres for juvenile delinquents). The hierarchical coercion as a biosocial phenomenon is known for validity, minimality and expediency. Provided, of course, there are some essential conditions. Animals have developed coercion in the course of their evolution to help their species survive. With them coercion is instinct-limited. Unmotivated excessive coercion is inexpedient since it leads to extinction. (The species that have failed to develop a system of instinctive restrictive reactions are doomed to dying out). A show of threat or a posture of submission are typical illustrations of the point. The better armed is the animal, the more formal and ritual is coercion. The more the situation prevents animals from going their way, the less the admissible degree of coercion, and vice versa. But this is true of natural conditions, of course. When at large, culvers will never peck one another to death, but if cooped up... If a wolf exposes his throat to its adversary, the latter gives up the attack instinctively. Before a fight, dogs normally growl and show their fangs. Reindeer clash with their horns, rather than thrust them into the adversary. With baboons a posture of submission has an immediate appeasing effect.

But things are more complicated with people. Our Stone Age forefather could hardly maim his fellow Neanderthal man. And small wonder, since their natural "armaments", as it were, were weak, each of the two could easily go his own way and, besides, their instincts restrained them from attacking each other.

But once people acquired higher nervous activity, they got a greater degree of behavioural freedom at the expense of their instincts. They used their mind effectively to invent weapons and the concomitant system of collective coercion, the army. People have, of course, created other coercion systems, like slavery or the system of state compulsion with the police and prison as its attributes. They partly made up for this kind of progress by transforming instincts into the defence mechanisms of traditions, morals, religion and culture. They likewise chose not to neglect other ways of social defence (attack), such as political institutions and the judicature. Of course, they could use weapons against predators, unwelcome arrivals or plunderers inside their own community. But they could likewise use their weapons to attack their tribesmen or the neighbouring communities. In short, weapons proved a powerful spur to developing the institution of government and the system of collective defence and attack. Unfortunately, the bowels of the earth are rich in metals, and the progress people made in manufacturing armaments was clearly more impressive than social progress (if we admit that it exists). The resourceful man would have created the H-Bomb, using but stone, wood and water. But this would have come about centuries later...

This is, of course, a simplified approach. Technological (scientific) and social progress both spur and hamper each other, growing retrogressive in their different aspects. In general, it is desirable that human evolution and history should be considered from different standpoints. The instinctive and conscious, the biological and social, the evolutionary and historic are both opposed to and complement each other through mutual enrichment and restriction, creating, in the process, a certain unity that's quite involved and is not just the sum total of the constituent parts. It is a totality of many, sometimes conflicting standpoints that can create a relatively true picture of the situation. But a simplified approach helps comprehend two important points. First, social organization helps society to survive, while simultaneously threatening this survival. Second, the determining factor in keeping this balance is the time that's required for social self-organization.

Sometimes military barracks are compared to a prison. Some people even claim that hazing is a replica of prison ways. This is wrong. Let me tell you responsibly that to serve a prison term is more comfortable. Especially if you know why you've been put behind bars. In prison one's treated harshly, but this is justified. It's taken the world community a long time to draw up the rules that convicts should go by to survive in the extreme conditions of starvation, cold, administration reprisals and the tyranny of jailers. It is the open hostility of the administration in the first place that makes the prison community establish and observe their convict code. This is the only way for the convicts to survive. Arbitrary rule, tyranny, even more so unmotivated collective violence are punishable in prison. If one obeys the convict code, one has nothing to fear. But, of course, one's got to be ready to defend oneself in individual conflicts. In prison all decent convicts have equal rights (and obligations, for that matter). But the "indecent" convicts are also entitled to some rights, and it is not allowed to treat them badly. True, there are numerous deviations, but it is not these that form the skeleton of the prison behavioural code. If the skeleton is insufficiently strong or too conservative, it may give way in the form of forced labour camp wars or the cropping-up of numerous "red" (administration-controlled) areas. I should emphasize two crucial points. First, the more seasoned are the convicts, the longer the term they serve, the better the convict code is observed. Things are at their worst with those who serve short terms or with juvenile delinquents. Second, the size of living space. In a camp it is easier to settle problems than at a prison, in a camp one is more likely to find some cold steel, like a sharpened bar of metal, which is a deterrent. If a group of convicts is transferred from a camp to a prison, they will kick up more and bigger rows for that reason alone. The habit to adhere to the convict morals leaves a mark on those who served prison terms. A hardened repeater is less dangerous to the man in the street than a sadist who's never been behind bars and will recognize no rules and regulations. Liberty and imprisonment are communicating vessels that exchange people, customs and culture. Although one should not, of course, idealize the world of convicts, one can certainly borrow some useful things from them.

What barracks resemble most is a press chamber, although the comparison is crude. With no organizing will of the administration the press chamber system will go to pieces like a house of cards. But hazing needs no commanders to thrive.

In the barracks one half of the contingent terrorizes the other one. This policy aims to intimidate conscripts, break their will, make them work for the soldiers in the second year of service, use the conscripts' food, clothing and money. But the brutality of terror forms and its scale are blown out of all proportion, in fact so much so that they make hardly any sense at all. The young draftees would have needed much less intimidation to be ready to do anything for the second-year servicemen, present them with whatever they have and stand humiliation. But conscripts can take a beating, or get crippled or even killed for no obvious reason, just because second-year servicemen fancied doing this. It is this unmotivated, excessive and inexpedient violence that makes hazing a unique phenomenon. The frequent rotation of the barracks contingent impedes rational self-organization. But then, the 18-year old school-leavers will hardly think of the need to get organized. When at liberty or in prison, they would form part of the community, while in the barracks they are a self-dependent isolated group that's compelled to make again the errors of animals and humans that once caused entire species and tribes to die out.

Actually, it's quite easy to generate hazing. Take a country that has only recently survived a period of unparalleled reprisals, the most savage that history knows of. Drive young, spiritually immature men into barracks, - actually children with no life experience, try to completely isolate them from the outside world, above all, from their nearest and dearest, their friends, the elevating influences of women, books and nature. Erase the realization of the importance of military service from their mind, so they would know for sure that honour, civic duty and the defence of Fatherland are but empty, hypocritical words. Bring it home to them that in a war they are cannon-fodder, while in the time of peace they are just free man power. Make their life maximally senseless so they would grow stupid from the nonsensical square-bashing, trench-digging from dawn to dusk, endless stool-levelling, bed corner-smoothing and beautifying themselves.

Burden them with the notorious hardships of military life: cold, heat, dirt, dampness, undernourishment and insufficient sleep. Make life in the barracks maximally uncomfortable, with the soldier having nowhere to warm himself and dry his clothing. Hand him a worn-out uniform, hastily-sewn boots, fill his dish with skilly. Better still, create a shortage of foodstuffs and outfit to add fuel to the flames of competition for every foot wrap and piece of bread. Let the officers adhere to the "Divide and Rule" principle, encourage violence, set the second-year servicemen against the draftees. Things would prove beyond perfection if the officers turned out to be malicious baboons who see the ranks as cattle. It is very important that the barracks should be taken out of any kind of control, whether state or public. Which is as easy as ABC in this state and this kind of society. So it's safe to elaborate on hazing on television, make interpellations, declare amnesties, call board meetings to discuss moves by the Directorate of Public Prosecutions. In this context hazing is impossible to extirpate, and the barracks as a communicating vessel will start pumping its ways through millions of demobilized servicemen over to Civvy Street. It must be high time we, too, started dying out.

And yet, there's some riddle behind all that. Why should one victimize so hard and senselessly their own folks? All right, they are young, but they're people; they could be even children, but they are human children. What great dissension between people, and within man proper, is it evidence of? So, who should be held responsible for hazing? Easy as a pie. One thing why the army is good is that you always know who is responsible for what. The Sergeant is answerable for his section, the platoon commander for his platoon with all the sections, the company commander - for his company with all the platoons and their sections, and so on down the line. The Supreme Commander-in-Chief, that's Russia's President, is responsible for the armed forces in general. What's still unclear is who and how is responsible for the President. But that, of course, is a different subject.

How can we get rid of hazing? It's pointless to look to the commanding officers, since they normally benefit from it. It's even more hopeless to look to the criminal justice system, which cares little, if anything, about human rights. If the justice system is determined to ignore torture at police stations, why should it care about torture at the barracks? There's likewise little hope that civil society with its control mechanisms will shape itself in the foreseeable future. The simplest solution is to switch over to a military service on a contractual basis, to switch over to a professional army. This type of army will, of course, boast hazing of its own. A newspaper reported recently about thriving hazing in an airborne regiment of contract soldiers. Two servicemen beat their fellow-soldier to death. Another indicative story is about Colonel Alexander Kozhendaiev, the garrison chief in the Chechen town Shali, who also commands the military unit 23132.

> On February 15th, 2003 Colonel Kozhendaiev got drunk and alleging that Senior Lieutenant of the military unit 98311 A. Mikakov boasted a sloppy outward appearance behaved dishonourably by first battering the latter and then humiliating him by ordering his subordinates to chain Mikakov to the porch of the unit headquarters' building and keeping him that way for five hours in full view of the garrison. Kozhendaiev continued to humiliate the Junior Officer by beating him up again at the duty officer's quarters later in the day and insulting him by using foul language. Then he ordered that Mikakov should be chained again and held this way until dawn... In keeping with the Government Amnesty Regulations we closed the Kozhendaiev criminal cas". [This is an excerpt from an interview that Military Justice Colonel S. Bugreiev granted to the "*Novaia Gazeta*" newspaper and that was carried in its issue n°67 of September 11-14, 2003.]

If there is no way to avoid hazing even in a professional army, this army will at least be manned by volunteers. Yet another radical solution is to get rid of the army altogether, since no enemy would have done to us what we have done to ourselves.

In conclusion I'd like to briefly comment on the frequently discussed issue of whether now we are better off than in Soviet times. It depends. Those in favour of the current situation, used to considering things through the prism of economic (this time market) relations, claim that today things are much better than in the past. Anybody can take the initiative and set up a business of their own. In short, today we enjoy many more freedoms. How very true, gentlemen! Some do have the freedom to freeze in their unheated flats, while others - to bask in the sunshine on Canary Islands. Some do have the opportunity to face the threat of eviction because of inability to pay rent, while the others - to use the situation to enrich themselves. There is indeed the opportunity to run a business and get a clinch shot in the head (mostly for the same social group). There is a freedom of speech and a freedom of silence because one's family can't feed on angry exposures. But, perhaps, society should proceed from the plight of most hapless and deprived of all civil rights when assessing its welfare standards? Of an orphan at an orphanage, of an old man at a shelter for disabled people, of a convict in a prison cell and a soldier in the barracks. If they are better off today living the way they are, then all of us are better off. But are we?

5 The Reasons for *Dedovshchina* and Ways to Prevent It: A Retrospective Analysis[1]

Igor V. OBRAZTSOV

One of the main problems, that troubled the Soviet Armed forces during the last three decades of their existence, were the so-called "relations violating the regulations" (RVR). Russian Armed forces, created in May 1992, also inherited this problem. "*Dedovshchina*" as a form of "relations violating the regulations" continues to ruin the Russian Army *ab intra*, takes toll to its image and lowers the prestige of military service. Not only physical mutilation and moral troubles, but also soldiers' deaths can be enumerated among other grievous consequences of "*dedovshchina*"[2]. Criminal acts due to *dedovshchina* account for 20-30% of total military crimes[3]. Effective ways of "relations violating the regulations" root-out (or at least minimization) may be outworked based on a good understanding of their core.

1. "*Dedovshchina*": what is it?

First of all, the terms should be clearly defined. The words "*dedovshchina*" and "relations violating the regulations" are often used as synonyms. The first is usually used in mass media and by common people, and the latter is used in official documents of the Military office and in scientific researches.

It is commonly known that the term "relations violating the regulations" was first introduced by A.D. Glotochkin, a military psychologist and tutor, who considered such relations as a kind of "abnormal" interpersonal relations in

---
[1] Translated from the Russian by Anastasia Turgiyeva.
[2] S. Rybkin, "Suitsidal'nye iavleniia sredi voennosluzhashchikh: problema i puti resheniia", *Voennaia mysl'*, no. 6, 2000, pp. 38-42.
[3] I. Plutagariov, "Udruchaiushchii oblik Vooruzhennykh Sil", *Nezavisimoe voennoe obozrenie*, 11th March 2005.

the form of deviant behavior of individual servicemen[4]. In other words, he did not admit that such relations were a mass phenomenon.

Such a view did not change until the mid 1980s when democratic changes in Soviet society (*perestroika*) contributed to wide discussions over the RVR problem in mass media and even in books[5]. At that time, there were two views on the problem: "wide" and "narrow". The "narrow" view treated the RVR problem as a negative phenomenon among soldiers serving conscript military service: for instance, "specific social relations between informal groups of conscripts (of the same service period or nationality) appearing in closed military societies in parallel with formal relations prescribed in the regulations and serving the functions of replacement, socialization, protection and social control"[6]. Further on, under this approach, "*dedovshchina*" was for the first time considered as an informal status system existing in the Armed forces next to the formal (prescribed by military regulations) status system[7].

The "wide" approach determined RVR as a negative phenomenon in the relations of all servicemen categories: officers, warrant officers, privates and sergeants serving as conscripts: "any violation of the comrade in arms' rights and personality, made by servicemen of all categories or their groups". Still, a massive character of this phenomenon was rejected as a fact. "RVR - are sporadic, individual or group organized perverted way of self-actualization, behavior, cooperation; adverse habits, false group and units traditions; nervous break-down and reactive condition of servicemen, resulting in humiliating comrades in arms"[8].

Thus, "relations violating the regulations" and "*dedovshchina*" aren't synonyms, but terms serving to name different phenomena. "*Dedovshchina*" is used to identify negative phenomena only among conscripts. Its mecha-

---

[4] A.D. Glotochkin, *Formirovanie vzaimootnosheniei v voinskom kollektive (vzvod, rota) na osnove trebovaniei voinskikh ustavov*. Dissertatsiia kandidata pedagogicheskikh nauk. Moskva: Voenno-Politicheskaia Akademiia imeni V.I. Lenina, 1964.

[5] Iu. M. Poliakov, *Sto dnei do prikaza: Povesti*, Moskva: Molodaia gvardiia, 1988.

[6] N.I. Marchenko, "K voprosu o genezise i sushchnosti neustavnykh vzaimootnoshenii", *Sotsiologicheskie issledovaniia*, no. 12, 1983, pp.112-115.

[7] S.A. Belanovskii, *Dedovshchina v Armii (Sbornik sotsiologicheskikh dokumentov)*, Moskva: Akademiia Nauk SSSR, 1991.

[8] S.I. S'edin, V.M. Kruk, *"Dedovshchina": v voinskikh kollektivakh: prichiny, puti vyiavleniia i iskoreneniia (Social'no-psikhologicheskii aspekt)*, Moskva: Voenno-Politicheskaia Akademiia imeni V.I. Lenina, 1990, p. 14.

nism is the functioning of hierarchic informal structure, based on the duration of conscription. Etymologically this word comes from the name of the most privileged informal category of conscripts - "*dedy*".

But it is necessary to keep in mind that in spite of the fact that "*dedovshchina*" is the most widespread form of negative relations among the conscripts, it is not the only one. There are also: 1. "conscripts' land communities" ("*zemliacestvo*") in two forms: "territorial land communities" (groups formed on loyalties derived from common regional origins) and "ethnic nationality communities" (groups formed on loyalties derived from common national origins); 2. "cult of force" ("*kult sily*", relationships - between servicemen of the same conscription term - based on force), among other forms... Therefore a number of informal status systems may coexist, compete or rival in the same military unit.

"Relations violating the regulations" - is a "wider" term, used to describe any negative phenomenon taking place between conscripts.

Some preliminary remarks are needed. According to us, this term does not reflect the meaning it usually implies. For instance, it can be used to explain informal servicemen relations during off-duty time (as a synonym for "free time" or "informal"). Therefore we consider the term "anti-regulations" (counter regulations) relations to better express negative elements of informal servicemen relations. As far as these relations are aimed at violating regulations and undermining military discipline. Hereafter we will use the commonly recognized expression "relations violating the regulations" (RVR). It is evident that such phenomena, influencing all categories of servicemen relations, more often arise among conscripts. So, conflict situations or clashes, based on social or social-psychological status of a person or a group, on physical or moral interests, form the essence of this negative phenomenon. That is why it is necessary to determine the degrees of this phenomenon.

Violations and conflict situations, arising on interpersonal level for the reasons of personal antipathy, insults or unreserved feelings are less socially dangerous (as far as they are temporary and situational) than those observed on intergroup or personal-group levels. Here we deal with phenomena that pose a real threat not only to normal functioning of a specific unit, but also to the whole military system as a social institute. It is explained by the fact that informal servicemen division (contrary to the formal one, implied by laws and military regulations: by position, by rank etc.), - when rival social groups are looking forward to obtaining the leading positions in elements or units -, form the basis of intergroup or personal-group conflicts.

Thereat getting a social status (position) for some groups inside the servicemen corps means they enjoy informal "privileges" and impose "duties" on the other groups, forcing them through the system of psychological and physical violence. "*Dedovshchina*" is a system of sophisticated forms of physical and psychological violence, which exists in all spheres of the armed forces, thus, providing the older servicemen with a dominant position over the young ones. So, the status-role system of "*dedovshchina*" is based on a stable and self-reproducing hierarchy, strictly obeyed by all "categories"[9] of servicemen.

Division of servicemen into "categories" with specific functions have been existing for a long time through the introduction of vicious rituals and traditions by older servicemen. Such rituals, as a spontaneously appeared mean of enforcing "*dedovshchina*," were "very different in form but equal in the general sense: to secure differentiation, division of conscripts by service terms, make each man know his role in the system of deformed intergroup relations, resulted in by the phenomenon of RVR"[10].

Thus, informal division of servicemen is quick spreading, stabile and self-reproducing due to its functionality, which is related to a real opportunity for the "humiliated" groups to later gain the same privileges of a dominant ("suppressing") group (improvement of status of younger servicemen after the older ones are dismissed or changes in the national structure of the unit, etc.). Such an opportunity for vertical social move results in accepting the rules of this forced "game" by the "humiliated" group members, thus, creating preconditions for further reproduction of negative traditions (that significantly affects the efficiency of current attempts to cope up with the problem).

---

[9] The categories correspond to the period of service [Editors' note].
[10] Iu.I. Deriugin, "Dedovshchina: sotsial'no-psikhologicheskiy analiz iavleniia", *Psikhologicheskii zhurnal*, vol.11, no.1, 1990, p. 113.

2. Why and when did this negative phenomenon appear?

RVR and "*dedovshchina*" are considered to have appeared in the late 1960s when the law "On general military obligation" decreased the service term in the army - from three to two years, in the navy - from four to three years. Therefore, long term servicemen and young conscripts found themselves together and it resulted in mass violence against the newcomers. Dissatisfaction with the "unfair" government decision found its expression in physical and psychological violence. The next generations kept those "traditions" from then on.

Yet, there is another explanation saying that "*dedovshchina*" appeared in the mid 1950s when Khrushchev's "thaw" replaced the cult of Stalin. Discipline, which had been very strict during the totalitarian period, loosened. Besides, many people with criminal past (with record of convictions) came to serve in the armed forces. They brought criminal traditions and culture.

The truth is that both abovementioned phenomena existed and contributed to the appearance and development of "*dedovshchina*". However, the roots of that phenomenon should be searched for in an earlier period - during World War I and the two Revolutions in 1917. There was no "*dedovshchina*" in the Imperial Russian army[11]. Conscription service was implemented in

---

[11] Strange as it may seem, before the Revolution of 1917, the Russian Army did not know "*dedovshchina*". It did not exist not because soldiers had a higher educational or cultural level; on the contrary, in comparison with European soldiers, their level was lower. The reason is that, before 1874, Russia basically had a professional army, and the recruits were long-service personnel. That is why the relations between young recruits and elder soldiers, e.g. veterans, were friendly, fatherly, knitted by brotherhood of arms. This fact could also be explained by the state of constant wars and conflicts of the 17-18th centuries, in which the Russian Army was involved (the Caucasus, Middle Asia). Call-up liability was introduced in 1874. Soldiers served 10-25 years. Absence of "*dedovshchina*" during this period was also explained by military engagements (in 1877-1878, 1901, 1904-1905, 1914-1917), and what is more important by the existence of well-prepared non-commissioned corps (noncommissioned officers). *Feldwebels*, senior and junior noncommissioned officers were elder companions in arms (a typical informal name of noncommissioned officers at that time was "*diad'ka*" ("uncle"), in the manner of blood relationship between uncle and nephews). The formal system of noncommissioned officers' activities was effective, that is why there were no prerequisites for a system of informal relations, such as "*dedovshchina*". "Relations violating the regulations" in the tsarist army could be observed between different categories of servicemen - be-

1874. Before that, the soldiers served 15 to 25 years, and were almost professional servicemen. When the conscript system was implemented, officers who much older than the young conscripts played the major role. Officers were like elder comrades to soldiers. They came from noble families and their relations with the conscripts were restricted to training time. In daily life, sergeants were the main regulators of the off-duty relations among soldiers.

During World War I, Russian armed forces increased from 1.320 men in 1914 to 6.900 men in 1917. Most professional officers were killed, but the remaining ones were absorbed in the great number of civilians recruited in the armed forces. The two Revolutions of 1917 finally weakened the Russian army that went out of the officers' control (the 48 thousands professional officers also grew into a huge formless 250-thousand mass of war time officers).

After the Russian Empire collapsed, the new government began to build the Workers' and Peasants' Red Army. Revolutionary freedoms resulted in elements of anarchy and disorder in this army. In the 1920s, the first sprouts of *"dedovshchina"* appeared. Formal status system of "junior commanders" (sergeants) had no rooted traditions. Red officers and sergeants were almost of the same age and their education level was the same as the Red Army soldiers. As a result, their authority among soldiers was very low. Formal status system was hardly able to fulfill its tasks. The "Revolutionary consciousness" of common soldiers was more a slogan than a real fact. Along

---

tween officers and soldiers -, and shown either by verbal (abuse) or physical (fight) violence from the officers toward the subordinate soldiers. Still, these negative events couldn't be characterized as large-scale phenomenon. "Relations violating the regulations" system, corresponding with *"dedovshchina"* existed in military training schools (officer schools - military and Junker training schools). This system could be observed in a special form of Junker (Cadet) relations of senior and junior courses. Junior Cadets had to defer senior Junkers (Cadets) and to carry all their whims. The humiliating treatment was rather moral than physical. This special form of relations was called *"zuck"* (from German) or "screw" (training of juniors means to screw up/to tighten discipline). The incidence of *"zuck"* was different (more often in cavalry schools, less often in infantry). Still, this phenomenon was of German origin, not Russian. German military education system of Cadet Corps, introduced by Peter the First, together with positive moments implemented in Russia the *"zuck"*. During the Soviet time, this negative phenomenon moved to compulsory military service in the form of *"dedovshchina"* - but it was the product of another social-political system. Some elements of "relations violating the regulations" could sometimes be observed in Soviet military training schools (military schools and defense institutes) between the Cadets of junior and senior courses. Though, these phenomena were a rarity and were severely checked in the bud by the authorities (including the dismissal from military training school).

with the formal system, an informal status system, which later grew into "*dedovshchina*", began to form.

Russian emigrant Semen Portugeis published (under the pen name of Stanistal Ivanovich) the book "Red Army" based on the analysis of Soviet newspapers of the 1920s. He concluded that there were many negative phenomena in the Red Army. According to him, the reasons for this were the poor cultural education of the soldiers and the inability of the Soviet government to rule the country and the armed forces in an effective way. He also paid attention to the reasons of the development of these negative phenomena in the armed forces.

We consider Portugeis to be the first who addressed RVR as a serious social problem for the military system:

> To gather by force young people, yet with an unstable morale and to make them obey under the threat of severe punishment may have psychological consequences of a very sad kind. The after-effects are inevitable whatever these gatherings are. In barracks, in an atmosphere of specific military discipline... suppressing an individual and ignoring his natural rights can take anarchic forms with all its disgusting moral consequences. [...] However, the higher the culture of a country is, the freer, the more independent and autonomous an individual is, and the easier it is to minimize sad results of barrack life[12].

Thus, "*dedovshchina*" appeared in the early Red Army and existed further on in many forms (from soft ones - in Stalin's cult period and World War II, to very severe ones - from the mid 1960s till the collapse of the Soviet Union). The Russian armed forces inherited this tradition and continue to fight aigainst it. "*Dedovshchina*" appeared as a reaction against low efficiency of formal status system (officers and sergeants). It has old roots, and it is a self-reproducing and quickly spreading phenomenon with various forms of physical and psychological (moral) violence.

---

[12] St. Ivanovich, S.O. Portugejs, *Krasnaia Armiia*, Paris: Izdatel'stvo "Sovremennie Zapiski", 1931, pp. 222-223.

3. Can we fight this evil?

Sometimes, especially in foreign research on this issue, statements asserting that *"dedovshchina"* is obviously a product of the Soviet system can be found. To prove this statement, the authors refer to the former socialist countries. In 1970-1980, this phenomenon really spread to some extent in the armed forces of some of the Warsaw Pact countries. In Poland, for example, *"dedovshchina"* is known as *"fala"*; the same phenomenon took place in Czechoslovakia. But at the same time, it did not spread widely in Eastern Germany.

However, *"dedovshchina"* has mostly spread in the countries where there is no contract military service and alternative civil service. Besides, we have already cited Portugeis' book on the pattern of negative phenomena appearance. In particular, he mentioned such factors as average level of culture of the population, level of citizens' legal protection, and political freedoms. So, *"dedovshchina"* is a product of not only the Soviet system, but of any totalitarian system.

Despite some opinions, the Soviet and Russian military officials have always been fighting against *"dedovshchina"*. The matter is that in 1980-1990, the problem was raised in Russian mass media. Earlier it had not been allowed to write about the issue. As for the fighting with the problem, the officials resorted to severe measures: sentence by a military tribunal and imprisonment or service in disciplinary military units (battalions).

In the late 1960-early 1970s, new attempts were made. Units (platoons and companies) where all servicemen started servicing the same year were organized. However, the problem of effective work of sergeants arouse. In such units, RVR took the form of the "cult of force" rather than *"dedovshchina"*. Physically strong soldiers took leading positions.

In the late 1970s-1980s, many conscripts from the Caucasus and Central Asia came to serve in the armed forces; "land communities" began to replace *"dedovshchina"*. Therefore, the commanders had to divide large national communities within the armed forces into smaller groups.

After the Soviet Union collapsed, the problem of "land communities" became less serious. Despite this, local problems, especially related to the communities from the Northern Caucasus (Dagestan, Chechnya, Ingushetia, etc.), still remained. But, in the Russian armed forces, the "classic" form of "*dedovshchina*" began to prevail again. However, due to social, political and economical changes in the country, mercenary trends in "*dedovshchina*" became stronger (taking money from young soldiers, extortion, etc.).

Thus, by 1990, a system of organized physical and psychological violence, affecting all sides of military units' life, had already formed in the Russian armed forces. A comprehensive system of countermeasures (instead of single organizational and pedagogic measures with a short-term effect) had to be set to cope with the problem.

Sociological research related to "*dedovshchina*" and "relations violating the regulations" began in 1967, when a Department of Military Sociological Research at the Main Political Department of the Soviet Army and Navy was established. However, the commandment ignored most of the research results.

Research is still being conducted at the present time. Based on research carried out over a long time, we can determine some patterns (trends) in RVR development and assess what activities the officers should carry out in order to resolve the problem. Preventive work demands deep analysis of the characteristics and essence of certain informal structures, formed and existing in military units along with the formal system. In this concern, research centers considered RVR as a kind of an "organized disorder" system with some military units functioning in its basis. In other words, it was approached as a form of social organization.

In order to analyze the informal structure of a military society, we should consider the following factors.

Firstly, informal structures were non-homogeneous: in each social group (both of older or younger servicemen, representatives of some social group, nationality, etc.), there were "leaders", "neutrals", "outcasts", etc. That is why informal structures in military communities were considered alltogether.

Secondly, along with the formal system, which is an ideal form of military organization, there has always been an informal system of servicemen relations. And it was not always affected by "*dedovshchina*" or "land community" problems - there were other reasons.

Thirdly, under the influence of many factors of social development, "*dedovshchina*" and "land communities" problem, as informal systems, better matched the situation in the armed, whereas the official system failed to secure effective functioning of the armed forces and to solve all social contradictions. Informal systems, supported by "shadow lawmaking", compensated disadvantages of the formal system. At the same time, the formal system and various informal systems could be in different kinds of relations: compete, conflict or complement each other.

Fourthtly, RVR, in particular one of its prevailing forms based on informal division of servicemen by the terms of service ("*dedovshchina*") has been functioning in the Army and Navy for many decades (it appeared not in the 1950s-1960s, but much earlier). During this time, stable negative traditions have taken shape.

Research showed that none of the analyzed forms of RVR (the most common "*dedovshchina*", "land communities", as well as rare ones, such as criminal subculture) as a rule exists alone. Each form could dominate in certain periods, but this did not mean that there were no other forms of RVR. They simply were not so obvious. RVR in groups and in between groups of servicemen took various forms and, besides, were influenced by interpersonal RVR.

Researches proved the hypothesis that a young man with a criminal record or from a difficult family, and a young man matured in a good environment have equal chances to become a bearer of RVR having experienced "*dedovshchina*". The difference between them will probably be only in the extent to which they would use the "privileges" for older servicemen (in the first case - utmost infringement of honor and dignity, in the second case - participation in formal performance of traditional "duties" of the older servicemen, necessary only to keep the status).

Thus, it would be unjust to state that there is only a small group of those who violate regulations (and that the problem can be solved simply by neutralizing these people): almost every older serviceman is a bearer of RVR to some extent. Because there is always a real risk to be punished for breaking the "traditions" of the older servicemen. The punishment includes lowering the status of an older serviceman back to the status of a younger serviceman. This circle turned out to be an extremely subsistent and widely spreading in the armed forces. Informal hierarchical structure ("*dedovshchina*"), existing almost in every military units, compensates the disadvantages of the formal system including the weakness of junior commanders. Similarly to the formal system, in the informal system there is disciplinary punishment and moral encouragement, which are supposed to secure its smooth functioning.

The informal system of moral stimulation mainly implies the idea that binding realization of younger servicemen "obligations" guarantees timely transition to new position of an older conscript with the adequate loss of "obligations" and gain of "privileges". This system proves to be well-organized, reliable and quite effective. That is why it is acknowledged by most servicemen as necessary and advisable in military conditions.

As for the system of penalty, it proves to be a quite effective (contrary to the system of disciplinary responsibility) regulator of servicemen behavior. It includes a complex of psychological and physical violence, covering almost all spheres of the armed forces.

Forms of physical and psychological violence are treated as steady, efficient for reproduction and quick distribution of different types of "relations violating the regulations". These different types of RVR may be seen in almost in every military unit. Such types of RVR are treated as social indicators of the real existence of RVR in this or that military unit (bodily harms of different gravity, unauthorized leave, suicidal behavior are the consequences of these types of RVR)[13]. The division of violent forms into acts of physical or psychological coercion is quite relative, because it is sometimes very hard to determine which component dominated in this or that RVR. For example, some forms of psychological coercion are very often transformed into physical coercion or turn to be part of it.

The analysis of the essence of different types of RVR (more than 80 typical forms were considered) made it possible to conclude that mechanisms of their acticvation were explained by a number of factors. Among them are: specific display of youthful psychology in conditions of closed masculine society, attempts to compensate for the deficit of free time, different types of al-

---

[13] Rybkin, 2000, *op. cit.*, pp. 38-42; I. Plutagariov, "Udruchaiushchii oblik Vooruzhennykh Sil", *Nezavisimoe voennoe obozrenie*, 11th March 2005.

lowances, difficulties of military life, procedures of cultural and leisure activities etc.[14]

The most important thing that united different types of RVR was the fact that both the younger and the older servicemen were obliged to fit in the roles ("bosses" and "subordinates") dictated by the informal structure. It is real because all the existing types of RVR, starting from "servicing", "limitation", "infringement" and other pervertive forms, imply active (and not only passive) participation in their realization by the "insulting" side. Here comes the problem of social danger of this negative phenomenon, finding its display in all types of armed forces activities.

Based on the results of our research, it is possible to make some conclusions:
- The dominating functioning mechanism among the existing types of RVR is based on the informal division of servicemen by the term of conscription. From 1989 to 1992, "*dedovshchina*" replaced RVR, based on informal servicemen division by national identification ("land communities"). At least untill 2007 (when a planned reduction of the conscription term to 1 year is going to be implemented), such form of RVR as "*dedovshchina*" will continue to exist. Still, in the near future, other types of RVR may come (and do come) to life, such as regional "land community", "cult of force", religious, criminal and other factors.
- Among all other spheres of the armed forces activities, the social-domestic one is mostly affected by negative phenomena. The actualization of negative phenomena happens due to the rise of servicemen load, explained by the degradation of social-domestic conditions (field conditions of military life, breakdown of elementary rights and refusal to meet servicemen needs) resulting in compensation of these problems by artificial growth of younger conscripts exploitation and their deprivation of physical and men-

---

[14] I.V. Obraztsov, *Neustavnye vzaimootnosheniia: sushchnost', formy proiavleniia i profilaktika*, Uchebno-metodicheskoe posobie. Moskva: Tsentr voenno-sotsiologicheskikh, psikhologicheskikh i pravovykh issledovanii, 1994; S.S. Solov'ev, I.V. Obraztsov, *Rossiiskaia Armiia ot Afganistana do Chechni: Sotsiologicheskii analiz*, Moskva: Natsional'iye Institut imeni Ekateriny Velikoi, 1997, pp. 339-345.

tal benefits through a number of forms of psychological and physical violence.
- The variety and the social dangerousness of different forms of physical and psychological violence are in deep relation with effectiveness and consistency of preventive measures held by the units' chiefs. The growing public interest in military discipline in the armed forces and in servicemen interrelations, openness in discussion of the military problems will contribute to activation of preventive work in the armed forces. As a result, the existing form of RVR will move from physical violence (the refusal from physical acts leading to heavy bodily harms) to forms and methods of moral and psychological influence (psychological violence) on younger conscripts, the number of which will increase.
- The non-conformity with social and legal guarantees and lack of social-domestic conditions will result in a real danger of activation of some forms of RVR among contract servicemen (the first signs have already been observed in some units).
- The problem of servicemen interrelations is based on the difference of material conditions and business activities before conscription. That is why a new type of RVR, based on property crimes, will come to life.

The following ways and forms of preventive measures were outworked on the basis of our research.

The strategy followed to fight these negative phenomena is based on the essence of social perversions (breaching the norms), their types, and the reasons of existence leading to their dispersion. The main theoretical precondition is that the overcome of immoral behavior is determined by a fight for its limitation ("minimization"). Cardinal changes in RVR prevention (dramatic reduction in number of these negative phenomena) demand a change in the social, economic, political situation of the country, as well as a switch to an army based on contract service, security of rights and personal dignity etc.

This does not mean that it is impossible to try to solve the problem of RVR prior to real social changes in the armed forces. Our experience indicates a significant reduction today of the RVR problem on the level of a unit. That is why the way to determine the aims of the fight against social perversions (NRV) should always be differentiated by place and time (how to influence, when and what for). An optimum combination of all methods of preventive work should also be implemented, the planning and organization of which should take into consideration the following traits of these negative phenomena:

Firstly, fhe functioning of a closed masculine society leads to the presence of negative phenomena in this milieu. The realization of specific tasks by that society (for example, the country's military defense milieu) and tough legal regulation of its activities raise the probability of negative phenomena displays in most pervasive forms.

Secondly, together with legal and formal (the regulations based) structures of an ideal type of military organization exists an informal organization of servicemen interrelations. This phenomenon has a long history.

Thirdly, it is vital to understand that even the most effective RVR preventing work can not guarantee total extinction of this multi-factors determined social and psychological phenomenon. It is transformed into a less socially dangerous form and in "good conditions", it revives again because it possesses a reproductive function. Real implication of the units' leaders in the fighting of "relations violating the regulations" can only lead to limitation ("minimization") of their display.

Fourthly, a certain number of causal relations have been noticed. The degree of RVR dispersion depends on the intensity of military trainings: the more trainings there are, the less RVR are dispersed. The worse the social-domestic conditions are, the more RVR are observed. So, the intensification of trainings and the improvement of social-domestic conditions are one of the human factors that will contribute to the extinction of RVR.

RVR prevention in the armed forces must be exercised with the use of the whole arsenal of forms and methods of organizational and educative work. The set of preventive steps constitutes a complicated system of counteraction. Effective strategy can be provided only through coordination of the above named theories.

Generalization of the experience would give potentiality to the formation of the most effective methods of preventive work:

- functioning and activity organization of the armed forces in cooperation with legal norms: execution of the responsibilities aimed at strengthening military discipline; all living premises are to be equipped according to the internal service Regulations' demands (maintenance of medical and sanitary norms, timely provision with ratio etc.)

- well-considered system of material and moral stimulation of the officer corps to reward a high level of discipline in subordinate units and for the conscripts to reward a fair work and personal discipline (including the use of non-traditional forms of encouragement);

- concrete aims and goal-setting in the sphere of preventive work. Unachieved aims inevitably result in disillusion and officers' neglecting the problem;

- full and detailed research and description of the existing system of RVR (forms of their display and functioning mechanisms as the subject of study), and quick trace of the development tendencies and "innovations" in this sphere; use of research data during the young officers' teaching on forms and methods of preventing these problems;

- stage-to-stage planning and realization of the preventive work (coordination of the place and time of all actions: when, what for, how and to what extent the issue should be influenced). From this perspective, RVR prevention can be planned according to the rate of its social threat and its spread. The urgent measures must be aimed at reducing those forms of physical and psychological violence which usually have the most serious consequences (death or injuries, escapes, suicides, etc.).

- optimal and creative combination of all preventive methods, including non-traditional ones (replacing negative rituals and traditions with positive ones: honoring older servicemen on the day their demobilization is issued; use of servicemen arts, etc.);

- identifying informal leaders in military units and set up special work with them (entrusting positively oriented leaders, promoting them to sergeant positions, involving them in the unit social life; discrediting and neutralizing negatively oriented leaders - the bearers and supporters of RVR)[15];

---

15   Obraztsov, 1994, *op. cit.*; D. Klepikov, *Dedovshchina kak sotsial'nii institut*, Dissertatsiia kandidata sotsiologicheskikh nauk. Sankt-Peterburg: Sotsiologicheskii institut, 1997.

- systematic teaching of the officers to use effective preventive methods, forming the right understanding of the social threat these negative phenomena pose to the normal functioning of the military system;
- getting up-to-date and comprehensive information from soldiers about the effectiveness of the taken measures and counter-measures taken by RVR supporters;
- good preparation of young conscripts (intensive physical training, preparing them to face negative phenomena;
- stable and effective introduction of preventive measures (even disappeared forms of RVR can be reactivated if preventive measures get softer).

As experience shows, these and other measures have a considerable effect if they are combined into a single system of preventive measures, considering the specifics of the branch and arm of service, actual tasks of the unit (ship), location, qualitative characteristics of the conscripts. Participation of civil institutions in preventive measures along with the state organizations should ensure this work to be public and effective.

II *Dedovshchina* Frameworks in Russia

6 Russian Army *Mat* as a Code System Controlling Behaviour in the Russian Army

Vadim MIKHAILIN

This text is a shortened (and based on somewhat different material) version of my article "*Russkii mat kak muzhskoi obstsennyi kod: problema proiskhozhdeniia i evoliutsiia statusa*", published in n°43 of *Novoe literaturnoe obozrenie*[1]. The aim is to show that the military milieu (and some other social strata structurally close to it), has always been - and remains - absolutely adequate for the "*mat*-speaking". Moreover, within these strata, *mat* has always carried on a rather specific function connected with creating a man's identity as a "military", i.e. a member of the armed forces. The adequate use of *mat* offers various and sometimes the only possible means of imposing oneself on an equal, a subordinate (or even a superior). As a matter of fact, *mat* is a basis for a whole code system that de facto controls different military behavioural practices.

I begin the discussion of Russian *mat* in its modern form and function by discussing its origins. The initial form of the key formula in modern Russian *mat* (*eb tvoiu mat'* from *pes eb tvoiu mat'* (fucked your mother from dog fucked your mother)) seems to meet no objections among modern scholars studying Russian obscene speech practices. After the basic articles by B. A. Uspensky later published as a whole fundamental chapter in his *Selected Works*[2], nobody has really tried to call it into question. Nevertheless, from my

---
[1] V.Iu. Mikhailin, "Russkii mat kak muzhskoi obstsennyi kod: problema proiskhozhdeniia i evoliutsiia statusa", *Novoie literaturnoie obozreniie*, no. 43, 2000, pp. 347-393.
[2] B.A. Uspenskii, *Mifologicheskii aspekt russkoi ekspressivnoi leksiki*, M.: Izbrannyie trudy. T. 2, 1997, pp. 67-161.

point of view, the very logic of Uspensky's argument, leading in its turn to the author's basic hypothesis concerning the genesis of Russian *mat* and the stages of its formation, needs rather serious adjustment.

For example, Uspensky derives the basic formula from the "widely spread motif" of a marriage between the Sky Deity (or the Thunderer) and Mother Earth; with the subsequent travesty of the replacement of the Thunderer by its eternal enemy, a chthonic deity in a form of a dog, and then the second replacement of the Mother Earth with the interlocutor's own mother. Then the acting subject is re-comprehended, due to the reduction of an initial formula, and since the verb form *eb* corresponds to any person singular, the third person (*pes*; dog) is replaced by the first one.

The total of the author's argumentation in support of each one of the above mentioned initial formula evolution stages is very impressive. But it is possible to ask: for what reason the Thunderer's eternal enemy whose traditional iconography connotes not dog but serpent, invariably takes the form of a dog in this particular context? Evidently trying to forestall the questions of the kind, Uspensky produced a special appendix - one of the two following his main text - to show the numerous serpent-dog parallels as reflected in very different mythological systems. Whilst not objecting to the bulk of the data, it proves nothing. Dogs seems to be the main figurative referent in all the Indo-European invective practices without exception (Uspensky even bases the etymological closeness of Russian words *pes* (dog) and *pizda* (cunt) tracing them back to the Pre-Slavonic verb *pisti* with a meaning *ebat'* (to fuck)), and it is the author's view that such an exclusive attention only to one same animal has to be based on more solid grounds, particularly as the serpent itself is represented in the obscene vocabulary in rather a humble way.

Evolving the "dog theme", Uspensky says: "We put no objective here to clearly find out more or less the reasons why the dog is perceived this way; the detailed discussion of this question would lead us too far astray. We only shall point out the possibility of serpent to dog associations, and to wolf also; the serpent, as well as the wolf, represent the incarnations of a "ferocious beast", i.e. the Thunderer's mythological enemy... and also embody a cruel and dangerous creature, inimical to a man. What is essential to us in this case is the idea of dog's uncleanliness, the idea that goes deep into history and far beyond the limits of Slavonic mythology"[3].

That very question of the obscene speech practices associated with a dog, associations so clear that even the respective speech behaviour forms in some Slavonic language traditions have the distinct "dog" etymologies, is, for the author, crucial. The following objectives - to look for a basis to the dog's magical uncleanliness and to the tabooing of the corresponding speech and other behaviour practices within the limits of a "human" territory, to examine the peculiarities of the obscene speech practices functioning in different social contexts - are logically bound to this.

1. "Dogs' barking". Russian *mat* as a territorial (and magical) based male speech code.

The key to the problem of Russian obscene speech practices system genesis is to be found through one of the most sufficient characteristics of Russian *mat* that makes it related to perhaps little but all the similar phenomena existent in other Indo-European languages and cultures. I mean here the strict - in its initial state and status - gender-conditioned character of the appropriate speech behaviour forms. Russian *mat* is an indispensable attribute of any group consisting solely of males, only recently beginning to get into the females-only groups, and the practices of *mat* speaking in the mixed groups are to be reduced to the last twenty or thirty years (if to exclude certain practices seen as the ritual ones). In fact, every scholar who has raised this problem has mentioned this peculiarity, but up to now nobody has tried to make a following step, namely to link fundamentally the genesis of Russian *mat* as well as its semantic peculiarities with the specific gender conditions of its social existence.

The majority of researchers are so much taken with, from one side, the idea of *mat* as connected to the archaic fertility cults, and on the other, the carnival mythology created by Mikhail Bakhtin, that in the majority of cases any material conflicting with this point of view is simply being cut off the main

---

[3]   *Ibid.*, p.117.

trend of research. Thus we read in the Uspensky's paper: "...they think at Polessye, that the *mat* is especially banned for women: *mat*-speak coming from a woman is considered as a sin from which the land suffers...; whereas it is hold as a more or less common everyday male behaviour pattern, taking in itself no sin at all"[4]; wherefrom the author comes right to *mat*'s connection to the cult of the earth, while dropping the question of it being a gender-determined phenomenon. And, to mention Vladimir Zhelvis' argument[5] basing the exceptionally male status of *mat* on the exclusion of women from some vague "strictly male" fertility cult rituals in antiquity, the only comment would be that this hypothesis is quite typical for the book's general standard.

Now, *mat* in domestic tradition is (or, rather, used to be) sharply defined by the speaker's sex; it is a kind of a male code, the usage of which till recently was conditioned by a set of rather strict rules. The changes that happened to *mat*'s status in the course of the 20th century are discussed elsewhere, so here mention of *mat*-ruling taboos refers to the traditionally prevalent speech situations.

Nobody seems to question the fact that *mat* (as a social phenomenon as well as a set of stable speech constructions and "forms of speech") bears relation to some magic-based practices. The problem seems to lie in other field: a) what magical practices exactly it goes back to and b) if we could try to reconstruct the practices in question, starting from the situation with modern *mat*.

What do we have? *Mat* is a prerogative of the male part of Russian (and Russian-speaking) population of the former Soviet Union. Therefore from the very beginning we can limit our search for the hypothetical ritual models to a sphere of male only rituals. The second essential premise is that any taboo-based magic is always strictly territorially conditioned (mention that the "territory" here is seen not so much in its topographic but in its magically significant connotations[6]). The things you can do in the woods are often subject to strict taboos in the village, not to mention the space where home magic is dominant. Hence, the sphere of our search is to be limited not only with the

---

[4] *Ibid.*, p. 71.
[5] V.I. Zhelvis, *Pole brani. Skvernosloviie kak sotsial'naia problema*, Moskva, 1997.
[6] See also: V. Mikhailin, *Izbytochnost': iskhodnyi sotsiokul'turnyi smysl, kul'tura, vlast', identichnost': novyie podkhody v sotsial'nykh naukakh*, Saratov, 1999, pp. 229-235.

mat speakers' gender characteristics but also with the territorial and magical conditions these practices exist in.

What magical (the term meaning the readiness of a human consciousness to see any item as burdened by the additional meanings, magic by origin) territories might and could be seen as the purely male ones, being opposed by this feature to the territories both "female" and "common" and thus producing the basis for the tabooistic systems? Agricultural ritual and the fertility magic linked with it are strictly bound to specific territories. Agricultural magic - due to its procreative character - supposes that both sexes are to be included into the magic rites. More than that, in a number of rather archaic agricultural traditions there are labours seen as strictly female ones (in the traditional Russian culture - cropping and any other harvesting). Agricultural magic is mainly female, connected with the "Mother Earth" cults beginning from the late Stone Age. Thus if any strictly tabooistic speech or behaviour practices were to appear as based on the agricultural magic ritual, then in no way they could be oriented onto the exclusively male part of the population. Rather the opposite, gynaeco-centric situation seems possible on these grounds. And if obscene male speech patterns are really used during some rituals having to do with the fertility cults (season rites, weddings), this usage seems to be of a relatively late origin, to be based on already existent taboo codes which one can use to emphasize the masculine status of the participants within the "exterritorial" situation of the festivity.

If to look for the strictly male zones, then the hunters' and the warriors' territory would answer these in the majority of known cultures - that is the territories of nature either not mastered but known, where the relations between the man and the land are based on the "agreement" and "parity" grounds (hunting), or those alien to the man, chthonic and magically inimical (war). These territories were always seen as marginal ones from the point of view of the (magically understood) cultural centre, surrounded by the "female" territories of a mastered land. This "frontier" originally was a male food territory, entering which a man was to drop automatically all his "family" magic roles, crucial for the "common" territories (those of a father, son, husband, head of a family), and instead to take upon oneself the strictly masculine roles, characteristic of the aggressive and unified from the gender point of view group (hunter, warrior, raider, hunter or war chieftain).

Supposing that the basic magistical territory for the rise of the male tabooistc code (that was seen thus as "obscene" at all the other territories in all the possible situations, except the strictly ritual ones) was the hunter/warrior territory, peripheral in respect of a cultural centre. The next question is - could we find any grounds for some special role played namely by the dog (or by the wolf, magically compatible with the dog) and namely within the limits of this territory - the grounds that would enable us to trace modern *mat*'s "masculinity" back to ancient male rites?

The fact is that the existence of male warrior unions, the members of which not only called oneselves dogs/wolves, but actually felt so, is long ago proven for the entire Indo-European habitat, from Celts to Indo-Iranians, and from Germans to Greeks and Romans (as well as for many other, non-Indo-European peoples). A. I. Ivanchik says in his article, provided with rather a good bibliography and significantly entitled "Dog Warriors. Male Unions and the Scythian Incursions into Asia Minor"[7]:

> The male unions and those rites and myths connected to them are well studied for Germanic, Indo-Iranian, Greek, Latin, Celtic and, also, Balto-Slavonic traditions. One of the results of this research was the ascertainment of that major role that was ascribed within these unions to the image of dog-wolf. The warrior god, the patron for the union was honored in this very image, but what's much more significant in our case is that all the members of the union was also considered as dog-wolves. Young warriors' initiation consisted of their becoming wolves [the narcotic or intoxicant matters were used during the rites], who had to live for some period outside the human settlements with a life of the "wolves". I.e. plundering and making war. In Spartan cryptia we see this custom especially well preserved; young Sinnfjotli in the Voelsungsaga passes the equal initiation as a wolf, murderer and plunderer, for to become a full value warrior. Irish hero Cuchulain's initiation resulting with his new name, meaning "the Culain's Dog" [the usual change of name during the initiation], consisted of his service as a

---

[7] A. Ivanchik, "Voiny-psy. Muzhskiie soiuzy I skifskiie vtorzheniia v Peredniuiu Aziiu", *Sovetskaia etnografiia*, no. 5, 1988, pp.38-48.

dog for Culain the godly blacksmith, i.e. he actually had to become a dog. This could be compared with the Ossetin Nart story about Ouryzmag turning into the dog and about the heavenly blacksmith who took part in Nart heroes tempering. Evidently the same idea gives birth to the Indo-European legal formula, according to which any murderer "becomes" a wolf, with the subsequent development of the notions like "outlaw" or "criminal" characteristic of this word and imparting a pejorative shade to it[8].

The examples of the kind could be cited ad infinitum, to begin with Romulus who founded[9] the strictly male (juvenile) and predatory town of Rome, and to finish with the Irish epic tradition, where, for one thing, Cuchulain is in no way the only hero bearing the root *cu* (dog) in his warrior's name, and, for the other, practices of different warrior (and juvenile warrior!) unions, initiations and peculiar tabooistic systems (*geis*) are abundant[10]. It seems appropriate to remind ourselves here about the statistical abundance of "wolf" names in Europe and in Russia. Indeed, there are many more (times and times) Volkovs in Russia than Medvedevs[11], while the bear is traditionally looked at as a national symbol.[12] And if we sum Volkovs to Biriukovs and Odintsovs[13], the statistic would become even more indicative. The traditional Indo-European plots based on the idea of lycanthropia are also of interest therein - especially as superstition accords that only the men tend to turn into werewolves.

---

[8] *Ibid.*, pp.40-41.
[9] It's worth remembering in this context about the most particular, magistically meaningful conditions of Rome foundation - about the fratricide, passing the furrow (i.e., in fact, both putting the magic border line and no less magic marking the act of ploughing - compare the traditional for many cultures figure of a ploughman warrior) etc. Besides, different ritual practices during the feast of Lupercalia could be also significant from this point of view.
[10] See also K.R. McCone, "Werevolves, cyclopes, diberga, and fianna: juvenile delinquency in early Ireland", *Cambridge Medieval Celtic Studies*, no. 12, Winter, 1986.
[11] *Volk* = wolf; *medved'* = bear.
[12] Incidentally, *"volk"* and *"medved"* are nicknames given to Fall conscripts in the Russian army [Editors'note].
[13] Both terms (*biriuk; odinets*) meaning a lone wolf with the specific accent on the animal living outside its pack.

2. Dog/wolf status as an age-conditioned phenomenon

In the vast majority of the above mentioned cases the matter concerns not just the warrior unions, but namely the juvenile warrior unions. Cuchulain passes his initiation at seven years old, makes his main feats of arms[14] at seventeen (i.e. at the year he have to prove his right to count as a rightful man) during the war of the Bull from Cualnge[15] and is killed at twenty seven due to breaking taboos. Sinnfjotli turns into the wolf for a time only before he becomes a full value man and warrior. Spartan cryptia precede the proper man's initiation, being in fact its first preliminary stage. Romulus becomes a city founder after killing his own brother who declined to refuse from the "wolf" total destructiveness. The "seasonal" attachment of certain activities in a number of cultures seems to be significant too. Thus the Irish fenians spent 1 May till 1 November (from Beltain to Samhain) "in the field", while living in peasant cottages during the remainder of the year[16]. There was also an institution of "summer" and "winter" chieftains in some North American tribes. As a matter of fact, the wolves live according to a similar pattern, half a year living as mated pairs and the other half "in pack". The difference is that the "natural" wolves pack period fall on the winter half of a year. Could it be so, in this case, that the respective human practices are a kind if magical "spheres of influence division" with the wild confraternities? Winter being a season of chthonic magic prevalence, the "neutral" marginal territory is given to the "natural" wolves; while in summer, when the "cultural" magic gets stronger, it is occupied by the human "pack", living in accordance to the same territorial and magical conditioned rules.

Within the tradition of male upbringing and class-to-class transition common to all the Indo-Europeans, every man had to pass through a peculiar "wolf" or "dog" stage. This stage was of an openly initiatiory character and the radical increase in social status is to be seen as a result of passing it - sup-

---

[14] Protecting the grown-up Ulad warriors fallen into the ritual state of feebleness.
[15] See also the pack of teenage Ulad youths holding the position for few days while recovering of the wounded Cuchulain, falling everyone of them on the border of their land not to let the enemy across it.
[16] Hence the decoding of an enigmatic phrase cited by Lady Gregory in her "Gods and Fighting Men": that every fenian along with the other privileges has right to "the fostering of a pup or a whelp in any (peasant - V.M) house from Samhaine to Beltain", i.e. any household has to upkeep one fenian ("dog") from November till May.

posing, evidently, the right for marriage, for self-standing household activities (i.e. creative and procreative ones), and, which is particularly important in our case, the right to carry arms within the precincts of a settlement. The franchise of all the men having right to bear arms within the precincts of a settlement is a basis for all the types of a primitive democracy. At the same time, the actions incompatible with the status of a grown-up man who must subdue and control his aggressive instincts (within the zone of a common, "family" rule), lead to the return to the "wolf" status, which in this aspect couldn't but to be seen as anti-social and infamous one. For all the period of their lycanthropic metamorphoses, the wolf-warriors live at the periphery of a culture space, i.e. within the borders of a strictly male magistical zone, disturbing no "human" borders, but protecting them from any outer perils. As a matter of fact, in accordance to the archaic model of the world, they are ousted into a chthonic zone, the zone of death: hence the particular importance of werewolf motifs. In this respect, any attempt of an unauthorised and ritually "uncovered" intrusion to the "human" territory is to be seen as a contamination, as the breaking of all existent human and cosmic norms, as violence over the "home-land", "mother-earth" etc. A "dog" can acquire his right to the "normal" life only by passing the initiation rites' final stage, equivalent to an act of purification. In Sparta, the ex-wolves had to pass through the painful flagellation while being spread on the altar of Aphrodite (!) - and only after shedding their blood over it they could get their right to a first manly status, opening way to the regular set of arms and to a place in phalanx. The place Spartans reserved for their "wolves" in their battle orders was before the phalanx, and the latter were armed (apart from "the wolves' rage" and lack of necessity to follow certain set of rules) with light and throwing weapons only. The age structure remained also the main principle of a phalanx formation: the first, the most dangerous ranks were occupied by the "recruits", the middle ones - by men "in their prime", and the rear ones, the closest to "home and temple" - by veterans, having the highest possible warrior status.

This kind of differentiation making a strict correspondence between the male/warrior status and the "time of service" is general to the Indo-European military and paramilitary structures - right up to the home army institution of "*dedovshchina*", where during the first half a year of service (of two years in total, as a rule), being in a status of a "*dukh*" ("spirit"[17]), the recruit in fact has no rights at all and is looked at as somebody less than human, while the last half-year, burdened with no duties at all (if not to take in view the ritual "upbringing" of the younger ranks) is dedicated to the hypertrophied idea of "*dembel*" (demobilisation), namely the distorted in a peculiar way idea of "home and temple".

Here it is worth remembering that the steady tradition that binds the warrior's valour with youth and pays special attention to a young warrior's death - regardless of how death is interpreted in different cultural and historical contexts. Within the modern European cultural tradition the motif of a young warrior's death becomes more and more bombastic, at the same time losing its "heroic" constituent and acquiring mournful features, for the motif of senseless sacrifice. A marked tendency towards the evolution of a young hero fearing neither pain nor death to the no less formula image of a boy-soldier, a miserable and innocent victim of war, is to be seen in the European culture of the last 200 years. But the very fact that the theme itself remains actual and active for the myth-creating lets us interpret these "emotional modifications" namely as modifications of a settled cultural schema.

3. The initial ambivalence of the wolf/dog status

Thus, the wolf/dog status is to be seen as an initially ambivalent one - from the point of view of its subjects as well as from the point of view of a community as a whole, whose marginal part the named age/gender group constitute. On the one hand, within the archaic IE cultures, any man has to pass through this stage if he wants and if he is able to acquire a "rightful", "mature" age status. From this point of view the wolf/dog stage, framing and forestalling the initiation rites and, in a sense, being an initiation complex in itself, have certain positive connotations, connected above all with the notions of youth, strength, aggressiveness and permanent combat readiness (and also with a specific "divine irradiation", the capacity to "run amok", contempt and readiness for death and pain). These qualities are characteristic of the very notion

---

[17] Also translated "ghost" or "soul" [Editors'note].

of masculinity, positive markers of a cultural tradition and seen as fitting - to some extent - for any possible male behaviour pattern.

On the other hand, for grown-up men these modes of behaviour are territorially and magically conditioned, and appear as unambiguously positive only within the limits of a strictly defined warrior/hunting territory of a "Wild Field"; displaying the same attitudes to those "foreign" to their territory of "home and temple" is fraught with the risk of breaking rules, with "hybris" that in some cases may lead to the deprivation of the higher male status.

Hence, the features of a "wolf" behaviour - speech patterns making no exception - can impart to their subjects some totally opposite characteristics. Within the limits of a "Wild Field" territorial and magical situation, any demonstration of a "wolf manners" or a "wolf-speech" is, undoubtedly, aimed at elevating the subject's situational status. Army culture being traditionally a male-only one (and marginal, from the point of view of the basic status culture zones) quite naturally is subject to the like behaviour models - as well as criminal and some other marginal cultures. This thesis is so obvious for anyone living in modern Russia that it needs nothing more than being just stated.

Of course, these forms of behaviour can take place not only at the "wolf territory" in a strict sense. The territory of a feast, being magically "fenced off" the common culture space, also permits - and sometimes even implies - the usually unacceptable modes of behaviour; being conditioned and constrained by ritual, any demonstration of an openly, "beyond the borders" masculine attitude, tabooed in "normal" life, can play a positive, beneficial, and even sacral role. Also in a conflict situation (male-to-male), when the subject is in sharp need of adequate ways and means enabling him to suppress his opponent, the "everyday" norms can recede to the background, giving way to the habitual forms of aggressive demonstration in their "barefaced", "wolf" forms. The usual tendency to exclude from the conflict situation all the participants and circumstances "magically incompatible" with it becomes apparent in the search for an adequate place where the conflict could be developed and settled (from the common "let's get out of here and have a talk" and up to the common and strictly observed ban on indoor duels, especially in respect of any kind of living quarters), as well as in the selection of the "adequate" participants (quantitative restrictions [tête-à-tête], the instituting of seconds in a traditional duel situation; qualitative restrictions - the equal by age and status participants are favored, while women and children are virtually excluded from the process). Thus conflict itself is ritualized, "played" according to certain rules and - just like a feast - "fenced off" from the everyday culture space to prevent damage, creating no peril for the "peaceful" magistics so crucial here.

On the other hand, the "dog" status is inadequate from the point of view of those norms active within the everyday culture space. "Wolves" and "dogs" lack a place of their own inside the "human" territory, which can be contaminated by the very fact of their presence: all the respective forms and norms of behaviour are strictly tabooed, and their subjects, if not passing through the purification rites and thus transforming from wolves back into men, lack elementary "civil rights". They are - by definition - the bearers of chthonic characteristics, they are "dead" from the magistical point of view and, as such, simply do not "exist". (Hence the practice of "excluding" members of warrior bands from the common law. Thus, an Irish youth wanting to become a fenian had to obtain his clan consent on that he would not revenge for his relatives even if they would be killed up to the last living soul. At the same time, if a fenian caused any kind of damage to anybody, his kin were unaccountable.) In this case, arrogating the "dog's" attributes to somebody appears to be rather a strong act from the magistical point of view - being equal to an opponent's obliteration, as having no right for existence.

The formula of Russian mat

Let's return now to the key formula of Russian *mat*. The phrase *"pes eb tvoiu mat"* seems to be a perfect formula of the opponent's social self magic annihilation, for from the point of view of the territorial and magical connotations, its meaning can be described as follows. The opponent's mother was defiled by a dog, the difference between a "wild" warrior and an actual animal in this context being insufficient. Therefore, the opponent is unclean, damned and - in fact - simultaneously dead in three senses: 1) because his father was inhuman (and so he is inhuman himself), 2) because his mother loses her right to be a woman by the very fact of her coitus with a dog, that makes her a bitch, and her son - a son of a bitch, and 3) because the territory where the coitus of the kind is possible cannot be "normal" and thus adequate for a human child conception - it is a "Wild Field" and as such opposed to any human space.

4. *Mat*-speech practices, their specificity, functions and status within their territorial and magical attachment and the peculiarities of the Russian army *mat*

I suppose that initially the "*maternaia laia*" ("*mat* barking") was a kind of territorially attached code, having no obligatory invective connotations but strictly tabooed within the limits of foreign to it, strictly "human" territories. Because of this not only really strong *mat* invectives, but the very "out of place" speech practices acquire openly invective connotations within these zones - owing to the destructive "dog" magistics' becoming even more destructive by being foreign outside the "prescribed" zone (in the earlier, magic-oriented societies) or at least to the fact that they simply "insult one's ear" (in the later societies, oriented sometimes on the same but losing their initial magical meaning sets of social tabooes).

In this case the denominations of those parts of a human body, that have to do with fertility and as such cannot be tabooed in (ideal) agricultural or pastoral societies whose welfare is based on the procreative magic procedures, are to acquire tabooistic status only in the case when they are associated with the key formula situation. In other words, *khui* in this case is in no way a membrum virile, but *pesii*, the dog's *khui*, *pizda* is a bitch's, *such'ia pizda*, and the verb *iebat'* denotes not a coitus between a man and a woman, but between a dog and a bitch (let me remind that the 'dog-warriors' not only named themselves so, but were the dogs from the magistical point of view). Hence, the corresponding terms applied to the "human" reality won't be denominative by character - they'd be a part of an encoding practice, conveying quite a specific "wolf" attitude.

Indeed, nobody just "cusses" using *mat*; up to the present moment people just speak it. Among the great quantity of lexical and grammatical forms derived from the three main and some more "auxiliary" productive roots, only insignificant number of words (nouns, mainly) could be determined as invectives. The verbs *iebat'*, *v"iebyvat'*, *vyiebyvat'sia*, *iebnut'*, *naiebnut'*, *naiebat'*, *ostoiebenit'*, *uiebyvat'*, *pízdit'*, *pizdít'*, *opizdenet'*, *okhuiet'*; nouns *khui*, *khuin'a*, *khuieten'*, *pizda*, *pizdiulei* (Gen., pl.), *pizdets*, *bliad'*, *iebar'*, *iebenia* (pl.); adjectives *okhuiennyi*, *okhuitel'nyi*, *kherovyi*, *pizdetskii*, *pizdanutyi*, *iebnutyi*, *iebanutyi*; adverbs *okhuienno*, *khuievo* etc. are extremely emphatic as compared to their non-*mat* synonyms, sometimes to the extent where they lack any adequate "translation" into "normative" Russian - but they are not invectives[18].

The everyday, "normative" speech is totally transparent for a *mat*-speaker; contrarily, the lack of corresponding speech practices makes *mat* absolutely obscure for a - hypothetical - "pure" Russian language speaker. Any attempt to speak in *mat* using the same rules that organize the usual "human" speech inevitably gives the experimentalist away. Here we come to the main problem of the Russian army *dukh*, a fresher, a newcomer - but before switching to it we have to specify the main characteristics of the army *mat* that make it different from the same patterns in the everyday speech practices of the majority of the modern Russian-speaking males (and more and more females also).

The first of the army *mat* basic characteristics is its totality. No "closed zones" where *mat* would be more or less tabooed exist within the army culture - with the possible exception of the officers' flats in "military towns" when the wives or the daughters are present: but recently even this narrow zone gets more and more eroded.

The second is the universality of army *mat*. No such situation exists in army culture that could not be "covered by *mat*" (*pokryt' matom* = *oblozhit' matom* = *vymaterit'*) (to cover by *mat* = to berate).

And the third one is the primacy of army *mat*, for it is the basis for all the behaviour and code practices existing in the Russian army. The necessity for any *dukh* "*vsasyvan'ie sluzhby*" ("suction of service") comes only through mastering the *mat* "army code", emphatic usage of which serves as one of the main markers for successful adaptation. Any - purely hypothetical - attempt to cling to "normative" Russian speech will inevitably lead only to the

---

[18] The peculiarities of the *mat* encoding and of the mat usage are discussed at length in the article mentioned in footnote 1.

experimenter being transferred to the pariah class of *chmo*[19]. At the same time, any other form of passive or active resistance to the system of the traditional self-organization of the levy soldiers[20] (the system of *neustavnye otnosheniia* ["out-of-regulations interrelations"] or *dedovshchina*) are due to "correction" within the limits of the system itself. This kind "defensive" reaction on the part of the system is the best evidence for the *mat* encoding being primary for any practices existing within its limits.

The first thing that the recruits from non-Slavonic peoples learned in the Soviet army (and learn now in the Russian one) was *mat*. Mastering *mat* emphasizes the high situative status of a speaker, and in the case of *inorodcheskii* ("other-peoples") staff-sergeant substitutes, in fact, the mastering of the "due-to-regulations" Russian language. Pronounced with a strong Uzbek (Azerbaijanian, Lezghin etc.) accent, the phrase *"Vas ne pízdishch - vi khuieiete"* is well-known to anybody, who used to be closely acquainted with the former Soviet army. After then, the *mat* encoding becomes the basis for the non-status male communication on the native languages - and for the communication with the representatives of the other nations - and goes hand

---

[19] A complex notion, meaning a pitiful, obnoxious and foolish person of the lowest possible status, untidy in his clothes and habits and subject to "everybody's" disdain and ordering about. Possibly, going up to the Yiddish *"schmok"* passing usual rather way through the criminal argot, where we meet *"chmo"* and *"chmyr'"* in the meanings close to the army ones, and *"shmu'* ("cunt") and *"shmokha"* ("whore").

[20] Any attempts to attribute the appearance of *dedovshchina*-like relations only to the late-Soviet army (See: K. Bannikov, *Antropologiia ekstremal'nykh grupp. Dominantnyie otnosheniia sredi voiennosluzhashchikh srochnoi sluzhby Rossiiskoi Armii*, Moskva, 2002, p. 41) are but the evidence of a certain "research naivity» (peculiar to the Bannikov's book as a whole - in spite of abundance of rather interesting field material). Not to mention the other national and historical traditions, which any researcher calling himself anthropologist just must be acquainted with, a lot of suitable data could be found in respect of the Russian army tradition: giving a striking resemblance to the ones existing in the late Soviet or modern Russian army. Comp. e.g. the abundantly described (See: V. Kozhevin, "Neformal'nyie traditsii rossiiskoi voiennoi shkoly kontsa XIX - nachala XX vv.", *Voienno-istoricheskaia antropologiia*, lezhegodnik, 2002. *Predmet, zadachi, perspektivy razvitiia*, M., 2002, pp. 195-215 and pp. 216-229; E. Komarovskii, "Vospitatel'nyie aspekty kadetskikh traditsii v rossiiskikh imperatorskikh kadetskikh korpusakh XIX - nachala XX vv.", *Voiennoistoricheskaia antropologiia*, lezhegodnik, 2002; N.K.M., *Tsuk*, Pedagogicheskii sbornik. 1908. Kn. 501, pp. 200-212; N. Kekushev, *Zveriada*, Moskva: Iuridicheskaia litteratura, 1991; E. Giatsintov, *Zapiski belogo ofitsera*, SPb., 1992; A. Ignat'ev, *Piat'desiat let v stroiu*, M., 1989) pre-revolutionary practice of so-called *"tsuk"* in the military schools (the reasons of this very military milieu being the best-described seem quite evident).

in hand with permissibility of other behaviour practices, tabooed within the "native" cultural context, like eating pork by the demobilized Moslems.

> - *Poslushai, Ruslan, a iz chego ty shashlyk delaiesh?*
> - *Iz svininy. Iz svininy shashlyk - samyi, bliad', vkusnyi.*
> - *Ruslan, no ty zhe musul'manin. Razve tebe mozhno svininu iest'?*
> - *Kakoi, na khui, mozhno - ne mozhno? Ia, bliad', v russkoi armii sluzhil.*
> (Saratov, 1996)

> [- Listen, Russlan, what meat do you take for shashlyk?
> - Pork. The pork shashlyk is the most, *bliad'*, tasty one.
> - But Russlan, you are a Moslem. Does it mean that you may eat pork?
> - What, *na khui*, may - not may? The Russian army is where I, *bliad'*, did serve].

The self-organized levy soldiers' milieu, just as any other marginal milieu, needs a rigid system of the behaviour encoding, openly manifested through a system of no less rigid code markers. Only the system of the kind, strictly ranged and marked, allows the hierarchical relations, immanent to this milieu, to be instantaneously established and maintained. Any group of soldiers, consisting of any number of people coming from any different units, if being left on one's own, will organize itself in the course of a day or two into a hierarchical system with strictly established status positions and gradations. The garrison hospitals could serve as the best example of the like self-organization - the privates and sergeants usually come here one by one and from different units, but at once fit in the pattern. "*Srok sluzhby*" (the length of being in service) and the potential status of the future "bedmates" are instantly defined by those soldiers already being given the hospital treatment, through the system of markers, conveyed in the behaviour patterns and in the peculiarities of treating one's uniform, absolutely transparent for all the participants of the situation. Nevertheless, sometimes the complicated situations are possible:

A student of the Saratov State University taking part in the summer military training, is brought late in the evening to the garrison hospital in Shikhany with a minor trauma. His clothing is rather specific: after coming to the unit location, the "cadets" were produced with the dingy [next to white] uniforms of the 1936 standard [knee-long soldier's blouses to be girded by belt and galife breeches]. As he is sitting in the casualty ward, two patient "*dukhs*", obviously sent by the "*deds*" for the reconnaissance, watch him from the dark corridor through the half-opened side door. The whisper comes:

- *Vrode, dembel'. A vrode, i net.*
- *A khui iego zneiet. Poidiom, Demida sprosim.*
- *Pizdy dast.*
- *Oshibems'a, khuzhe budet.*
- *Nu, na khui, poshli.*
Dukhs are away. A few minutes later a loud voice comes from behind the door.
- *Vy cho, mudaki, bliad', okhuieli? Da ia vas, bliad', na khui, vyiebu I vysushu! Kakoi, na khui, dembel', eto zhe, suka-bliad', salaga letniaia.*
[Privolsk, Sartatov region, 1985]

[- Seems to be a ded. But who knows.
- *Khui* knows. Let's go and ask Demid.
- *Pizdy dast* (He'll beat us blue).
- Make a mistake and get worse.
- Well, *na khui*, let's go.
- You, *mudaki, bliad', okhuieli?* I'll, *bliad', na khui, vyiebu I vysushu* you (I'll fuck and squeeze you dry)! What, *na khui*, kind of a *dembel'* is he, he's just a *salaga letniaia* (specific term for the students passing their summer military training)].

The *a priori* presence of a behaviour encoding and code markers system in a form of the army regulations distinguishes the army milieu from other marginal - say the criminal - ones. This primarily established system serves are basic for the army milieu self-organisation. On one hand, the knowledge of the regulations is necessary for mastering the inner code systems. On the other, the regulations serve as a kind of foundation, on which the whole structure of the army "out-of-regulation" self-organisation erects itself, and the degree to which this or that person is free to treat the regulations is the best marker for his place within the "out-of-regulation" hierarchy. *"Vsosat' sluzhbu"* means to master the fundamentals of such re-coding, giving one an opportunity to manoeuvre between the "up to regulations" and "out of regulations" codes.

The recruits' behaviour transformation, necessary for the army mechanisms' adequate functioning goes first of all through the regulations-bound speech practice system (e.g. the specific "normal", "free from *mat*" officers' speech, that M. Bakhtin would call a sociolect). The re-coding of this system also goes through the speech practice system - the *mat* one. Thus, one of the constitutive elements in the "education of the young" is a peculiar re-coding training, where any "wrong" from the point of view of the official army regulations phrase pronounced by a *dukh*, produces a *mat* rhyme on the side of a *ded* - or even an officer.

- *Saveliev*!
- *A?*
- *Khui na*!

- *Dneval'nyi!*
- *Cho?*
- *Khui cherez plecho! Tashchi stanok iebal'nyi!*

- *Mozhno voiti?*
- *Mozhno Mashku, bliad', za liazhku! A v armii - "razreshite"!*

- *A kak!*
- *Da khuiem ob kosiak!*

The communicative act of the kind carries out several functions at once. Apart from "teaching the regulations", it naturally demonstrates the difference in the warrior status that exists between the participants - through the demonstration of difference in level, to which they master the codes and are free in treating them. Violation of the regulated communication through ignorance at once provokes an openly out-of-regulations speech act, putting the interlocutors "on different sides of the regulations".

At the same time, among those servicemen mastering the codes, any demonstration of a strictly up-to-regulations behaviour may be interpreted as a sign of refusing communication. The usual threat of a senior by rank to the inferior ones: "*Ne khotite zhit' po-khoroshemu, budem zhit' po ustavu*" (As you don't want to live well, we shall live according to the regulations) has this very meaning. Here, as it seems to me, the reasons for the famous dislike that field marshal Suvorov had to "*nemoguznaiki*" is to be found. The demonstration of a traditional warrior "*schweinbruderlei*" which Suvorov used to exploit when dealing with inferior ranks was not evidence of him wishing to demonstrate any real equality of status. It was only to flatter - and it flattered - the soldiers' self-esteem, as an act of acknowledgement of equal rights to master a code. In this case, the up-to-regulations answer "*Ne mogu znat'!*" (I don't know!) to any, even the most provocative question of the *otets-komandir* (father-commander) was equal to breaking up the communication. On the contrary, any dashing and spirited answer, even absolutely absurd (even preferably, absurd), was an evidence for unanimity in the acceptance of the code, mastering it and readiness to "play according to the rules" - and keeping the hierarchical relations untouched[21]. It is hard to doubt that the basis for Suvorov's code speaking could be nothing else but *mat*.

Lev Tolstoi, himself a former battle officer, made an excellent presentation of the like situation in the famous scene at the road, in the evening of 5th November, after the first day of the Krasnoie battle narrated in "*War & Peace*". Kutuzov begins his speech addressed to the soldiers of Preobrazhenski regiment as a commander-in-chief and then Tolstoi brings the reader's attention to the change in Kutuzov's manner: now he speaks like a "simple old man, wanting to inform his comrades of something important". And after he ends his speech with a *mat* phrase, all the men who are present let themselves go, "buck-up' and become at once a group of comrades. In the Russian army code system of 1812, this speech act could have one more

---

[21] On the combination of the "brotherly", "comrade" terminology and feeling with the strict hierarchical relations as an inborn characteristics of a male warrior band, see a very strong in some aspects Enright's book: M.J. Enright, *Lady with a mead cup. Ritual, prophecy and lordship in the European warband from La Tène to the Viking Age*, Chippenham, 1996.

meaning: it emphasized the continuity of a "glorious" tradition, coming right from victorious Suvorov. The tradition of admiring with "*krepkoie soldatskoie slovtso*" (hard-boiled soldiers' little word), often without the direct "citation" but with a mute implying of mutual (on the writer's side, as well as on the reader's) knowledge of the code, comes down in the "high" Russian literary tradition from Tolstoi, through the writers dealing with the wars of 1914 - 1920s, like Babel or Serafimovich, and 1939 - 1945, like Viktor Nekrasov, up to the modern texts dealing with modern Russian army and modern armed conflicts.

But it seems that the traditions of *mat* functioning within the XVIII or XIX Russian army and those of the Soviet Army were somewhat different. The codes existing in the professional army of the Russian Empire offered a recruit some kind of a military initiation, having a life-long importance for him and providing him with an adequate set of behaviour patterns (seen as marginal by the rest of society, but nevertheless in this very quality fitting in the social interrelations net, for the quantity of those veterans coming back to their villages was insignificant if to compare it to the rest of male population)[22]. The same codes functioning in the Red (and later in the Soviet) Army in the lower ranks based on the short-term levy principle, had quite a different social impact. The task of marginalizing a recruit, making him forget the ways of his native village and fit into the "wolf/dog" behaviour patterns of a lower warrior rank was done no less successfully. But a recruit was no longer condemned to a life-long marginal role and after spending his two or three years in the army, a *dembel* had to return to the "normal" life passing no real initiation to a grown-up status. All the initiatiory practices existing inside the self-organized army milieu are - by the tradition - aimed at acquiring a high marginal status. After returning home, all the code markers of *dembel* status become useless trinkets, and his real social status remains the lowest possible.

---

[22] Situation hardly changed after Miliutin's army reform of 1870. Although the general levy system was proclaimed the main principle of army complectation, in fact, hardly 20 to 25 per cent of recruits really went to the ranks - and the whole social strata were totally excluded from the conscription system. Thus, in 1914, the Russian Empire, having on paper the hugest army in the world, could promise to its allies to mobilize "at once" only about 800 000 soldiers, of which, actually, only 400 000 were in time to begin the war activities against the German and Austro-Hungarian forces. In 1941, the Red Army units, concentrated at the USSR western borders, had ten times more men, while there was no growth of population.

Here we come to the main task of the Soviet Army: to marginalize the male population of the former Russian Empire. The pre-revolution levy system left the vast majority of male population outside the army training - and thus outside the training in those marginal behaviour practices that were basic for the army culture. The new one reduced the term of service but became total, aimed at instilling the new forms of behaviour in the vast majority of the most socially mobile age strata of the traditionally rigid "country-side" population (peasants of different categories, mestechko Jews etc) that constituted up to 85% of the new USSR citizens. Peasant community, dictating the traditional life strategies to the majority of population, used to be the main stumbling block for any reforms and reformers of imperial Russia. Even Stolypin reforms, the most purposeful and pragmatic attempt to destroy the peasant community and to plant the new economic relations in the country-side, really failed.

Bolsheviks, being one of the weakest political forces at the Russian political scene in 1917, could succeed only by utterly slackening the situation, provoking the wave of violence - and then by saddling it. The four-million army of former peasants clad in the soldiers' tunics, armed and supplied with totally new to them models of behaviour formed a necessary critical mass for the explosion. The success of the October revolution of 1917 in St. Petersburg was due to the number of reformed regiments quartered in the capital - having no itch to return to the trenches and at the same time acquiring the habit of the "soldiers' self-rule", the practice very much alike the primitive warrior band "armed democracy". The three years showed the limits of this "cavalry attack at capitalism", as Lenin phrased it - for these four millions were enough to change the situation "in the city", but as compared to the mass of not-marginalised country-side population, they were too little. While the main enemy was the defenders of *ancien régime*, while the main campaigns of the Civil war were deployed along the railway lines, taking and loosing the main junctions and towns with the warehouses, the success was on the bolsheviks' side. The former peasants were ready to pass through this bloody initiation, and the phantom of total marginalisation seemed quite real. But when the Whites were beaten and the great numbers of mobilised peasants returned to their villages - and then the real Civil war began to unfold itself with Tambov uprising, with Kronshtadt revolt etc. For now the peasant community became aware of a real threat. And this community showed inclination to defend itself against "the city". So Bolsheviks had to change their politics radically, forgetting for a while about the immediate World Revolution and letting the New Economy Politics to re-create the very "proprietorial" relations that were one of the main targets for the early Bolshevik propaganda.

The task changed also. The peasant community was to be destroyed not at once, by the "cavalry attack". It was to be taken "by starvation", by implanting the forms of behaviour alien to it - and by doing so totally. The collectivization couldn't begin just after the end of the Civil war. Any attempt to force the peasants into kolkhoz in 1922 would mean the immediate end of Bolshevik rule. It took six years more and about 6 millions of young peasants passing through the Red Army training - and massive recruiting the demobilized from the ranks to the new Soviet structures[23] - to begin the process. It is worth remembering that it was not the literate urban intelligentsia that became the main victim of Stalin's repressions. The majority of the urban intelligentsia somehow managed to find their way to the new ways of living and new behaviour modes[24]. The peasants proved to be much more rigid. And those who were not "reforged" in the ranks of the Red Army or killed by the same army during the neutralisation actions formed the main contingent of the army-guarded concentration camps: the natural habitat for the third of the main Soviet *mat*-based cultures, the camp/criminal one.

Thus the task was successfully fulfilled. The two main bolshevik aims were being solved: destruction of any social structure able to resist to a new system and creating a bottomless reserve of living force for the "future fights for the World Revolution". The second aim was forgotten in the 1940s, as a result of the Second World War. Then Soviet socialism tried to become creative and thus to forget the first aim - or at least not to mention it too openly. But the army has always been one of the most rigid social structures. And the principles, on which the Soviet army (and the code systems operating in it)

---

[23] Not to mention the massive ideological pressure, the propagation of literacy that made it easier to create the unified educational and cultural space, etc.

[24] Including the Party codes "for the inner use" - also *mat*-based. *Mat* was strictly censored from the everyday official usage and from "Soviet culture" that tried to appear a stable and a status one. But any first secretary of the regional party committee who wanted to control his subordinates and - at the same time - to create a "comrade" atmosphere, had to master *mat*.

were based, bore little difference from those of the Red Army. The marginal warrior *mat*-based code systems became "inborn" for the vast majority of the male population. *Dembelia* coming from the army taught their younger brothers up to the ways that could help them to pass through the army initiatory practices - and quite naturally *mat* was the basis for such a knowledge (compare the fatalistic proverb, concerning the "inevitableness" going to prison: *"ran'she siadesh' - ran'she vyidesh"* [the earlier you get there, the earlier you get out] - taking in view that the code systems of the criminal milieu are also *mat*-based).

Within the modern cultural situation in Russia, when the marginalization of the speech practices (and, naturally, not only the speech ones) becomes total, army *mat* in some aspects loses its specific character, preserving some peculiarities which are to be looked at rather as the features of a professional argot. This process might seem equal to the process of the post-war liberalizing the speech practices within the English-speaking communities, but it seems to me that the reasons for taking down the taboos for the obscene speech are common only in some aspects. Although these very aspects seem to have to do with the army inner code practices.

7   Dedovshchina and the Committee of Soldiers' Mothers under Gorbachev

Julie ELKNER

> Hundreds, thousands of lead coffins are soldered annually in every large army—a phenomenon so normal that in America at least, the press is silent about it, and the chatterbox-orators, who do nothing but wait for sensations, are silent. —
> *Kommunist vooruzhennykh sil*, November 1990[1]

> [Military service] is a compulsory state service. And [*dedovshchina*] is in actual fact a crime against the individual ... It's exactly the same as if someone were attacked on the street, or beaten up, or tortured. So there is no such thing as a separate crime of 'non-statutory relations'[2]. That's a mask, a lie. And for long decades this lie concealed the fact that mass crimes were being committed. —
> Valentina D. Mel'nikova, Committee of Soldiers' Mothers[3]

> For the military establishment, which is unquestionably implicated in the crimes committed behind the impenetrable green fences, the movement of soldiers' mothers represents no small danger. The fact is that ... the overwhelming majority of the country's citizens are in solidarity with the movement ... This means that the movement's potential strength is huge. And, realising this, the USSR Defence Ministry and the Military Procurator's Office dependent upon it ... have organised a mighty counter-action against the soldiers' mothers. — *Rossiiskaia gazeta*, August 1991[4]

The culture of the Soviet military was imbued with and sustained by a distinctive sentimentalism. Nowhere was this more evident than in the official rhetoric surrounding universal military service. Read the Soviet military press, or the Soviet mainstream conservative press for that matter, from the spring or autumn of any year, when the twice-yearly call-up of new conscripts was conducted, and you will find a series of standard articles containing a set of standard images: the romance of the young conscript serving in far-flung sections of the country, fulfilling his sacred duty to the Motherland, attaining

---

[1] V. Uspenskii, "Tainyi sovetnik vozhdia", *Kommunist vooruzhennykh sil*, no. 21, November 1990, p. 84.
[2] The euphemistic term for *dedovshchina* favoured by the military.
[3] V.D. Mel'nikova, author's interview, Moscow, 21 October 1998.
[4] S. Kornilov, "Dvizhenie soldatskikh materei: ne v nogu, no soobshcha", *Rossiiskaia gazeta*, no. 173, 17 August 1991, p. 3.

manhood by facing hardship, sustained by the memory of his home and most importantly his mother. A key moment in such narratives was the conscript's separation from his mother. Such separations paid tribute to the sublimation of maternal instincts and the poignancy of the mixed feelings of the mother, sad but proud to see her son become a man and fulfil his mission of defending the Soviet state, and ultimately happy to entrust him to the care of the Soviet military.

Cracks in this idealised image of military service were already beginning to become visible by the time Gorbachev came to power in 1985; by the end of his rule, the image was on the point of shattering altogether. In the erosion of the legitimacy of the universal military service and of the Soviet military itself, the Committee of Soldiers' Mothers (henceforth the CSM)[5] played a crucial role. Under Gorbachev, the Committee emerged as a mass movement aimed at exposing and eradicating the violence endemic in Soviet military barracks, violence which had hitherto been masked by sentimentalism and taboo[6]. In particular, the Committee played an important role in drawing public attention to *dedovshchina* — the widespread systems of informal power hierarchies that operated in Soviet barracks, and the associated violence in which senior conscripts bullied and victimised new recruits[7].

---

[5] Currently the organisation's full title is the Union of Committees of Soldiers' Mothers of Russia.

[6] The initial impetus for the soldiers' mothers' movement was the issue of deferments from military service for tertiary students, which had been restricted in the early 1980s. After a group of mothers successfully lobbied the USSR Supreme Soviet and attained the re-institution of educational deferments in spring 1989, it was decided to give the movement a concrete organisation base, and the CSM was formally established in April 1989.

[7] Strictly speaking *dedovshchina* is a quite specific term referring to the informal power hierarchies governing relations between conscripts based on their length of service. In this article I follow the practice widely adhered to in the Soviet media of using the term more loosely to refer to the associated violence in the barracks, and as shorthand for the tyranny inherent throughout the Soviet military hierarchy. It should be noted that barracks violence also often took the form of *zemliachestvo*, or *gruppovshchina*, whereby conscripts from particular regions or republics banded together and persecuted rival ethnic groups. Levinson makes a convincing case that these ethnic divisions amongst conscripts were drawn as a survival mechanism in response to *dedovshchina* and its associated violence, which indirectly created a sense of ethnic identity between people who may not have felt any commonality in civilian life; A. Levinson, "Ob estetike nasiliia. Armiia i obshchestvo v SSSR/Rossii za poslednie 10 let", *Neprikosnovennyi zapas*, vol. 2, no. 4, 1999.

Controversy over *dedovshchina* played a significant role in eroding the Soviet military's authority from 1988 onwards[8]. Claims that the military was incapable of maintaining order in its own barracks in peacetime cast doubt on its overall defence-capability and efficiency. At the same time, revelations about *dedovshchina* ushered in a dramatic shift in public perceptions of military service. Official rhetoric on the beneficial nature of military service for young men's physical and moral development was displaced by the widespread acknowledgement that for many conscripts, military service was in fact a profoundly damaging and traumatic experience. By the same token, the validity of the hitherto unquestioned notion that it was every male Soviet citizen's "sacred duty" to undergo military service was eroded, as the controversy over *dedovshchina* brought into question the legitimacy of the state's claim to exact military service from its male citizens. For many, in fact, *dedovshchina* provided a reasonable justification for draft evasion, and was one of the causes of the conscription crisis of the late 1980s-early 1990s.

The Soviet military put up staunch resistance to what the prominent pro-military conservative writer Prokhanov described as "the myth of the degradation of the individual in the army"[9]. This article traces the military's attempts to control and to set limits upon debate over barracks violence in the face of the

---

[8] The public controversy over *dedovshchina* can be traced to a July 1988 article in *Komsomol'skaia Pravda*, describing an incident in which a conscript who had been the victim of ongoing abuse in the barracks eventually snapped and turned his weapon against his fellow servicemen, killing eight; M. Mel'nik, "Intsident v spetsvagone", *Komsomol'skaia pravda*, 20 July 1988, cited S. Solnick, *Stealing the State: Control and Collapse in Soviet Institutions*, Cambridge: Harvard University Press, 1998, p. 185, and Levinson, *Neprikosnovennyi zapas*, 1999, *op. cit.* The taboo on mentioning *dedovshchina* had first been broken in works of fiction on the pages of the so-called "thick" literary journals, despite attempts on the part of the military to prevent their publication. The first of these, a novella by Iu. Poliakov, was published in the journal *Iunost'* in November 1987; Iu. Poliakov, "Sto dnei do prikaza", *Iunost'*, no. 11, 1987, pp. 46-68. *Iunost'* received numerous readers' responses to the story, both positive and negative, a selection of which were published in "Skol'ko dnei do prikaza?", *Iunost'*, no. 5, 1988, pp. 90-1. For an account of the debate over Poliakov's work see S. Zamaschikov, "Insiders' Views of the Soviet Army", *Problems of Communism*, vol. 37, nos. 3-4, May-August 1988, pp. 110-16. Another highly controversial novella on this theme was S. Kaledin's "Stroibat" which dealt with *dedovshchina* in the military-construction units, S. Kaledin, "Stroibat", *Novyi mir*, no. 4, April 1989, pp. 59-89.

[9] A. Prokhanov, "Zametki konservatora", *Nash sovremennik*, no. 5, 1990, reprinted in L. Dobrokhotov et al, *Nesokrushimaia i legendarnaia: V ogne politicheskikh batalii 1985-1993 gg.*, Moscow: Terra, 1994, p. 211.

CSM's campaign to increase public scrutiny of the previously hidden sides of military life.

1. Soldiers' Mothers' strategies

> There isn't anybody who knows this problem better than the Committee of Soldiers' Mothers. Because we come into contact with this problem every day. We live and breathe these military units, we know their routines, we know what goes on there behind the fence, because the boys tell us much more than they tell their own parents. — CSM member Liudmila N. Zinchenko[10]

One of the CSM's main objectives was to raise public awareness of violence and peacetime deaths in the barracks. Soldiers' mothers' press conferences and demonstrations were an important counterweight to military attempts to deny or downplay barracks violence. In particular, the participation in these demonstrations of grieving mothers whose sons had been killed in peacetime provided eloquent proof of the problem's existence, greatly weakening the military's position. Grieving mothers threw into relief the disjuncture between the mothers' pain over the deaths of their sons on the one hand, and the regime's treatment of conscripts as so much expendable manpower on the other. Public representations of maternal grief were a key aspect of soldiers' mothers' demonstrations during this period, and will be examined in more detail below.

Organised soldiers' mothers' activism on barracks violence took on mass proportions in the spring and summer of 1990, after the CSM widely publicised claims that fifteen thousand peacetime or non-combat deaths had occurred in the Soviet armed forces during the preceding four-year period, and that the military was actively engaged in covering up these deaths[11]. Mass soldiers' mothers' demonstrations over this issue were held in Moscow and elsewhere in early summer 1990[12].

---

[10] Liudmila N. Zinchenko, author's interview, Moscow, 20 October 1998.
[11] This figure appears to have originally been put forward by Vladimir Lopatin, USSR Supreme Soviet Deputy and one of the most high-profile young reformist officers, who was later to work closely with Yeltsin; see V. Marchenko, "Pravoporiadok v armii - glazami pravozashchitnikov", *Za mimuiu Rossiiu*, vol. 2, no. 20, March 1999.
[12] See S. Foye, "Moscow TV: 15,000 Soldiers Dead over Last Four Years", *RFE/RL Daily Report*, 5 June 1990. The Committee of Soldiers' Mothers had a particularly

The fifteen thousand figure would mean that non-combat deaths over the preceding four years exceeded the official number of Soviet deaths in almost a decade of fighting in Afghanistan, an irony which was not lost on democratic commentators[13]. In August 1990, a spokesman for the General Staff declared that the widely cited fifteen thousand figure did not "correspond to reality"; he refused, however, to provide alternative figures, on the grounds that this was classified information[14]. By the same token, the military refuted claims that 75-80 per cent of peacetime deaths were attributable to *dedovshchina*, maintaining that only just over 1 per cent of deaths in the army fell into this category[15]. Accidents arising out of conscripts' lack of discipline, carelessness, and drunkenness were cited as by far the most common cause of peacetime deaths[16].

Whatever the real figures may have been, for my purposes it is public perceptions of barracks violence that are of interest. Public opinion was obviously a matter of great concern to the military, too, whose attempts to shape perceptions of barracks life will be examined below.

---

high media profile in summer 1990. For other reports on their public campaign during this period see RFE/RL Daily Report, 5 June 1990; 2 July 1990; 17 July 1990; 20 July 1990; and 24 July 1990. See also G. Zhavoronkov, "'Spasi i sokhrani!', - shepchut soldatskie materi, provozhaia svoikh detei v armiiu", *Moskovskie novosti*, no. 29, 22 July 1990, p. 11; St. Foye, "Non-Combat Deaths: Latest Gorbachev Decree Reflects Army's Woes", RFE/RL Report on the USSR, 13 September 1990; and Shreeves, "Mothers against the Draft", pp. 3-8.

[13] In August 1989 the General Staff stated that 13,833 Soviet troops had died in Afghanistan from 25 December 1979 to 15 February 1989; cited A. Liakhovskii, "Na afganskoi vyzhzhennoi zemle", *Kommunist vooruzhennykh sil*, no. 22, November 1990, p. 62. The Committee of Soldiers' Mothers estimated that thirty-eight thousand noncombat deaths had occurred in the Soviet army during the same period; cited M. Galeotti, *Afghanistan: The Soviet Union's Last War*, London: Frank Cass, 1995, p. 97. For an example of democratic commentary highlighting the irony inherent in the fact that soldiers were more at risk in peacetime conditions at home than they had been in combat in Afghanistan see A. Demchenko, letter to the editor, *Ogonek*, no. 29, July 1989, p. 5.

[14] "Zhertvy dedovshchiny?", *Krasnaia zvezda*, no. 199, 30 August 1990, p. 4.

[15] *Ibid.* The 75-80 per cent figure appeared in the newspaper *Kuranty* in 1990; cited Galeotti, *Afghanistan*, 1995, *op. cit.*, p. 97.

[16] See V. Kaushanskii, "Osennie pikety", *Krasnaia zvezda*, no. 258, 10 November 1989, p. 2, and I. Ivaniuk, "...I strakhovoi polis", *Krasnaia Zvezda*, no. 5, 8 January 1991, p. 1. On occasion soldiers' mothers were directly implicated in such deaths by the military press; see Iu. Bychenkov, "Dve sud'by", *Krasnaia zvezda*, no. 264, 16 November 1990, p. 4, which recounts the case of a conscript who died in an accident while drunk on vodka sent to him in a parcel by his mother.

In addition to raising public awareness of the plight of victimised conscripts, the CSM lobbied for various concrete mechanisms to be put in place to protect conscripts and to prevent barracks violence. These demands were summarised in the Committee's official address to the USSR Supreme Soviet in April 1990, in which the mothers called for a number of measures to be taken with a view to improving the procedures governing investigation and prosecution of cases of barracks violence. In particular, they proposed that the Military Procurator's Office be abolished and replaced by an independent civilian body[17], and that an independent commission on peacetime deaths be established. The mothers also insisted that the practice of drafting ex-criminals be discontinued[18] and that statistics on peacetime deaths be declassified[19].

Later that year the Committee addressed the Supreme Soviet again, expanding its list of demands to include public access to barracks, compulsory state insurance for servicemen, legislation decriminalising desertion on self-defence grounds, abolition of the *stroibat*[20], and new medical examination

---

[17] Formally the Military Procurator's Office was part of the Office of the Procurator-General. Financially, however, and in numerous informal ways, the Military Procurator's Office was dependent upon the Defence Ministry, and military procurators were reportedly frequently willing to register violent deaths as suicides or natural deaths in exchange for housing and other resources; see W. Odom, *The Collapse of the Soviet Military*, Yale University Press, New Haven, 1998, p. 366. On the relationship between the Defence Ministry and the Military Procurator's Office see further "Konets revoliutsionnym tribunalam", *Moskovskii komsomolets*, no. 172, 10 September 1991, p. 1; "Femida zhdet resheniia", *Trud*, no. 29, 2 October 1991, p. 3; V. Vyzhutovich, "V kakom zvanii zakon?", *Izvestiia*, no. 246, 15 October 1991, p. 3. *Krasnaia zvezda* denied that the Military Procurator's Office was in any way compromised by its links to the Defence Ministry; see for example L. Zaika, "Na prestupnost' - edinym frontom", *Krasnaia zvezda*, no. 217, 21 September 1989, p. 2.

[18] The practice of drafting youths with criminal records, partly to compensate for falling birth-rates in the Slavic republics and difficulties meeting the draft quotas, was one of several factors contributing to the singular scale and brutality of bullying and initiation rites in the Soviet military. Other such factors include structural features of the Soviet military (such as the principle of *edinonachalie*; the entrenched culture of *krugovaia poruka* or "collective responsibility" at the lower levels; the low number of non-commissioned officers); and other demographic factors.

[19] G. Zhavoronkov, "'Spasi i sokhrani!',—shepchut soldatskie materi, provozhaia svoikh detei v armiiu", *Moskovskie novosti*, no. 29, 22 July 1990, p. 11.

[20] The popular term for the military-construction units (detachments) (VKOs) located within various Soviet civilian ministries and departments. Mortality and crime rates were especially high in the *stroibat*, which were notorious for their harsh conditions, poor safety record, corruption, and general neglect of the welfare of the conscripts.

regulations and procedures preventing the drafting of conscripts in poor health[21].

Meanwhile, pending the institution of legislative measures "from above" to remedy the situation, the Committee developed practical strategies aimed at preventing and counteracting barracks violence from below.

2. Knocking down the military's Potemkin villages

In the late 1980s, the Soviet military came under growing pressure to open up its barracks to public scrutiny. The Defence Ministry responded by stepping up construction of "show military settlements", Potemkin villages which bore little resemblance to the overcrowded and dilapidated military barracks in which most conscripts were housed[22]. As of 1989, as the Committee's criticism over *dedovshchina* mounted, the focus of this public relations campaign shifted to target soldiers' mothers in particular. A series of "gatherings" of soldiers' mothers were organised by the Defence Ministry, whereby soldiers' mothers from across the country were invited to visit individual units[23].

Such events lasted several days at a time amidst a frenzy of highly-orchestrated Soviet-style hospitality and gallantry. The mothers were greeted at the stations and airports with bouquets of crimson carnations and military bands. They would then witness training displays and be taken on guided tours of the units, and in the evenings concerts and banquets were held in their honour[24].

In spring 1989, one such attempt to woo the mothers backfired disastrously. The Moscow Military District's Political Administration had invited soldiers' mothers to view training demonstrations by the famous Taman Guards Division, followed by a concert and a special banquet honouring the mothers.

---

[21] N. Nikolaev, untitled, *Argumenty i fakty*, no. 46, November 1990, p. 8.
[22] M. Tsypkin, "The Soviet Military: Glasnost' against Secrecy", *Problems of Communism*, vol. 11, no. 3, May-June 1991, p. 59.
[23] See N. Polianskaia, "Slet soldatskikh materei", *Krasnaia zvezda*, no. 230, 6 October 1989, p. 2; "Mosty doveriia", *Krasnaia zvezda*, no. 237, 15 October 1989, pp. 1-2; V. Kaushanskii, "Osennie pikety", *Krasnaia zvezda*, no. 258, 10 November 1989, p. 2; "Slet soldatskikh materei", *Krasnaia zvezda*, no. 258, 10 November 1989, p. 4; and N. Gusarov, "Gotovnost' k dialogu", *Krasnaia zvezda*, no. 16, 20 January 1990, p. 2.
[24] See for example Polianskaia, 1989, *op. cit.*

Subsequent anonymous tip-offs informed the media that several soldiers had been killed during the training display when a shell exploded. The organisers had made no mention of these deaths, and next day the soldiers' mothers' programme had continued in a festive atmosphere[25]. Obviously this debacle only reinforced the impression of the military's callous attitude towards conscripts which such events were designed to dispel.

Even when these events ran smoothly, however, the Committee of Soldiers' Mothers remained unconvinced that the model units which the mothers were permitted to visit were in any way representative. Indeed, most Soviet citizens would surely have been familiar with this sort of window-dressing (*pokazukha*). *Krasnaia zvezda*, however, went to considerable effort to advertise the relief experienced by concerned soldiers' mothers after such visits. Throughout the late Gorbachev period, *Krasnaia zvezda* published numerous letters from soldiers' mothers in this vein. These letters were remarkably consistent in format and content. They all began by describing the mothers' initial anxieties over the media reports on *dedovshchina*, which were subsequently allayed upon visiting the units in person. The letters invariably ended with glowing descriptions of the barracks and the commanders, often with a word of advice to other mothers not to listen to those spreading rumours about the state of affairs in the barracks[26].

The Committee was not satisfied by the formal soldiers' mothers' visits organised and controlled by the military. It demanded genuinely open access to military units, and developed tactics aimed at breaking through the façade of the military's Potemkin villages. Committee member Liudmila Zinchenko relates:

---

[25] Mamicheva, letter to the editor, *Ogonek*, no. 21, May 1989, p. 7. See also Deputy Military Procurator Nagibin's comments on this incident; V. Nagibin, letter to editor, *Ogonek*, no. 29, July 1989, p. 5.

[26] See for example letters to the editor, "'Teper' my spokoiny za synovei", *Krasnaia zvezda*, no. 202, 2 September 1989, p. 3; "Opaseniia byli naprasny", *Krasnaia zvezda*, no. 270, 25 November 1989, p. 1; "Esli slushat' "znaiushchikh" liudei...", *Krasnaia zvezda*, no. 118, 24 May 1990, p. 5; and "My spokoiny za Andreiia", *Krasnaia zvezda*, no. 22, 29 January 1991, p. 2, all of which take the form described above. See also two articles summarising and paraphrasing similar letters received by soldiers' mothers; V. Yermolin, "Diapazon pliuralizma", *Krasnaia zvezda*, no. 275, 1 December 1989, p. 1, and G. Barnev, "Neizvestnaia armiia?", *Krasnaia zvezda*, no. 265, 20 November 1991, p. 3.

> The first time we went to a military unit, we were told 'Oh, now we'll show you this, and we'll show you that...' And then we started to implement 'dispersion' tactics—that is, we would arrive at the unit, two or three of us would engage the commander in conversation, and the rest would scatter throughout the unit. And then when we came together again, we'd ask one another 'What did you see? And what did you see? I saw a bruise. I saw a boy crying. I saw such and such.' And this general information, as it happened, gave us a complete picture of what was going on in the unit. Because otherwise, previously, all this was veiled, it was concealed from outside view[27].

Such practices enabled the Committee to build up profiles on individual units, instituting an alternative monitoring system and sharing this information with other Committee branches. The physical presence of the mothers in the units also combated the isolation of conscripts and acted as a deterrent against violence.

---

[27] Committee of Soldiers' Mothers member Liudmila N. Zinchenko, author's interview, Moscow, 20 October 1998.

3. The dangers of *glasnost'*

> Her eyes were burning with rage. She rose up above the crowd and hurled down ... scathing, merciless words, exposing the army: 'They're carving tridents on our sons' chests! They're burning the words "Glory to Ukraine!" on our sons' backs with cigarettes![28] They're mocking our sons!' And she also spoke of how the soldiers should go home, and mothers should take their sons away from the army, and should picket the *voenkomaty* (military commissariats) ... Ah, how appealing Natal'ia Nikolaevna Kovalenko found herself at that moment" [29].
> 'Give us facts, concrete names, addresses', the military men from the Ivano-Frankovskii garrison rejoindered.
> But what do names have to do with it? The most important thing is the rush of the rally, the roar of the crowd and the tears of the mothers... — from a 1991 *Krasnaia zvezda* article "If Your Son is a Deserter..." [30]

The military was unhappy about mothers intruding into the barracks, and argued that this often led to problems, undermining discipline and thwarting commanders' efforts to transform the conscripts into men[31]. It was difficult, however, to ban the mothers from entering the barracks without creating the impression that the military had something to hide.

The mothers' spontaneous inspections of military units were just one aspect of their incursion into the military sphere. Even more alarmingly for the military, the mothers were transgressing other boundaries governing the acceptable limits of public debate on military affairs by commenting on barracks violence in the media. In its struggle to reinforce the old boundaries cordoning

---

[28] Whether such a slogan would have been used by or against Ukrainian conscripts is unclear. In general, the inclusion of this line seems odd in the given context; this may be a case of creative misquoting on the part of the military press.

[29] Protesting soldiers' mothers were frequently depicted as motivated primarily by vanity and exhibitionism; see for example the semi-fictional description of a mother whose son had been killed in Afghanistan and who publicly refused to receive a medal on his behalf. The mother is portrayed as acting purely out of self-interest (the author claims that she had made herself up specially for the TV cameras), seeking attention and 'cheap popularity'. The author berates her, "so the glory of your hero-son is alien, incomprehensible to you—then return the medal without making a noisy spectacle under the floodlights, without insulting the honour of the dead soldier"; Uspenskii, 1990, *op. cit.*, p. 84. The mother's action is also attributed to the democrats' campaign to "whip up anti-Afghan [war] ecstasy".

[30] V. Popov, "Esli syn—dezertir...", *Krasnaia zvezda*, no. 9-10, 12 January 1991, p. 3.

[31] On the dangerous effects of parental visits see for example V. Salmin, "S etim nel'zia ne schitat'sia", *Krasnaia zvezda*, no. 252, 2 November 1989, p. 2, and the case of private Gelashvili described in V. Usol'tsev, "Za gran'iu razumnogo", *Krasnaia zvezda*, no. 269, 24 November 1989, p. 2.

off the military from the civilian world, the military employed a number of methods aimed at undermining the legitimacy of the mothers' commentary on the military.

One favoured line was to depict protesting soldiers' mothers as fuelled by female hysteria[32]. Women's propensity to hysteria and over-reaction was cited as necessitating restrictions on *glasnost'* in media coverage of military affairs. In 1990 the prominent military figure Colonel General Rodionov asserted that media coverage of *dedovshchina* was "sowing panic amongst mothers whose sons are going to the army"[33]. Military spokesmen frequently argued that issues like *dedovshchina* should not be discussed publicly, and that information on such internal military problems should be restricted to the military itself. For example, one officer conceded that *dedovshchina* should be discussed, but argued that "only military people should read this, they understand it and are in a position to draw the correct conclusions; but there's no need to frighten the mammas and grandmothers"[34].

The idea of women presuming to comment on military affairs was viewed as particularly disturbing, and was ridiculed by many commentators[35]. One broadside on non-specialist meddling in military affairs referred contemptuously to "unbalanced ladies" (*baryshni),* who demanded the abolition of conscription on the 'democratic' model but who were uninformed and failed to realise that so-called democratic armies in the west also contained "base-

---

[32] See for example *Krasnaia zvezda*'s coverage of the founding All-Union Congress of Servicemen's Parents which states that "more than once, the fever pitch of emotions drowned out common sense" and describes the women speaking at the congress as "tearing the microphones away from one another"; A. Vorob'ev, "Po antiarmeiskomu stsenariiu?", *Krasnaia zvezda*, no. 208, 9 September 1990, p. 1.

[33] I. Rodionov, "Kogda perestanut glumit'sia nad armiei i derzhavoi?", *Molodaia gvardiia*, no. 9, 1990, reproduced in Dobrokhotov et al, *Nesokrushimaia i legendarnaia*, 1994, *op. cit.*, p. 63.

[34] S. Martynov, *Soviet army officer*, cited N. Andreev, V. Litovkin, "Tri pis'ma iz armii. 3. Gotovy vypolnit' prikaz", *Izvestiia*, no. 40, 15 February 1991, p. 3.

[35] In a 1989 *Krasnaia zvezda* interview with "army sports master" Tiurin, for example, entitled "How to Become a Real Man", Turin complains about critics of the military, concluding "But male journalists aren't so bad; I am less able to understand those ... women who are attacking our army"; cited A. Goncharov, "Kak stat' nastoiashchim muzhchinoi", *Krasnaia zvezda*, no. 191, 19 August 1989, p. 3. When reformist forces within the military later proposed appointing a woman as Russian Defence Minister, misogynist rhetoric reached new heights of emotional intensity; see A. Lanshchikov, "Shtrikhi", *Literaturnaia rossiia*, no. 43, 23 October 1992, p. 11.

ness"[36]. Media representations of the soldiers' mothers generally portrayed them as ignorant, politically illiterate and concerned only with their personal, emotional interests[37].

The potential dangers of *glasnost'* in introducing new concepts and sensitive material to the public were illustrated by a November 1989 *Krasnaia zvezda* article entitled "The Boomerang: How a Mother Got Her Son out of Military Service"[38]. The article recounts a mother's cynical attempt to exploit the *dedovshchina* controversy in order to obtain her son's discharge, by attributing wounds sustained by her son in an accident to beatings by his fellow servicemen, thereby casting a slur on an innocent commander's reputation[39].

"The Boomerang" typified the general slant put on the issue of barracks violence by the military press. Numerous articles recounting cases of "fake" *dedovshchina* charges laid by soldiers' mothers were published in *Krasnaia zvezda* in the late Gorbachev period[40]. Such narratives reinforced ideas of women's emotions, particularly maternal instincts, as 'out of control' and having no place in a military environment. Furthermore, 'The Boomerang' demonstrated that mothers should not be exposed to information on barracks violence and other internal military problems. Finally, *Krasnaia zvezda*'s repeated publication of such stories cast doubt on the integrity of the CSM's claims regarding barracks violence.

What the author of "The Boomerang" finds most reprehensible is the fact that in her attempt to keep her son at home, the mother took shelter be-

---

[36] A. Fomenko, "Predannaia armiia", *Literaturnaia rossiia*, no. 4, 26 January 1990, p.9.
[37] For example, one article regarding a recent survey of women's attitudes towards military service and other related issues stated, "It is significant that the number of [respondents] who had difficulty answering questions connected with the service of their own sons in the army was minimal ... although up to 50% of the women were unable to answer a series of current political questions"; G. Sillaste, "Zhenshchiny zashchishchaiut svoikh synovei", *Narodnyi deputat*, no. 18, 1990, p.56.
[38] V. Kaushanskii, "Bumerang: kak mat' syna ot sluzhby izbavliala", *Krasnaia zvezda*, no. 259, 11 November 1989, p. 2.
[39] *Ibid*. The "boomerang" in the title refers to the criminal charges faced by the mother after she was found out in her deception.
[40] See for example V. Kovalev, "Za chto zh ty nas opozoril, synok... Pochemu daleko ne kazhdaia mat' skazhet eti slova sbezhavshemu iz armii soldatu?", *Krasnaia zvezda*, no. 236, 14 October 1989, p. 4; V. Evgen'ev, "Nespravedlivye upreki", *Krasnaia zvezda*, no. 258, 10 November 1989, p. 1; Iu. Gladkevich, "Za shirmoi 'dedovshchina'", *Krasnaia zvezda*, no. 27, 2 February 1990, p. 2; A. Volk, "'Derzhis', my dobivaemsia...", *Krasnaia zvezda*, no. 38, 15 February 1990, p. 2; and "Fantazii na temu 'dedovshchina'", *Krasnaia zvezda*, no. 12, 16 January 1991, p. 2.

hind "the eternal trust in sacred maternal feelings"[41]. This comment highlights the difficulties faced by the military in responding to protesting soldiers' mothers. In its campaign, the Committee played on the Soviet cult of motherhood. The semi-sacred status of the soldier's mother ruled out open attacks on the Committee, since this would undermine the foundations of the Soviet military ethos.

There were also more strictly pragmatic reasons why it made sense for women rather than men to organise such a movement. As Karklins points out with regard to the Latvian equivalent of the CSM, the League of Women,

> men were seen as being more vulnerable to retaliation. Most men in Latvia had served in the Soviet armed forces and could be recalled to active service or otherwise harassed more easily than women. The women activists also felt that they had the psychological and moral upper hand when dealing with Soviet military authorities. Many officers did not know how to react to assertive women confronting them in such unexpected ways[42].

For the most part, then, the military press avoided direct criticism of the Committee of Soldiers' Mothers. As we might expect, it was also conspicuously silent with regard to the concrete services offered by the Committee. The sole occasion on which *Krasnaia zvezda* mentioned the Committee's provision of assistance and advice to conscripts and their parents appears to have been the January 1991 article "Fantasies on the Theme of '*Dedovshchina*'"[43].

---

[41] Kaushanskii, 1989, *op. cit.*
[42] R. Karklins, *Ethnopolitics and the Transition to Democracy: The Collapse of the USSR and Latvia*, Washington, DC: The Woodrow Wilson Center Press, 1994, p. 73. Parallels could be drawn here with the bab'i bunty, Russian and Ukrainian peasant women's protests during collectivisation. Viola's study of these protests argues that the women, conscious of the fact that the authorities were less likely to use force against them than against the men of the village, manipulated stereotypes of women as irrational and hysterical in order to further their own political ends; see L. Viola, "Bab'i Bunty and Peasant Women's Protest during Collectivization", in B. Farnsworth and L. Viola, eds., *Russian Peasant Women*, Oxford: Oxford University Press, 1992, pp. 189-205.
[43] "Fantazii na temu 'dedovshchina'", *Krasnaia zvezda*, no. 12, 16 January 1991, p.2.

The article recounts the story of a mother who was anxious about *dedovshchina* and visited her local Committee branch seeking advice on obtaining her son's transfer to a unit closer to home. The author asserts that the Committee pressured the mother into falsely declaring that all sorts of horrific tortures were being inflicted on the conscripts in her son's unit. A Committee member is cited as having told the mother, "Here's a sample [declaration] for you, write a declaration!... This never happened? No matter. Your situation is different? Never mind. Write it. That's how it's done"[44].

On such an account, the Committee was motivated not by a genuine concern for truth and legality, but by an irrational and vindictive anti-army bias which led its members to seek out and if necessary fabricate negative phenomena in the military[45].

Another tack was to hint that more sinister political forces were at work, suggesting that the soldiers' mothers movement were part of a wider conspiracy to destroy the military. It was frequently argued that soldiers' mothers' emotionality made them particularly vulnerable to "certain forces", who were hinted at here and there in dark tones. In the non-Russian republics, soldiers' mothers' activism was generally presented as being masterminded by nationalist-separatist extremists[46], while in Russia, it was the democrats, or, as they were commonly referred to in the military press, the "loudmouths", who were seen as the main culprits. Conservative military writer Prokhanov later

---

[44] *Ibid.;* the mother in question had reportedly since recanted and begged pardon of her son's military collective for offending them.

[45] Protesting soldiers' mothers were also frequently represented as being so blinkered and hostile towards the military as to be gratified by any abuses that they uncovered. For example, one military commander was cited in November 1991 as saying that he had the impression that some of the parents visiting his units had in fact been disappointed to find that everything was in order; G. Barnev, "Neizvestnaia armiia?", *Krasnaia zvezda*, no. 265, 20 November 1991, p. 3. This suggestion that protesting soldiers' mothers were only interested in the negative side of army life was also made on other occasions. See for example Zieminysh's account of a demonstration of Latvian soldiers' mothers. He claims that the mothers responded "with restraint, if not coldly" to servicemen speaking at the rally who maintained that they had not come into any contact with *dedovshchina* during their military service, since "this was not what [the mothers] wanted to hear". Zieminysh contrasts this to the mothers' enthusiastic applauding of two servicemen who spoke of their harsh treatment in the military and their eventual discharge for health reasons; M. Zieminysh, "Strannye prizyvy", *Krasnaia zvezda*, no. 220, 24 September 1989, p. 3.

[46] For example, one article about a Latvian soldiers' mothers' demonstration asserted that the demonstration had been secretly organised by Latvian nationalists; *Ibid.*

claimed, for example, that the soldiers' mothers' movement had been "created by the 'democrats'" who were intent on "setting the [soldiers' mothers] against the army"[47].

The positing of a democratic/nationalist conspiracy to destroy the Soviet Union by attacking the army's reputation meant that criticism of *dedovshchina* could be dismissed as nothing more than a ploy in this campaign[48]. Thus one 1990 *Krasnaia zvezda* article described the military's enemies as "hiding behind the screen of '*dedovshchina*'"[49]. Soviet Defence Minister Iazov also argued that the issue of *dedovshchina* was being used "to conceal both unlawful actions and far-reaching political goals"[50].

4. The "feminisation" of Soviet society

Another method commonly employed to undermine the legitimacy of the claims of soldiers' mothers protesting barracks violence was to present these

---

[47] A. Prokhanov, "Pod Argunom", *Sovetskaia rossiia*, no. 26, 10 March 1995, p. 3. Publications like *Moskovskie novosti*, *Moskovskii komsomolets* and *Ogonek* came in for particular criticism, as the military accused them of printing vastly exaggerated and uninformed articles about army life designed to frighten soldiers' mothers. *Ogonek* was seen by the military as the main villain in the *dedovshchina* controversy, or as one critic put it, the "guiding spirit" in the campaign to weaken and destroy the Soviet army; I. Dynin, "Sviatoe delo i krivaia ten", *Kommunist vooruzhennykh sil*, no. 22, November 1990, p. 6. *Ogonek*'s coverage of *dedovshchina* was the subject of frequent criticism from the military during this period; see for example N. Medvedev, "S poslednei nadezhdoi na pomoshch", *Pravitel'stvennyi vestnik*, no. 39, September 1990, p. 12, and N. Medvedev, "Prizyvniki, piketchiki, otkazniki...", *Pravitel'stvennyi vestnik*, no. 48, November 1990, p. 12 (Medvedev was a representative of the Defence Ministry's press service).

[48] See for example a 1989 *Pravda* article which stated that "anti-Army manifestations often feed parasitically on speculations concerning existing shortcomings in the Army, above all on 'hazing' [i.e. *dedovshchina*]"; "The Defense of the Fatherland Permits no Regionalism, Selfishness, or Self-Seeking", *Pravda*, 13 November 1989, translation in *The Current Digest of the Soviet Press*, vol. 16, no. 6, 1989, p. 3.

[49] The author also dismisses talk of people "becoming aware of their rights" as "abstract" and all part of the wider plot; Iu. Gladkevich, "Za shirmoi 'dedovshchina'", *Krasnaia zvezda*, no. 27, 2 February 1990, p. 2. In M. Zieminysh, "Skol'ko shansov pobedit'?", *Krasnaia zvezda*, no. 268, 23 November 1989, p. 1, the head of the *politotdel* of the Latvian military commissariat also describes the Latvian League of Women as playing a "dishonest and dirty game" and "striving to further ideas alien to socialism under cover of slogans of democratisation [and] *glasnost*".

[50] Cited "Vesennii prizyv", *Izvestiia*, no. 71, 12 March 1990, p. 3. One November 1990 article claimed that soldiers' mothers picketing the Moscow *voenkomat* had been paid (the author does not specify by whom) to go there and "yell"; N. Krivomazov, "Voenno-polevoi sabotazh", *Pravda*, no. 321, 17 November 1990, p. 4.

women as 'bad' mothers who were unwilling to separate from their sons. This strategy allowed the military press to shift the blame for *dedovshchina* onto overprotective mothers who had raised infantilised sons incapable of meeting the demands of military service and of attaining manhood.

In 1988, military sociologist Deriugin claimed somewhat enigmatically that *dedovshchina* should be attributed at least in part to 'the feminisation of men' in contemporary Soviet society[51]. Precisely how or why the "feminisation" of conscripts should lead to barracks violence remains unclear; in any event, questioning the masculinity of conscripts who reported instances of *dedovshchina* conveniently enabled the military to sidestep the issue of the violence itself.

After the first fictional account of *dedovshchina* was published in late 1987, the military press dismissed it as "the flight of imagination of a mamma's boy"[52]. The epithet "mama's boy" (*mamen'kii synok*) was to become a catchphrase in military commentary on *dedovshchina*. Yazov himself stated in 1989 that many conscripts were "mama's boys", who "don't know how to do anything" [53]. Similarly, a letter published on the front page of *Krasnaia zvezda* in 1990 entitled "I Don't Understand Those Parents", asserted that young men complaining about the hardships of military service had been raised as "mama's boys"[54]. The prevalence of this phrase in military accounts of *dedovshchina* takes on added significance in light of the Committee's campaign with its focus on the protective function of the mother.

---

[51] From an interview published in *Argumenty i fakty*, 27 August-2 September 1988, reproduced in Dobrokhotov et al, *Nesokrushimaia i legendarnaia*, 1994, *op. cit.*, p. 41. Here Deriugin was engaging in the ongoing public debates on the "feminisation" of men and "masculinisation" of women in Soviet society which dated to the 1970s. For more information on these debates see L. Attwood, "The New Soviet Man and Woman—Soviet Views on Psychological Sex Differences", in B. Holland (ed.), *Soviet Sisterhood: British Feminists on Women in the USSR*, London: Fourth Estate, 1985, pp. 54-77, and E. Waters, "Sex and Semiotic Confusion: Report from Moscow", *Australian Feminist Studies*, no. 12, Summer 1990, pp. 1-14.

[52] Cited S. Zamascikov, "'Insiders' Views of the Soviet Army", *Problems of Communism*, vol. 37, no. 3-4, May-August 1988, p. 114.

[53] E. Agapova, "Vremia stavit voprosy. Kak ikh reshat'?", *Krasnaia zvezda*, no. 173, 28 July 1989, p. 2. See also Khorev's attack on "spoilt and pampered" conscripts; A. Khorev, "Dolg i chest'", *Krasnaia zvezda*, no. 297, 27 December 1991, p. 2.

[54] The writer goes on to conclude that "I do not understand those parents who strive, using truths and untruths, to protect their offspring from the difficulties of military service"; V. Pankov, "Ne ponimaiu tekh roditelei", *Krasnaia zvezda*, no. 73, 29 March 1990, p. 1.

Mothers were heavily implicated in the process of "feminisation" of Soviet men[55]. The dominant role played by mothers in raising sons had, it was commonly argued, rendered many young men ill-equipped to adjust to life away from home[56]. In 1989 Colonel Soluianov, Hero of the Soviet Union and veteran of Afghanistan, noted that "no few young men come to the army today with a 'lady's' upbringing"[57]. These sentiments were echoed a month later by Kovalev who argued that:

> Among conscripts there are more and more youths who have received ... as we say, a 'lady's' upbringing, who are not accustomed to labour and physical loads... To an infantile young man [who is] not prepared for all this, the unavoidable and generally ordinary difficulties of [military] service seem perfectly intolerable, and he, forgetting about duty and honour, rushes to flee from this 'penal servitude', from this 'horror', to under the warm parental wing[58].

---

[55] Attwood writes that in the late Soviet period inadequate mothers increasingly served as scapegoats for a range of Soviet social problems such as hooliganism and alcoholism. She points out that "It is easier to blame the mother for not bringing up her children properly than to examine the very fabric of Soviet life for clues to the genesis of antisocial behaviour"; Attwood, "The New Soviet Man and Woman", 1985, *op. cit.*, p. 72. The ways in which inadequate Soviet mothers served as scapegoats for Soviet social problems is also addressed in A. Phizacklea, H. Pilkington and Sh. Rai, "Introduction", in Sh. Rai, H. Pilkington and A. Phizacklea (eds.), *Women in the Face of Change: The Soviet Union, Eastern Europe and China*, London: Routledge, 1992, pp. 5-6. The predominance of female teachers in the Soviet education system was also seen as having a negative effect on the masculinity of young Soviet males; see Mary Buckley, "The 'Woman Question' in the Contemporary Soviet Union", in S. Kruks, R. Rapp, and M. Young, *Promissory Notes: Women in the Transition to Socialism*, New York: Monthly Review Press, 1989, p. 256.

[56] At the same time, the poor quality of conscripts was elsewhere blamed on the lack of maternal attention, as in the case of one soldier whose mother had deserted him at an early age; A. Khorev, "Chto s nami?", *Krasnaia zvezda*, no. 276, 2 December 1989, p. 3.

[57] A. Soluianov, "Ya protiv 'damskogo' vospitaniia", *Krasnaia zvezda*, no. 214, 17 September 1989, p. 2, in which he argues that conscripts should be put through more rigorous physical training. He goes on: "I foresee the objection: ... today's conscript is yesterday's schoolboy, often spoilt by excessive attention". While Soluianov concedes that this is a problem, he argues that it is important to realise that men are not "born" soldiers. He cites the case of Afghanistan where 'weaklings' were excluded from important missions: "Cruel? But fair. We couldn't pay in blood for a 'lady's' upbringing".

[58] V. Kovalev, "Za chto zh ty nas opozoril, synok ... Pochemu daleko ne kazhdaia mat' skazhet eti slova sbezhavshemu iz armii soldatu?", *Krasnaia zvezda*, no. 236, 14 October 1989, p. 4.

This juxtaposition of "duty" and "honour" to weakness and self-interest was a recurring motif in attempts to defend the principle of universal military service as the draft system moved into crisis. Contemptuous references to conscripts who hid behind their mothers' skirts can be read as oblique responses to the growing power of the Committee of Soldiers' Mothers.

5. *Glasnost'* and grief

> They brandished photographs of their sons and [their] black headscarves, saying 'Here is our mandate!' [59]

This was the response of a group of soldiers' mothers asked for their credentials by doormen at the October 1991 Congress of Servicemen's Parents in Moscow. In a sense, their grief, as signified by their black headscarves and the photographs of their dead sons, can also be viewed as their license to enter the public sphere. Maternal grief was the source of the mothers' legitimacy—their right to speak and to be heard; it was also arguably their most powerful weapon. A mother who refused to give up her son for military service was one thing; a mother who had trustingly fulfilled her duty only to be betrayed was quite another.

Portraits of their dead sons in black mourning-frames provided the main visual focus of this and other soldiers' mothers' protests under Gorbachev. The public display of maternal grief and loss was a method that had been used very effectively by other mothers' activists groups, most notably by Las Madres de Plaza de Mayo in Argentina[60]. These public performances of mourning were not only symbolically powerful, but disarming—there could be no justifiable response to this grief other than respect and sympathy. The discussion below examines the ways in which maternal grief escaped state strictures under Gorbachev and came to acquire new political valency.

6. Soldiers' Mothers' grief and the war in Afghanistan

The immensity and significance of the outpouring of soldiers' mothers' grief under Gorbachev becomes clear if we compare it to the experience of moth-

---

[59] A. Vorob'ev, "Materinskie nadezhdy", *Krasnaia zvezda*, no. 236, 15 October 1991, p.1.

[60] For discussion of the ways in which such portraits functioned in Las Madres de Plaza de Mayo's protests, see A. Malin, "Mothers Who Won't Disappear", *Human Rights Quarterly*, vol. 16, no. 1, 1987, pp. 187-213, and S. Ruddick, "'Woman of Peace': A Feminist Construction", in L. Lorentzen and J. Turpin (eds.), *The Women and War Reader*, New York and London: New York University Press, 1998, pp. 216-17.

ers whose sons were killed in Afghanistan before *glasnost'*, at a time when public expressions of maternal grief were repressed and controlled by the state.

Consider for example the case of Zinaida Chivileva, a Russian mother whose son was killed in Afghanistan in 1982. After receiving notification of her son's death, Chivileva visited the local military authorities to obtain further information. Chivileva says that the commander told her briefly the date and location of her son's death, and then attempted to cut the meeting short, asking, "Now, is there anything else I can help you with?" At this point Chivileva became angry, and retorted, "Give me back my son!" The commander responded by committing Chivileva to a psychiatric hospital, a place where, he informed her, ways would be found to "moderate [her] ardour"[61].

Nor was this attitude restricted to the military—Chivileva's subsequent experience in her workplace, where she was subjected to a disciplinary campaign by colleagues who declared her too-visible mourning to be selfish, abnormal and detrimental to the collective, indicates that entrenched social mechanisms of controlling inappropriate responses to Afghan war losses operated in wider civilian society, too[62].

Chivileva's case would appear to be an extreme example of the way that the Soviet regime dealt with maternal grief during the Afghan War. The underlying principle of rendering invisible the losses incurred in Afghanistan, however, also governed more widespread practices during that war. Bereaved mothers were frequently bullied into keeping silent about their sons' deaths. For example, one mother has recounted how, like Chivileva, she visited the local *voenkomat* and asked for information on the circumstances of her son's death only to be shouted at by the military commandant: "That [information] cannot be divulged. And you're going around and telling everyone that your son has been killed. You must not advertise this"[63].

---

[61] Sh. Zhaksybaeva, "'Mat' soldata", *Izvestiia*, no. 217, 4 August 1990, p. 6.
[62] *Ibid.*
[63] Cited A. Adamovich, "Spriatannaia voina", *Moskovskie novosti*, no. 33, 19 August 1990, p. 14. There are many stories of such cases; in a 1990 interview, for example, a mother whose son was killed in Afghanistan describes a 'shadow of secrecy' surrounding information about her son's death; see L. Ovchinnikova, "Svet lampy vospalennoi...", *Komsomol'skaia pravda*, no. 157, 11 July 1990, p. 2. Frequently parents were not informed when their sons were sent to Afghanistan; see for example Monakhov's account of an incident in 1980 when a female colleague whose son

Other aspects of grieving and remembrance were also tightly controlled. In the early years of the war, for example, the headstones of the graves of soldiers killed in Afghanistan bore only the dates of birth and death[64]. As of 1984 the inscriptions read "Died heroically in the performance of his internationalist duty", but still did not state the place of death[65].

7. Harnessing maternal grief: the regime changes tack

Clearly, the grief of soldiers' mothers was viewed by the late Soviet regime as something dangerous, which needed to be hidden and contained. This was in stark contrast to the official veneration of maternal sacrifice and loss that was so central to the Soviet World War Two iconography.

But there were limits to the extent to which deaths in Afghanistan could be concealed. Attempts to do so ran the obvious risk of alienating the relatives and friends of the dead. Furthermore, official security-related reasons for censoring information on the war notwithstanding, this silence could be interpreted as an admission of the illegitimacy of the Soviet military intervention in

---

had been called up to the landing troops was worried because a parcel she had sent to her son had been returned. Monakhov rang his colleagues at the *Krasnaia zvezda* editorial office to ask for information; they checked the son's details and then told Monakhov: "You understand... He's THERE..." "Where's 'there'?" I said, bewildered. "Well, where?..." — they coughed meaningfully into the receiver. "Where are the landing troops now? Got it?"— V. Monakhov, "Afganistan v nashei sud'be", *Narodnyi deputat*, no. 10, 1990, p. 114. Mothers whose sons were taken prisoner in Afghanistan were similarly kept in the dark; see the account of one mother who, upon making an inquiry to the Defence Ministry when her son's letters stopped arriving in the early 1980s, was told "What POWs? What are you talking about? There is no war in Afghanistan". She received notification that he was officially missing only several years later; I. Lagunina, "Call from a Mother's Heart", *New Times*, no. 30, 1989, pp. 36-38.

[64] See Galeotti, *Afghanistan*, 1994, *op. cit.*, pp. 85-86.

[65] See A. Simurov and P. Studenikin, "Returning to what was Printed: 'There is no Gratitude in their Hearts'", *Pravda*, 25 November 1987, translated in *The Current Digest of the Soviet Press*, vol. 39, no. 48, 1987, p. 7. The controversial documentary about the war in Afghanistan, "Pain", released in 1988, included an interview with a mother who had lost two sons in Afghanistan and who lost a battle with local bureaucrats who refused to authorise the headstone she had selected for one of her son's graves; see V. Dashkevich, "Careful! This was Paid for in Blood", *Krasnaia zvezda*, 21 October 1988, translation in *The Current Digest of the Soviet Press*, vol. 11, no. 44, 1988, p. 9. Moscow's first memorial to soldiers killed in Afghanistan was erected (by a group of veterans) as late as 1992; see A. Oliinik, "Simvol skorbi i pamiati", *Krasnaia zvezda*, no. 39, 18 February 1992, p. 1.

Afghanistan. This was particularly so after Gorbachev came to power, as grieving mothers sought out and received the attention of the democratic media. Eventually, the military press appears to have arrived at the realisation that if it did not mention the grieving mothers, the democratic press certainly would, and that the plight of these mothers was a potentially damaging weapon able to be used to discredit the regime.

The first sign of the change in the official line on maternal opposition to the Afghan war was handed down by Gorbachev in 1985. According to Cherniaev, a "flood" of letters (mostly from women) opposing the use of conscripts in Afghanistan had come into the Central Committee and to Pravda as soon as Gorbachev became General Secretary[66]. At a Politburo session in October 1985 when Gorbachev declared that a decision had to be taken on Soviet involvement in Afghanistan, he illustrated his point by reading aloud from a number of bereaved soldiers' mothers' letters which questioned the validity of 'internationalist duty' and criticised the Soviet leadership harshly for using untrained new recruits in the conflict[67].

As Afghanistan came to be discussed more openly in the late 1980s, the regime made attempts to control and harness maternal grief for official state propaganda purposes. Expressions of concern for the plight of mothers whose sons had been killed, wounded or were missing in Afghanistan became a commonplace in the military press[68]. In October 1989 the USSR Defence Ministry officially endorsed the new Council of Mothers and Widows and Warrior-Internationalists Killed while Fulfilling their Military Duty in Af-

---

[66] The unprecedented nature of this protest is indicated by Cherniaev's own admission of his amazement at the fact that almost all of the letters were signed rather than anonymous; see A. S. Cherniaev, *Shest' let s Gorbachevym. Po dnevnikovym zapisiam*, Izdatel'skaia gruppa Progress - Kul'tura, Moscow, 1993, p. 37. At the 19th CPSU Conference in summer 1988 the writer Grigorii Baklanov also described the numerous letters he had received from mothers of sons killed in Afghanistan, citing the letters to support his argument that "We must create a mechanism that will prevent such things happening again"; cited A. Pumpyansky, "Defeat or Victory?", *New Times*, no. 30, July 1988, p. 13.

[67] Cherniaev, 1993, *op. cit.*, pp. 57-58.

[68] See for example one journalist's comment that "Every Afghan bullet that killed a Soviet soldier struck in the heart of a mother", V. Miasnikov, "Dom na ulitse Sovetskoi", *Krasnaia zvezda*, no. 159, 11 July 1989, p. 2. For similar articles in this vein see V. Ziubin, "'Zagorsk. Evdokii Koriavinoi...", *Krasnaia zvezda*, no. 191, 19 August 1989, p. 3; O. Bar-Biriukov, "Mozhno li prostit' predatelia?", *Krasnaia zvezda*, no. 20000 (special edition), 16 September 1989, p. 6; and "Zakon dolzhen 'rabotat'", *Kommunist vooruzhennykh sil*, no. 20, October 1990, p. 40.

ghanistan, thanking them publicly for their sacrifices and for "raising worthy sons of the fatherland"[69].

The regime manipulated the mothers' desire to keep their sons' memories alive and to make sense of their deaths by mobilising bereaved mothers to give lectures on their sons' heroism at local schools and other institutions. These ritualised public performances aimed to reactivate the figure of the stoic soldier's mother of World War Two, transforming maternal grief and despair into pride.

One Afghan mother has told of her initial collusion in such a scheme and subsequent realisation of her own complicity and blindness:

> What did he die for? Why him?... I force myself to be with people, I take Sasha with me, I talk about him. Once I gave a talk at the Polytechnic and afterwards a student came up to me. 'If you'd stuffed less patriotism into him he'd be alive today,' she told me. When I heard that I felt ill and fainted. I gave that talk for Sasha's sake. He can't be allowed to just disappear like that... Now they say it was all a dreadful mistake—for us and for the Afghan people. I used to hate Sasha's killers... now I hate the State which sent him there. Don't mention my son's name. He belongs to us now. I won't give him, even his name, to anyone[70].

---

[69] See A. Oliinik, "V neoplatnom dolgu", *Krasnaia zvezda*, no. 243, 22 October 1989, p. 1. According to Pinnick, who interviewed members of this group in 1994, many of these mothers and widows later came to "regret that they acted on requests to make a contribution to the state's military socialisation programme, as they are now sceptical about the authorities' objectives at the time and feel they were exploited in their grief"; K. Pinnick, "When the Fighting is Over: The Soldiers' Mothers and the Afghan Madonnas", in M. Buckley (ed.), *Post-Soviet Women: From the Baltic to Central Asia*, Cambridge: Cambridge University Press, 1997, p. 149.

[70] Cited S. Alexievich, *Zinky Boys: Soviet Voices from a Forgotten War*, trans. Julia and Robin Whitby, London: Chatto and Windus, 1992, p. 66. Alexievich's book consists of a series of interviews conducted primarily with Soviet veterans of the Afghan war and their mothers. The interviews focus on the brutality of the war and its effects on participants and their loved ones. Extracts from Alexievich's book were first published in the USSR in *Komsomol'skaia pravda* and *Druzhba narodov* in early 1990. Alexievich was subsequently excoriated in the military and conservative press and accused of having fabricated the interviews. Attacks on Alexievich made on the pages of *Krasnaia zvezda* included the following letter from a soldier's mother castigating Alexievich: "I, the mother of an internationalist-soldier ... am outraged to the depths of my soul by those attacks with which Aleksievich is trying to shame our sons ... Misanthropy [and] cruelty have never been inherent in our children ... I

This woman's response was to retreat into private grief again; many others opted instead to bring their grief into the public sphere on their own terms.

The Afghan war was not an easy war to sell. The World War Two iconography of the soldier's mother bearing her grief stoically was clearly not applicable, primarily because the main rationale for the mother's sacrifice (the need to protect the homeland from an external invader) was absent. The contrast between the two wars was articulated by one mother whose son was killed in Afghanistan:

> When my son was taken, it was particularly difficult for me because I had nothing to lean on emotionally. I couldn't say to myself: this is essential, the country needs it, the people [need it]. The Afghan War is not the Great Patriotic War, such as it was for our fathers. That was a people's war, everyone understood it. But in this war I didn't find any logic, [or] commonsense, and so it was doubly hard.[71]

8. Peacetime deaths under Gorbachev

"Internationalism" had been shaky enough as a justification for soldiers' deaths in Afghanistan, but it goes without saying that no even remotely plausible "meaning" could be found in peacetime deaths. As we have seen, the military press attempted to make sense of this phenomenon by presenting it as a symptom of social decay and the erosion of Soviet values in wider civilian society. But even were this interpretation accepted, it could bring no solace.

The Committee of Soldiers' Mothers' widely publicised claims that fifteen thousand conscripts had been killed in peacetime during the past four

---

consider that those who are trying to shame our soldiers [and] our army, are shaming their own Motherland..."; "Kto otvetit za klevetu?", *Krasnaia zvezda*, no. 80, 7 April 1990, p. 2. Another critic described Alexievich as a "lady intellectual" (intelligentnaia damochka) who had "made up stories" about the war; see *Krasnaia zvezda*, no. 103, 5 May 1990, p. 2.

[71] Cited V. Monakhov, "Afganistan v nashei sud'be", *Narodnyi deputat*, no. 10, 1990, pp. 114-15.

years lent fresh impetus to the movement. The previous taboo on peacetime deaths had served to isolate mothers in their grief; now they became aware that their situation was part of a large-scale phenomenon, and that they were not alone. The peacetime deaths issue also mobilised many mothers of conscripts currently undergoing military service.

The Soviet military, which had felt so threatened by angry outbursts from isolated individual mothers during the Afghanistan war, now found itself faced with a mass outpouring of maternal grief, as thousands of mothers of soldiers took their anger and grief to the streets for the first time in Soviet history—an outpouring which the regime was no longer able to contain. Mass soldiers' mothers' rallies over peacetime deaths were held in Moscow's Gorky Park in early June 1990, with bereaved mothers demanding Yazov's dismissal and the abolition of conscription[72]. A series of hunger strikes and other protests by grieving soldiers' mothers to draw attention to peacetime deaths continued throughout 1990 and 1991[73]. The impact of these public representations of maternal suffering was compounded by the military's ineptitude in managing and responding to the peacetime deaths issue.

9. Military responses to maternal grief

The military proved highly resistant to demands for more *glasnost'* in the reporting of peacetime deaths and revelations of military cover-ups added to public outrage over the deaths themselves. Isolated calls from within the military for de-classification of statistics on peacetime deaths as a means of rebuilding relations with the community appear to have fallen upon deaf ears[74].

---

[72] RFE/RL Daily Report, 5 June 1990.
[73] See for example RFE/RL Daily Report, 22 April 1991, 6 May 1991 and 10 July 1991; "Kak khotel ya zhit'", *Moskovskii komsomolets*, no. 130, 10 July 1991, p. 1; "Vopiiushchie ob otmshchenii", *Moskovskii komsomolets*, no. 134, 16 July 1991, p.1; *Express-Chronicle*, no. 31, July 1991; T. Ivanova, "'Svoi' i 'chuzhie'", *Krasnaia zvezda*, no. 231, 9 October 1991, p. 1; and Iu. Iogov, "Soldatskie materi uzhe ne golodaiut, a 'dedy' vse vyiasniaiut otnosheniia", *Moskovskii komsomolets*, no.197, 16 October 1991, p. 1.
[74] In autumn 1989, for example, Zolotukhin pointed out how damaging repression of mortality rates among conscripts was for the army itself, given that this generated rumours regarding the number of deaths, and he argued that the only way to

An important point of contention was the non-transparency of procedures governing the investigation of peacetime deaths. The CSM expressed its lack of confidence in the Military Procurator's Office on numerous occasions[75], and one of its central demands was that this body be replaced by independent civilian investigators[76]. Many soldiers' mothers were politicised precisely by their exposure to the military procurators' incompetence and sometimes clear corruption, to which they were alerted by discrepancies in the documentation related to their sons' deaths[77]. Bereaved parents had very few rights when it came to obtaining access to information about their sons' deaths, which was classified, or to their sons' remains, which were usually buried at their place of service[78].

The Military Procurator's Office was generally obstructive, and at times resorted to outright intimidation of troublesome soldiers' mothers, most notoriously in the case of Liubov' Lymar'[79]. After Lymar' demanded that her son's body be exhumed in order to ascertain the cause of death, the Military Procurator's Office had her son's corpse decapitated before returning it to her for burial. Upon demanding that the head be returned to her, Lymar' was reportedly told, "You yourself wanted an exhumation, and the head has been added to the criminal case as material evidence[80]"

---

[75] counter such rumours was to begin to publish the relevant statistics; cited V. Kosarev, "Domysly i real'nost'", *Krasnaia zvezda*, no. 241, 20 October 1989, p. 1.

[76] See for example "Kak khotel ya zhit'", *Moskovskii komsomolets*, no. 130, 10 July 1991, p. 1.

[77] See for example the CSM's April 1990 address to the USSR Supreme Soviet, cited G. Zhavoronkov, "'Spasi i sokhrani!', - shepchut soldatskie materi, provozhaia svoikh detei v armiiu", *Moskovskie novosti*, no. 29, 22 July 1990, p. 11.

See for example V. Vyzhutovich, "V kakom zvanii zakon?", *Izvestiia*, no. 246, 15 October 1991, p. 3, and V. Zhitarenko, "Vsego strashno teriat' syna", *Krasnaia zvezda*, no. 100, 6 May 1992, p. 4.

[78] On the withholding of inquest details from parents see V. Vyzhutovich, "V kakom zvanii zakon?", *Izvestiia*, no. 246, 15 October 1991, p. 3. On burials, see P. Poloz, "V garnizonakh i karaulakh", *Krasnaia zvezda*, no. 247, 27 October 1989, p.2.

[79] Lymar' was the leader of the Soldiers' Mothers of Russia group which was established in July 1991.

[80] On the Lymar' case, see "And the Head will be Kept as Evidence", *Express-Chronicle*, no. 23, 1991, and S. Kornilov, "Dvizhenie soldatskikh materei: ne v nogu, no soobshcha", *Rossiiskaia gazeta*, no. 173, 17 August 1991, p. 3. Note also that one 1991 *Krasnaia zvezda* article expresses strong disapproval of another mother calling for exhumation of her son's corpse. The author urges the mother not to disturb her son's corpse, and to resist falling prey to those who were "shamelessly"

Publicly grieving mothers were a loud reminder to the military of something that it would much rather forget. Public sympathies were clearly on the side of the mothers and there was no way in which the old methods of idealising the soldiers' deaths or suppressing the protests could comfortably be employed.

The military thus found itself backed into a corner, and occasions inevitably arose in which it came into open conflict with the protesting mothers. In September 1990, for example, troops were sent in to disperse a soldiers' mothers' picket at the Defence Ministry building in Moscow. Moscow Military Commandant Major General Smirnov, who led the operation, reportedly tore up one of the dead soldiers' portraits, saying: "You yourselves brought up such mongrels, [that's why] they get killed"[81]. Obviously, occasional outbursts and retaliations in this vein could not be reconciled with the military's traditional image as a benevolent and paternal force.

Such cases were rare, however; for the most part the military appeared to follow a course of avoiding direct mention of these protests[82]. Instead, the military press aimed to discredit publicly grieving mothers obliquely, challenging their claim to moral authority by running profiles of exemplary bereaved soldiers' mothers. Such mothers kept their grief private, and were not seduced by what was generally presented as a 'fashion' for showy protests and general troublemaking[83].

---

[81] casting doubt upon the accidental nature of her son's death; V. Usol'tsev, "Kogda nevmoch' peresilit' bedu", *Krasnaia zvezda*, no. 196, 29 August 1991, p. 2.
Moskovskie novosti, no. 39, 23 September 1990, p. 2. Troops were also used to break up another soldiers' mothers' protest outside the Defence Ministry building in December 1990; see V. Zhitarenko, "Na podnozhke 'demokraticheskogo ekspressa'", *Krasnaia zvezda*, no. 35, 13 February 1991, p. 3.

[82] On the rare occasions when such protests were mentioned in *Krasnaia zvezda*, the articles in question focused on the infighting and scandals within the soldiers' mothers' movement; see T. Ivanova, "'Svoi' i 'chuzhie'", *Krasnaia zvezda*, no. 231, 9 October 1991, p. 1, and A. Vorob'ev, "Materinskie nadezhdy", *Krasnaia zvezda*, no. 236,15 October 1991, p. 1.

[83] See for example the portrait of archetypical "good mother" Evdokia Koriavina, mother of a Hero of the Soviet Union who was killed in Afghanistan, who is described as "not one of those people who complain about their fate"; V. Ziubin, "Zagorsk. Evdokii Koriavinoi...", *Krasnaia zvezda*, no. 191, 19 August 1989, p. 3. See also V. Zhitarenko, "Vsegda strashno teriat' syna", *Krasnaia zvezda*, no. 100, 6 May 1992, p. 4, in which the author praises a mother whose son was killed in peacetime in suspicious circumstances but who, "to her honour" is bearing her cross quietly, without organising demonstrations or taking her anger out on her

As we have seen, one of the military's standard moves was to deflect responsibility for the mothers' suffering by attributing peacetime deaths to the 'poor quality' of the conscripts (who were undisciplined, foolish, drunken, and so on). Occasionally the military press blamed peacetime deaths on the soldiers' mothers themselves. For example, one article related the case of a soldier's mother who had publicly implicated the military in the suicide of her son. The article maintained that the soldier's suicide had in fact been prompted by his receiving a letter from his mother in which she threatened suicide herself. The mother was said to be 'speculating' on her son's death, and salving her conscience by shifting the blame onto the military[84].

Furthermore, it was often implied that the 'real' victims of peacetime deaths in the barracks were the military commanders implicated in these deaths and the reputation of the military in general. Rather than focusing on developing mechanisms to prevent peacetime deaths, military debate on the issue tended to focus on the fact that commanders were being 'persecuted' and 'indiscriminately punished' for crimes committed by their subordinates[85].

Finally, the military press attempted to take the sting out of the mounting corruption charges levelled against the military and the Military Procurator's Office by the CSM. Responding to allegations of cover-ups of violent peacetime deaths, the military press argued that the lack of openness regarding the details of conscripts' deaths was in fact motivated by a desire to protect the feelings of bereaved mothers. One article on peacetime deaths thus emphasised that it was a common and accepted practice of commanders to bend the truth in conveying circumstances of soldiers' deaths to their loved ones. The author drew an analogy to the World War Two practice whereby commanders would comfort parents by recasting their sons' deaths as heroic, even if they had in fact died cowardly deaths—missing the point that the cur-

---

son's commander. Similarly, see the case of a mother whose son was killed in a parachuting accident, but who cannot bear the idea of any of her son's fellow servicemen facing punishment for his death. She sends the following telegram to the fleet: "I request and beg as a mother to lift the punishment [if any] arising from the death of my son from the unit"; V. Massal'skii, "Osobym svetom", *Krasnaia zvezda*, no. 1, 3 January 1991, p. 2.

[84] V. Usol'tsev, "Kogda nevmoch' peresilit' bedu", *Krasnaia zvezda*, no. 196, 29 August 1991, p. 2.

[85] See O. Vladykin, "Tochku stavit' rano", *Krasnaia zvezda*, no. 265, 19 November 1989, pp. 1-2.

rent wave of soldiers' deaths was shocking precisely because the deaths had occurred not in the course of a war, but during peacetime[86].

In general, the military seems to have failed to appreciate the fact that what was required was an attempt at an honest appraisal of the situation and an acknowledgement of the military's own responsibility for the welfare of conscripts in its care, followed by a clear undertaking to increase accountability. Instead, military responses showed greater concern for saving face than anything else. Occasional expressions of sympathy extended to the mothers by military spokesmen were always heavily qualified and outweighed by the defensiveness which characterised discussion of this issue.

Conclusion

There were good reasons for the late Soviet regime's nervousness regarding the political potential of grieving soldiers' mothers. The deaths of conscripts, both in Afghanistan and at home, were an issue that galvanised anti-military and anti-regime public opinion. Ultimately, by attempting to keep these deaths quiet, the regime succeeded only in alienating further a large sector of the population and unwittingly creating a new class of martyrs with considerable moral and symbolic authority.

Grieving soldiers' mothers symbolised the growing rift between the 'people' and the Soviet army, giving the lie to the often repeated slogan that, in contrast to the situation in bourgeois states, "the Soviet army and the people are one". In 1988 a screening of the controversial documentary "Pain" which focused particularly on the suffering of mothers of soldiers killed in Afghanistan, was held at a cinema in Moscow. When speakers in the post-film discussion session praised the film for showing "the people's truth about the Afghan war", a general in the audience rose to his feet, declaring, "Mothers are not the people"[87]. The general's response seems to me to encapsulate something of the tone colouring military responses to the soldier's mothers'

---

[86] V. Zhitarenko, "Vsegda strashno teriat' syna", *Krasnaia zvezda*, no. 100, 6 May 1992, p. 4.

[87] Cited A. Adamovich, "Spriatannaia voina", *Moskovskie novosti*, no. 33, 19 August 1990, p. 14.

criticism. The military's stubborn refusal to accept or adapt to the changing climate of public opinion under Gorbachev made the prospect of reconciliation between the militarist and maternalist camps a slight one.

The military's attempts to deny and downplay the existence of barracks violence were largely counterproductive, only reinforcing the impression of conscripts' vulnerability. For the most part, the Soviet public appears to have been unconvinced by the military's counterattacks on the CSM. A survey of 1,898 people undertaken in early 1991, for example, found that 62 per cent of respondents believed that it was unfair to accuse critics of the army of "insufficient patriotism". Only 8 per cent of respondents accepted the notion that the military's complaints about criticism of the army represented attempts "to preserve ideals and traditions for young people". Thirty-one per cent of respondents, on the other hand, viewed the military's attacks on its critics as motivated by the desire "to preserve [the military's] political influence in the country". Crucially, the survey indicated that 60 per cent of respondents believed that 'the army itself, commanders who allow and encourage violence amongst subordinates' were responsible for *dedovshchina*[88].

The ramifications of the *dedovshchina* controversy extended beyond the issue of conscripts' welfare—in a sense this debate was about breaking down the barriers which separated the military from the civilian world. The public outcry over barracks violence illustrates the ways in which the forces of *glasnost'*, once unleashed, proved impossible to contain. Independent organisations like the CSM seized the opportunity provided by Gorbachev's reforms to take *glasnost'* much further than was acceptable to conservative forces within the Soviet establishment. The military's ultimate failure to quash public debate over barracks violence was in large measure the result of the soldiers' mothers' dogged campaign to raise public awareness of this issue.

This article leaves the CSM at a high point. In the wake of the failed coup of August 1991, the CSM's dealings with the authorities took place in a climate of receptivity and sympathy to maternalist thinking. Yeltsin's regime seemed to offer the promise of genuine military reform, a new approach to military service that took the rights of conscripts into account, and renunciation of the use of coercion against Russian citizens.

---

[88] "Otnoshenie naseleniia k armii", *Narodnyi deputat*, no. 3, 1991, p. 87.

This promise, however, was not fulfilled; indeed, Yeltsin's relations with the CSM would never be so good again. The period covered in this article was only the first stage in an ongoing struggle against human rights abuses in the Soviet, and now the Russian military. The post-Soviet Russian army has inherited most of the problems which plagued the Soviet army, including *dedovshchina* and the problem of dealing with secessionist regions within the Russian Federation[89]. Soldiers' mothers continue to fight the same battles over the same issues. Meanwhile, the advances of the Gorbachev era continue to be eroded by the war in Chechnya. Overall, the resurgence of militarist discourses under Putin shows just how fragile the soldiers' mothers' achievements have been.

---

[89] Indeed, CSM members frequently use the metaphor of the post-Soviet Russian army as the decomposing corpse of the Soviet army. Thus in October 1998 CSM member Ida Kuklina said of the post-Soviet Russian army: "The situation with ... peacetime deaths has not changed, because the Russian army is the skeleton of the Soviet army in decay. All the processes are continuing"; Ida N. Kuklina, author's interview, Moscow, 29 October 1998. Similarly, CSM member Liudmila Zinchenko stated that, "we always say that the Russian army is the fragments of the Soviet army, which was dismembered. And this corpse is stinking. That is, it has all the problems that the Soviet army had; it's stayed the same"; Liudmila N. Zinchenko, author's interview, Moscow, 20 October 1998.

III *Dedovshchina* in the CIS

8   The Kyrgyz Republic: Is Desertion a National Tradition?[1]

Bakyt KATCHEKEYEV

> *Vis consilii expers mole ruit sua*
> [Force without judgement fails by its own weight]
> Horace

Along with its Central Asian counterparts, the Kyrgyz Republic is now reforming the army with a view to bringing it closer to the model of modern mobile forces. Nonetheless, the problems encountered on this path are not only tied to insufficient funds, equipment and military technology and training, problems which can be found in many countries, but they are also due to authorities' lack of determination to implement reforms.

1.   An army in transition

The Kyrgyz Republic's military doctrine pursues the political goal of rapprochement with the Shanghai Cooperation Organization[2] and the states

---

[1] Translated from the Russian by Zoé Andreyev.
[2] The Shanghai Cooperation Organization: the Charter of the SCO was drafted following the creation of the Shanghai Organization on June 15th, 2001. The Charter was ratified on June 7th 2002 in St-Petersburg. The documents determine the aims and purposes of the organization, membership, bodies, and the privileges and immunities of the SCO and its representatives. The Member States of the SCO are Kazakhstan, Kyrgyzstan, the People's Republic of China, Russia, Uzbekistan, and Tajikistan. In the Moscow declaration signed by the heads of the SCO's member states in May 29, 2003, it is said that "the Member States of the SCO consider that no country in the world is immune from modern terrorism, drug trafficking and other transnational challenges, in the context of the growing globalization of political, social and economic issues [...] The Member States of the SCO, recognizing the

party to the CIS Collective Security Treaty[3]. In parallel, the Kyrgyz army working on a project of integration into international peace-keeping operations, including the multinational peace-keeping forces of NATO[4] countries. However, due to insufficient funding, the Army is unable to upgrade weapons and military technology and provide adequate training, and these limitations are hampering reform.

The military doctrine of the Kyrgyz Republic[5] is not directed against any specific government or military-political formation; its purpose is to defend the country against external aggressors, in other words to avoid the situation of 1999-2000, when several terrorist groups penetrated the south of the Republic and entirely paralyzed the armed forces of the Kyrgyz Republic. Today the military forces are made up of border guards, rapid reaction forces, as well as

---

[3] transnational nature of modern terrorism, being on the front line in the fight against terrorism and its concrete manifestations, are pursuing their cooperation and active participation in the context of the global alliance in the war against terrorism, including uncovering and stopping their sources of funding. In this respect an important role is conferred upon the cooperation of the judicial bodies and the intelligence services, as well as the defense ministries of the member states of the SCO"

[3] "The CIS Collective Security Treaty Organization" originated in the Tashkent Agreement on collective security, signed in 1992 by Azerbaijan, Armenia, Belarus, Kyrgyzstan, Kazakhstan, Russia, Tajikistan. In 1999, Azerbaijan and Tajikistan left the treaty and in 2002 Uzbekistan also left. In 2002, in Moscow, the Tashkent Agreement became the Collective Security Treaty Organization (CSTO) on the legal basis of the previous agreement. The main goals of the CSTO were the creation of a system of collective security on the post-Soviet territory and the military and political integration of the member countries, that is Armenia, Belarus, Kazakhstan, Kyrgyzstan, Russia and Tajikistan, in order to counter security threats. Measures were taken to create (regional) groupings of coalition troops and to equip their staff with necessary weapons and military technology. The Member States of the CSTO coordinate their forces in the fight against international terrorism and extremism, the trafficking of illegal drugs and narcotics by organized international criminal groups. The CSTO is funded by the contributions of the Member States. Field and command post exercises "The Southern Shield of the Commonwealth" are conducted every year; the parties to the Treaty have set up the "Rapid Reaction Collective Forces", the Antiterrorist Centre of the CIS and antiterrorist exercises and command training are regularly organized on the territories of the Parties to the Treaty.

[4] The Kyrgyz Republic joined to NATO Partnership for Peace programme in 1994; during that period bilateral events were conducted for the extension of cooperation in compliance with the Framework Document of Partnership for Peace. The Kyrgyz Republic is not a member of the Alliance.

[5] The military doctrine of the Kyrgyz Republic was adopted by decision of the Security Council of the Kyrgyz Republic "Concerning the Military Doctrine of the Kyrgyz Republic for the transition period lasting up to 2010" on 23 March 2002.

regular troops. Its potential foes are: terrorists, religious extremists, drug traffickers.

The army is being built progressively, in accordance with security goals and financial means.

The reform will be implemented in three phases:

1 - The first phase (from 2002 to 2003) will consist of the following: setting up an effective legal basis in the field of military security, completing operational planning, providing material and technological equipment for the army, and training rapid reaction forces.

2 - The second phase (from 2004 to 2007) will be devoted to training the army to ensure its battle-readiness and ability to solve problems during low-intensity armed conflicts either independently or in the framework of the Rapid Reaction Collective Forces of the Central Asian region of the CSTO and the SCO.

3 - The third phase (from 2008 to 2010) [will be devoted to] the military preparation of the army, in order to ensure its ability to carry out missions in armed conflicts on a regional scale, either independently or in the framework of the Coalition Armed Forces of the member states of the CSTO and the SCO. The armed forces of the Kyrgyz Republic are made up of military troops and units which report to:

- The Ministry of Defense;
- The Interior forces of the Ministry of the Interior
- The National Security Services
- The Ministry of Ecology and Emergency Situations
- The National Guard
- The Government Protection Services
- The Border Troops
- The Protection and Escort Department of the Ministry of Justice

2. A weak officers' corps

While the Kyrgyz Republic is trying to reform its armed forces and bring them to a modern level of professionalism and quality, many problems still require special attention, from a both military and civilian point of view. If the problems of mutual interaction with the SCO, the CSTO and NATO can be solved through planned exercises, military contacts, military cooperation, if the lack of weapons and military technology can be made up for thanks to military-technical cooperation and aid from foreign governments, internal reform issues, however, are not always as accessible or understandable. Thus, for example, the transition to the brigade system did not change much in the army's unit structure or in the commandment of troops and units and it certainly did not solve the problems linked equipment, training, communication and planning. The staff policy of the armed forces is far from being consistent, logical and has no methodological basis.

The fact that the Kyrgyz forces are unable at the present to purchase modern weapons and military technology without aid is only the visible part of the problem. Despite recent salary hikes, given the inadequacy of social and financial compensations, a large number of officers' and sergeants' posts are vacant and filled by inexperienced young officers or reserve officers. Certain subdivisions are understaffed, with less than 70% of the officers' posts filled. Professionalizing the army does not seem realistic given the near-crisis situation of the country's economy. To be fair, the arrival of contract servicemen has improved the situation overall, for instance at border points, for air defense systems, however the use of contract men has been limited due to the financial strain on the country. At the same time several studies conducted by military specialists and economists have shown the comparative advantage in switching to an entirely professional army.

The plan to gradually reduce the number of officers and increase the number of professional sergeants is a step in the right direction in the reform process. For this purpose the creation of a modern school for professional sergeants is under way. A professional army is one of the goals advocated in the Doctrine and in other documents, but it is still a future project, earmarked for 2010[6].

---

[6] See footnote 4.

3. From criminal subculture to desertion

In this context, it is necessary to say a few words about the moral climate that prevails in the army. It is probably difficult for an outsider to imagine today's Kyrgyz soldier - most often dressed in a Chinese military jacket, Turkish shoes and an American kepi.

The training is based on the Seven Commandments of Manas (the Kyrgyz national epic poem)[7]. Even though it is true that these commandments only resemble modern values, nevertheless they have practically replaced Constitutional values. These commandments have been already included in the military pledge. Such is the present situation in the Kyrgyz armed forces. What we have is a crisis of values in the ideological and educational work of the military institution and as a result the democratic values enshrined in the Constitution are replaced by the archaic values of a medieval epic. The situation is becoming worse due to the criminal hierarchical subculture inherited from the Soviet army known as "*dedovshchina*" (hazing). According to official data of the Ministry of Defense of the Kyrgyz Republic and the military tribunal, every year, about 600 persons desert the army due to these "unauthorized relationships"[8*]. In comparison, in Russia, according to the data of the Ministry of Defense of the Russian Federation, about 1,800 persons desert the army every year[9]. Nevertheless, the total number of troops of the Kyrgyz army amounts to 15,000 men in the context of full recruitment and every year about 8,000 conscripts are called in. Among the 600 deserters who are amnestied every year, about 100 return to their unit. Criminal proceedings are dropped when they return to their unit. This practice is repeated every year. This could be a form of Kyrgyz "know-how" as concerns the building of their

---

[7] Manas is a Kyrgyz epic hero, - main acting hero of the Kyrgyz National epic poem. This epic poem is more than 1000 years old. Although the "Manas" is a genuine epic creation, it reflects not only historic events, but also all sides of human life: social, economic, political situation, struggle for independence, relations with other states. The epos widely depicts life, goodness and evil, friendship and humanism, love for the homeland, care for people's well-being.

[8] "Military statistics: more than 600 deserters are in an illegal situation", *Kyrgyzinfo*, 11 January 2004.

[*] Official expression for "hazing" [translator's note].

[9] H. Ivanov "Quality, not quantity", Country briefing: Russia - JDW 2003.

own armed forces. The following newspaper stories represent daily occurrences in Kyrgyz society:

> He deserted his unit...[10]
> Today more than six hundred soldiers of the emergency services who had deserted at one time their military units are in an almost illegal situation.
> Desertion. During peacetime, it is one of the most common military crimes and one of the most serious according to the country's penal code. The sanction is quite severe: from 3 to 7 years, and if the soldier goes AWOL with a weapon or with other soldiers, the sentence is ten years. There is no prescription for this crime. Deserters are deferred to the Criminal investigation department, like ordinary criminals.
> The only way to avoid criminal sanction is to benefit from the amnesty law. But even there deserters try to avoid this option, for the same reason: they are afraid of having to answer for their desertion.
> According to Galina Afonina, president of the association "Mothers of Soldiers", many of the 600 deserters had no choice but to leave their unit. Hazing, racketeering, the cruelty of the commanders — not everyone is strong enough to endure such treatment.
> In 1992, Private Khalilov, unable to bear the taunts of the "*dembels*"[11] deserted his unit and had no intention of returning. Neither did he take the risk of returning when one of the amnesty laws was adopted. For 10 years, he was wanted by the Criminal Investigation Department. Last year, he was arrested by the police. After a long inquiry, Khalilov was sentenced to three years in prison. After the intervention of the "Mothers of soldiers" association, the sentence was reduced to two years on probation. Had he gone to the military tribunal or the military registration office in due time, he would have escaped trial entirely.
> According to Kubanych Alyshbaev, deputy military prosecutor: "Here we can give only one piece of advice, - while the amnesty law is in force, a person can either come and see

---

[10] *Vechernyi Bishkek*, 11 February 2004.
[11] Soldiers who have received their demobilisation papers [Editors' note]

us or return to his military unit. Only in that case will criminal responsibility be withdrawn."

The Ministry of Defense is also implementing its own specific measures. At present the rights of citizens who have deserted because they were unable to stand the hardships of the army are being determined at the local level by the military registration offices.

As concerns "unauthorized relationships" in the army, unfortunately, they do exist. The military court is now investigating a criminal case concerning an unit officer who, being drunk, beat up a soldier for the sole reason that he made the mistake of calling himself an orderly instead of a sentry.

In this context it is not surprising for soldiers to flee the violence of officers and *dedovshchina*...

Other problems and difficulties are tied to the level of professionalism and training of the officers and sergeants, who is in turn responsible for the education and training of young soldiers, as well as of older soldiers. Despite public actions of the Ministry of Defense and other military institutions, and despite media intervention, hazing has harmed the army's reputation. For many young people of more wealthy families, who are able to afford higher education in a city university or institute, military service is limited to taking officers' courses in their institute and receiving the rank of officer. On the other hand, the underprivileged youth, in some cases young people who already have a criminal background, must do their military service in the armed forces. These young men are usually from rural backgrounds and their educational level does not exceed middle school; they are not very familiar with technology and often are not in very good physical condition. This is not very good for the country's defense capabilities or for army morale.

A count is made every year of murders, suicides, woundings and maimings not linked to military training and service. For example, in 2003, in the border guard service, there were two cases of suicide, four cases of death, 2 cases of using weapons against comrades (1 of which was fatal), five soldiers wounded, all of which had causes that were not linked to military duties[12]. Every year more than 50 soldiers go AWOL, and all the while the military court considers that the situation is satisfactory, reporting that it investigates

---

[12] "Situation of the border guards", *Vechernyi Bishkek*, 5 December 2003, part II.

12 to 17 cases of "unauthorized relationships" every year. These cases are reported only in elite divisions where the level of training of the officers, sergeants and soldiers is much higher than in ordinary units, and where the day's schedule leaves practically no free time to the soldiers[13]. In addition these cases are not related to existing "special initiation traditions" among soldiers of special elite units.

---

[13] "Ministry of Defense of the Kyrgyz Republic: Hazing has sharply declined in our national army", *Kyrgyzinfo*, 20 April 2004.

4. The mobilisation of civil society

Why are there so many deserters in the Kyrgyz Army, and why hasn't the situation changed since the independence of the Republic? There is no doubt that the Army is a specific organization with specific traditions, history and rules. The army is of course influenced by the same factors as society at large. Nevertheless, who is responsible for the situation in the armed forces? Society, the government, the army itself? And why can't the military function without persecutions or physical punishment?

The first answer to this question has come from civil society. The "Soldiers' Mothers' Fund", an organization created in 1994, has raised questions concerning the problems of military recruits. The aim of this organization is to fight hazing and work towards improving the moral climate in the army, in reaction to soldiers' complaints. Thanks to the efforts of this association, the number of complaints has significantly declined since 1994.

The office of the Ombudsman of the Kyrgyz Republic also investigates complaints made by soldiers. Some commanders, deputy commanders in charge of education, as well as the military court also look into these complaints. In addition to this there are Parliamentary committees and commissions. Nonetheless, despite all these organizations, hazing has remained a stable and persistent practice in the Kyrgyz Army.

In order to change the situation, the President of the Kyrgyz Republic introduced an amendment to the law on military service, reducing the duration of military service from 18 to 12 months. The law will enter into force in 2006, and the aim is to eliminate the presence of "older soldiers" who are the source of hazing. Of course this will not be sufficient to eliminate hazing entirely, because it is not enough to change the soldiers' habits; their commanders must also change their ways, and this is not an easy task. It is no secret that the commanders are responsible for their division as a whole and for each soldier personally. It is no secret either that some commanders are for various reasons the initiators of illegal actions, such as racketeering, coercion, exploitation of soldiers for commercial purposes (construction work, farming, transportation services and others) that are not directly connected to military service, or by committing abuses within the service, such as extortion of funds, theft and the fictitious billing of military supplies, equipment, the unjustified use of automobiles etc. There have been cases when commanders themselves assaulted and beat their subordinates. This confirms that some commanders and sergeants practice and transmit the hazing tradition. In addition, they do not consider their military function as including the defense of the country's constitution and of the law in the military sphere.

5. Economic criminality in the army

Despite the fact that the material situation has improved since 1999 and that the soldiers are now fed, there have been some delays in funding and irregularities in the purchase of supplies. As a result the military units often have to solve their own problems. Unfortunately, sometimes entire military units thus become hostage to self-management in terms of food supplies and construction materials, to the detriment of their service; military authorities like to speak publicly of such achievements, but this in itself has had a demoralizing effect on soldiers who must perform domestic and other chores instead of military tasks. The reason for this is not so much lack of funds from the government, but mainly their inadequate distribution. For example, there have been cases when instead of performing tasks connected with military service, soldiers had to collect firewood and manure for heating the units in the winter. If one considers the fact that these units are supposed to protect the country's borders, the situation is quite horrifying.

Due to the low morale of the forces, the low level of control on the part of senior officers due to ill-will or incapacity, and the low level of educational work, there have been cases in recent years where servicemen belonging to elite divisions have been caught in criminal acts or acts of conspiracy. For example, in 2004, soldiers of the special unit of the Ministry of Defense and the Ministry of Ecology and Emergency Situations of the Kyrgyz Republic took part in the murder of a successful businesswoman. Servicemen of the antiterrorist unit of the National Security Service organized the kidnapping of businessmen, conspiring with former and present employees of the Ministry of the Interior. In 2004, officers of the National Guard were arrested for having sold explosives and detonators to religious extremists, which were used in two terrorist attacks in the country. Many more facts revealing the low level of morality in the Kyrgyz Armed forces are now known to the public. Nevertheless it is necessary to underscore that the situation of the capital city of Bishkek is much better than it is in the surrounding regions.

Another specific issue is that of training — the training of soldiers and servicemen is rather nominal and consists in learning by heart regulations on internal and sentry service, which doesn't help improve the situation. There are no courses explaining democratic values and the civil rights of servicemen and citizens, and the institutions which guarantee their protection. Servicemen are not informed that they have the right to refuse to obey an illegal, anti-constitutional order, or an order that goes against military ethics - such information is not given and even discouraged. In this context, it is obvious that the army is not yet integrated into civil society. Servicemen of all categories are unprepared and are practically unprotected by law if they do not obey an illegal order, or an order that has nothing to do with their military obligations, or which is contrary to human dignity. This allows senior soldiers to show abusive behaviour towards junior soldiers, sergeants can abuse privates and officers can abuse their subordinates. Servicemen have no information concerning the procedure of removal from command and the countermanding of an order. In addition, the officers' training is also completely archaic. The officers who have had basic training in elite foreign academies are very few and they have no influence on the present situation. The level of training of military staff in the Republic leaves to be desired. Officers receive professional training on a subjective basis and in most cases those who benefit are officers with professions that are close to the military, such as members of international departments or managers of special units.

Of course, corruption is rampant in Kyrgyz society, but one must not forget that the army is made up of specially trained and armed military specialists, which should not only receive adequate funding but also be under the control of civil society. It is the duty of civil authorities to encourage reform in the army. In their present state the Kyrgyz armed forces represent a potential danger for the state itself. Parliamentarians agree with this and consider that it is necessary to set up more mechanisms of civilian control over the army. According to a Member of the Parliament, V. Dil, the state should not be putting the army in a position to have to solve its problems on its own. According to V. Dil, the first step would be to get rid of corruption which is blossoming in the army due to the "opacity" of the army and of the judicial services[14].

Conclusion

In such a context of transgressions of all types, with hazing becoming more and more widespread, not to mention other problems within the army, one has the impression that the military authorities are deliberately ignoring the problems; either they consider them unimportant, or as natural phenomena which cannot be changed. Despite repeated meetings between military authorities, representatives of civil society and parliamentarians, despite the fact that measures have been taken to punish the culprits, the overall situation is not looking any better. It is difficult to understand what is preventing military authorities from finding solutions these problems once and for all —possibly habit, familiarity with such forms of command and control, possibly the lack of determination to make decisive changes in the army. Perhaps it is also due to the chronic dearth of professional commanders with modern training, ready to implement reforms. Reform begins with quality human resources. Nevertheless it must be emphasized that today, in the Kyrgyz army, there are many military professionals who are willing and ready to do something about the situation; desertion must not remain a permanent, shameful phenomenon, close to becoming a national tradition in the Kyrgyz Republic.

---

[14] "The MPs are not satisfied with the army", *Vechernyi Bishkek*, 27 May 2003.

9 Hazing in the Georgian Army: The Association "Justice and Liberty"[1] Reports on Non-Statutory Relations

Irakli Sesiashvili

Building the armed forces was quite a complex process in Georgia. During the Soviet period, the Georgian people had little interest in military service[2]. After the collapse of the Soviet Union, several internal conflicts occurred in the country[3] and stability was achieved only in 1995. The organization and control of the draft for the compulsory military service started. In 1997, the law on "Military Responsibility and Service", which determined and regulated

---

* The editors wish to express their gratitude to Dany Héricourt for help with editing this article for publication.

[1] The "Justice and Liberty" Association is a nongovernmental army watchdog group that campaigns for the protection of the rights of conscripts and soldiers. It is the first NGO to monitor the Georgian armed forces. The organization received permission to visit individual military installations to monitor their conditions. This led to the publication in 2001 of a book entitled "The Georgian Army between Law and Reality" which looked at the situation in the army and highlighted certain abuses. The Association lobbied the Georgian Parliament to help formulate legislation seeking to improve conditions in the military. The NGO continues to provide free legal consultation to conscripts, soldiers and their families and regularly provides the public with information about the state of the armed forces [Editors' note].

[2] The reason for this low interest in military service comes from the fact that Georgia never developed a steady tradition of the military service: in the 19th century Georgians were not called up to a regular army. It was only at the end of the century that the 1886 regulations enabled conscription of the Georgians. During the country's independence (1918-1921), the government initially had no intention of building an army and when it finally did create one - that could hardly be considered efficient -, it suffered desertion and corruption. At this point a negative attitude towards the regular army was obvious. During Soviet rule, ethnic-based armed detachments were created and the army's popularity increased thanks to Stalin's Georgian origin. But in 1956, Kruchtchev abolished the ethnic-based armed units and post-Stalinistic regimes became increasingly anti-Caucasian. Consequently, between 1985 and the end of the USSR, very few Georgian officers graduated from Soviet Military Academies and most of the serving Georgian officers occupied posts in logistics. (On the history of military service in Georgia see D. Darchiashvili, *The army-building and security problems in Georgia*, Caucasian Institute, June 1997; on the Georgian army see: Th. Gordadzé, "Les nouvelles guerres du Caucase (1991-2000) et la formation des Etats post-communistes", in P. Hassner & R. Marchal, *Guerres et sociétés*, Paris: Karthala, 2003) [Editors' note].

[3] In Abkhasia and Ossetia [Editors' note].

compulsory military service and call-up, was approved[4]. Because of the Soviet heritage and post-Soviet conflicts, the Georgian army had to face a serious lack of qualified personnel. Only a relatively small portion of men educated in Russia's high military institutions were interested in becoming officers[5]. One of the ways to solve this shortage of officers was to fill the positions with people from other professions who had gone through the compulsory military service and fought in the country's wars. When these people became officers, they had practically no qualifications for such a position.

In 1994, General Nadibaidze, a Soviet army officer, was appointed Minister of Defense of Georgia[6]. His policy was to build the Georgian army on the Russian model[7] - a model where "hazing" was but one of the serious issues.

In the Georgian army, the syndrome similar to "hazing" is "non-statutory relations". It is important to note that hierarchy in the Georgian army was founded by the "informal laws" created by the servicemen, not by the men's experience as soldiers or the amount of years they had served.

Non-statutory relations with critical consequences have been observed from officers to soldiers as well as between soldiers themselves. There is no doubt that the country's social-economic crisis partially drove such behavior. Indeed, prior to 2004, military units were poorly resourced[8]. Officers failed to receive even the most modest of salaries for months on end. This aggravated tensions in the military units; the psychological situation worsened and the immediate outcome was bad treatment of soldiers.

From our point of view, the situation only started to improve when the professional army was established and when soldiers saw their wages increase. After the "Rose Revolution", in November 2003, military development of the country was declared a top priority. The military budget received sub-

---

[4] Conscription in the Georgian armed forces takes place twice a year for a period of 18 months or 12 months for conscripts with higher education [Editors' note].
[5] See note 2.
[6] Nadibaidze served as Minister of Defense from 1994 to May 1998 [Editors' note].
[7] As in the Russian army, there is no intermediate rank between sergeants and officers in the Georgian army. Sergeants are 18-year old conscripts trained for six weeks and sent to units where they are supposed to maintain order over the other conscripts aged up to 27 years old. [Editors' note].
[8] Before 2004, the army experienced a severe financial crisis: soldiers and officers faced harsh conditions in the military barracks with poor diet, shortage of uniforms, shoes, sleeping bags, pillows, medical supplies and inadequate plumbing [Editors' note].

stantial resources and by early 2005 it had practically multiplied by eight[9]. Furthermore, special attention is now being focused on discipline and improving the actual selection process of servicemen. Although recent reforms in the Georgian army appear to have reduced the amount of non-statutory relations, the problem is still not thoroughly solved.

The present article, based on reports drawn up by "Justice and Liberty", will discuss the different forms of non-statutory relations in the Georgian army and their motives both before and after the Rose Revolution.

1. Types of non-statutory relations in the Georgian army

Forms of non-statutory relations involving officers
The term "non-statutory relations" defines all actions that defy legally stated standards and all abuses of other peoples' rights during military service. While it is impossible to list all the different forms of non-statutory relations, the author has attempted to describe the non-statutory relations commonly found in the Georgian army. Several cases of criminal offence have also been included.

Widespread forms of non-statutory relations involve officers mistreating soldiers in the following ways:

- <u>Private use of power</u>: the commander imposes upon the military subdivision a task that is not within its area of duty. For example, the commander forces a soldier to wash his private car; the commander sends the subdivision to the forest to collect firewood that he uses personally, etc... Such behavior is commonly referred to as "grey labor" and was widespread in the Georgian army when the social-economic situation was extremely hard.

- <u>Oppression, humiliation and beating of a soldier by an officer</u>. In this case, the military commanders apply strict punitive measures in the aim of advancing their name and status. They declare such methods are effective for discipline and contribute to "turning the men into soldiers". The methods

---

[9]   In 2003, the military budget amounted to 38 million Laris, in 2005, it reaches 317 million Laris (*RFE/RL Caucasus Report*, no. 24, 22 July 2005) [Editors' note].

focus on humiliating the soldiers and ignoring their basic rights. Such cases are sometimes followed by disputes and conflicts within the units.

According to our observations, repression and/or beating of soldiers by officers often took place without reason. At times, violence was simply the result of an officer's psychological disorder. Should a soldier transgress discipline in any way, the widespread form of punishment was beating. Officers failed to impose duties upon the soldier according to existing legislation and military regulations. On the contrary, the officers spoke the verdict themselves and in most cases it was a beating, or a punishment directed at the entire subdivision.

- <u>Officers demanding kickbacks from soldiers.</u> Prior to 2004, owing to the Ministry of Defence's limited budget, even the officers went through long periods without receiving any payment. Officers tried to escape this situation by obliging soldiers to give them money and home-produced food, alcohol, or basic necessities in exchange for a day off. Soldiers who could not respect the deal faced terrible work conditions and cruelty.

> Case no. 1
> From July 18, 1999 to April 2, 2000, Captain M. K., Commander of the platoon, allowed his subordinate soldiers, Mamuka and Vazha, to go home without official leave. In exchange, the men were to bring the captain food, wine and money from their homes. When the soldiers could not fulfill the captain's demands, they were insulted and beaten. One particular incident was acted out for 38 hours: between December 10, 6 pm to December 12, 8 am the captain illegally deprived Mamuka S. of freedom. Having forcefully placed Mamuka in the barracks lavatory, the captain tied him to the water and sewerage pipes with a belt, locked the door and left him for 38 hours without food, standing on his feet, hands tightly tied behind the back and completely isolated from the outer world. The captain warned Mamuka that if anything was said, he would kill and bury him in a place where nobody would find him. After treating him pitilessly for several months, the captain forced Mamuka to attempt suicide. In April 2000, with the intention of killing himself, private Mamuka drank ammonium chloride and severely damaged his health.

In October 2000, the case was filed against the captain at the Kutaisi regional court: captain M.K. was sentenced to 5 years imprisonment.

Bribing also took place when a soldier had committed a crime: in several cases, officers demanded money from soldiers in return for not informing the military prosecutor of the soldier's misdeed. Cases were reported where officers blackmailed soldiers and threatened to hand them over to the prosecutor for a crime they had never committed. Aware of the soldiers' lack of knowledge about legal matters, officers regularly extorted money in this way.

> Case no. 2
> Roman D. was called up for military service in 1999. According to him, the unit management made him work in the barracks as an alabaster plasterer and obliged him to bring alabaster from the nearby alabaster factory together with two other privates. The unit commander let him go home once a week to clean himself up. After one of these days off, he was captured by officers and placed in the unit's former guardhouse. As Roman later learned, certain individuals had stolen non-ferrous metals in the factory and he and the above-mentioned privates were being accused of the theft. One of the privates managed to escape; the other was so severely beaten by the officers, all his ribs were broken. As for Roman, he spent 11 days in the "guardhouse" where he was visited every day by officers who beat him with truncheons. He was obliged to declare in writing that he had stolen the non-ferrous metals. He finally managed to escape from the guardhouse. His case was then handed to the military prosecutor on the grounds that he had deserted the military unit.

- Illegal seizure of personal property. Owing to the difficult socialeconomic factors mentioned above, officers were constantly seeking additional means of income. With this in mind, officers from several military units collected the salaries allocated to soldiers. Declaring the money would be used to buy personal items for the soldiers concerned, they were in fact appropriating the funds for their own needs. Other reports show that senior officers "borrowed" personal items such as mobile phones from junior officers then proceeded to keep the items for good. The junior officers were too afraid to demand return of their possession and accepted the loss in silence.

Forms of violence among soldiers

- Abuse of command position: This is when one person imposes his duties on another. For example, a commander orders a soldier to clean the lavatory or barracks; this soldier then obliges another soldier to do the task in his place. He threatens the "victim" with beating or another humiliating punishment should he refuse to comply.

- Humiliation of soldiers: Oppression, humiliation and beating of a soldier or group of soldiers by another soldier or group of soldiers. During military service, "leaders" generally appear in each military subdivision. These "leaders" try to advance their status and gain privileges by oppressing others.

- Being cast aside: Another critical type of non-statutory relation is that of casting aside a soldier. Alone, rejected from any form of military society, the majority of men attempt to desert their units. Even the risk of being arrested seems less terrifying than staying in the unit without any type of brotherhood. As a rule, soldiers are cast aside for refusing to comply with the army's "tacit" rules. For example, the unwritten law states that soldiers are never to reveal un-disciplinary behavior. Should a man oppose this law, he is both severely punished and rejected by the rest of the group.

- Disgrace. This type of non-statutory relation is the ultimate form of humiliation and recognised by the soldiers themselves as a crime. Disgrace - or rape - is often performed by a group of men. It is not caused by homosexual needs but by the desire to achieve humiliation and submission. Victims of such violation rarely reveal the abuse for fear of being insulted publicly. For young men, the violation leaves huge psychological trauma that deepens over the years.

- Non-statutory relations based on "regional" or ethnic differences. Prior to 2003, though most soldiers served in the closest military unit to their home, some were sent to more distant units. Hence, in the military units located in the "regions" there were so-called "regional minorities", mainly Kakhetians, Svans, Mengrelians, Imeretians and men from Tbilisi, Kutaisi, etc. Sharing common values and traditions, these men communicated quite easily. But disagreements among certain individuals easily turned into group conflicts based on regional differences.

Non-statutory relations in special units
Non-statutory relations were particularly intense in the disciplinary military units and guardhouses.

The soviet model directly inspired the disciplinary military units, guardhouses, and all rules determining the sentence for wrongdoings in the Georgian army. The conditions in the disciplinary military units and guardhouses failed to meet satisfying standards and being sent there equated torture. Although the Constitution of Georgia demands court approval before sentencing a member of the army to jail, in reality soldiers were condemned to the guardhouse upon mere order of the commander.

"Justice and Liberty" monitored several guardhouses and discovered a level of hygiene so terrible it frequently caused sickness. The association also revealed inhumane treatment of the soldiers by the guardhouse chiefs: i.e. beatings, torture and humiliation.

In addition, single cells often contained over 30 soldiers at one time, which led to non-statutory relations between the prisoners. In each cell, so-called "observers" used various methods to control the other soldiers, thus recreating a form of hierarchy. In a great number of cases, the observer ordered other soldiers to beat newcomers to gain their immediate submission. Should a man resist the observer and his supporters, he would be beaten so badly he ended up in hospital. Of course, nobody favored the idea of revealing these facts. The guardhouse chief hid the truth because he was supposed to prevent conflicts in the guardhouses under his command; the observer's supporters said nothing through fear of being labeled "informers" and thus receiving severe punishment; as for the victims, they preferred to be sent to hospital than go through further torture in the prison cells.

> Case no. 3
> On June 28, 2000, the military prosecutor's office of A-khaltsikhe region filed a case against two riflemen of the guardhouse of Akhaltsikhe garrison. The two men, T.M.

and G.G., were accused of torturing Suleiman A. S. to such an extreme that he attempted suicide.

According to the enquiry, Suleiman served as a private in the military unit N 10245 located in Akhlatsikhe. In February 2000 Suleiman A. was placed in the guardhouse for three days because he had left the military unit for 2 nights. On March 06, he was placed in the guardhouse for three days. On March 08, around 11 o'clock, the chief of the guardhouse, T.M., told him to leave the cell and clean the territory and the lavatory. Suleiman, claiming he was sick, refused to follow the order.

T.M. repeatedly hit Suleiman on the head and in the belly, then led him into the cell, told him to remove his uniform, poured water over him and all over the floor and finally locked him in. 30 minutes later, T.M and his assistant, G. G., pulled the prisoner out of the cell and beat him. When they tried to push him into the sewage canal bordering the commandant's office, Suleiman tried to defend himself. Both men reposted by attacking him with the handle of a spade. Suleiman was then locked in the damp cell. In June 2000, Suleiman A. was twice sent to the guardhouse to perform guard duties, and in both cases was beaten by T. M. and G.G. Before returning for a third time to perform guard duties, in fear of further beatings, Suleiman tried to commit suicide using his personal automatic machinegun. He did not die but his health was heavily damaged. In July 2000, T. M and G. G. were sentenced by the Tbilisi regional court to two years' of imprisonment for committing criminal offences as laid down in Article 115 of the criminal code. Their sentence was subsequently altered and both men were released on probation.

Because the laws regulating military guardhouses did not meet the constitution's standards, and having witnessed the illegal events performed in such places, our association repeatedly filed requests to suppress guardhouses, or to exclusively use them in accordance with constitutional law (stating that cases be processed in a constitutional court in presence of a public attorney).

In 2003, before the court had examined our request, President Shevardnadze abolished the system of condemning military servicemen to guardhouses for violations of discipline (presidential decree 337 of July 10, 2003).

In disciplinary military units, conditions were even worse than in the guardhouses. Cases of tuberculosis were reported. Owing to the fact that the government could not cover the expense of providing protection squads within the units, these places were also abolished by presidential decree 310, in July 2003.

2. Consequences of "non-statutory relations"

An unofficial hierarchy of privates

Non-statutory relations divide military servicemen. Research conducted by "Justice and Liberty" allows us to define four categories:

- The "Boss" category. Commanders, seeking to escape their duties, oblige sergeants to maintain order in the companies and units under their control. The sergeants, in turn, coerce particular soldiers to play "boss". Within this status, the "boss" is both responsible and accountable for discipline. In return, he receives particular benefits such as better food, rest periods and good relations with the officers. He is encouraged to beat and humiliate the other soldiers.

- The "Servant" category. These soldiers are particularly subject to being humiliated by officers and "bosses". They are obliged to perform the most unskilled labor (although the soldiers are supposed to share all such work). The servant's tasks include: washing the bathroom, cleaning the barracks and the yard, buying food in the shop, etc. Of course, these men frequently suffer from psychological trauma. Many attempt to leave their units, even at the expense of imprisonment. In the last resort, they commit suicide[10].

- The "Brave Men" category. Men gain this status before starting military service, or through fighting with the "bosses" and the "*dembels*" (soldiers who have served for more than a year and are soon to be released from military service, - this term comes from the Russian word "demobilisation"). If the "brave man" shows enough will and endurance, he will not be bothered by his

---

[10] See K. Liklikadze, "Why soldiers die in peacetime", *The Army and Society in Georgia*, March-April 2001 [Editor's note].

superiors and doesn't have to do jobs considered humiliating in the army (e.g. washing the lavatory, cleaning the barracks, etc.).

- The "Honest" category. These men generally try to avoid fights. They sometimes act as conciliators. More intellectual and unbiased than the other men, they are generally left alone. However, certain tacit laws in the army state that if a soldier is under repression, one should not interfere because one could become the next object of repression. Officers treat "the honest" just like other privates. The honest receive no special privileges.

From non-statutory relations to suicide

While forms of "hazing" existed virtually everywhere, suicide was not reported in all the armed units. According to official data, 26 suicide cases and 26 homicides were registered in the armed forces between 1996 and 2000. All these cases were related to hazing and other forms of humiliation. Between 2000 and 2001, "Justice and Freedom" interviewed soldiers for a survey about violence in the army.

> Extracts:
> - Do you know of any cases of beating, insulting, inhumane treatment or torture in the army?
>   Yes - 18%   No – 82 %
> - Were there any cases of homicide, suicide or serious physical humiliation in your unit?
>   Yes – 13%   No – 82 %.
> - Have you ever had a fight with your co-servicemen?
>   Yes – 13%   No – 87 %
> - Do the officers always treat you in compliance with military law?
>   Yes – 23%   No – 12%   Partially – 65%

From non-statutory relations to desertion.
During confrontations between soldiers and officers, the oppressed sees but one way out: desertion. He attempts this alone or with the help of his family. He then either moves to another unit, hides and/or attempts to buy his freedom with bribes. Prior to 2003, men frequently bribed officers in order to stay at home. Some men even obtained their military cards with backhanders. In

1996, the office of the military prosecutor officially searched for 3 000 deserters, i.e. 10% of the total amount of military forces[11].

Here is a typical scenario involving a victim of non-statutory relations: a private argues with a sergeant and is consequently beaten by the sergeant and his circle. At this point, the private is obliged, by decree, to inform his immediate superior of the hazing that has taken place. However, as mentioned above, such action is deemed unacceptable according to the "unwritten law". Hence, the soldier has to leave the military unit. If the officials manage to capture him, the private's circumstances further deteriorate. The commander of the military unit will demand the private's motive for running away (despite the fact that most commanders already know when hazing has taken place). To avoid being branded an "informer", the soldier does not voice his difficulties. Therefore the unit commander judges that the soldier has attempted to abandon the unit and sentences him to beating or imprisonment in the guardhouse.

If the soldier is not caught while escaping, he makes for home. In some cases, he tells his family what has happened; in others he remains silent. Generally, he only tells part of the story and omits pronouncing any names. In the meantime, the soldier's close friends try to find connections or give bribes to help the soldier transfer to another military unit. It was difficult to get a transfer because soldiers couldn't give the true reason they wanted to change units.

When a soldier deserts for the first time, he generally returns to his unit within four weeks. But when continued hazing obliges him to leave again, he does not return. The commander of the military unit subsequently sends the case to the military prosecutor's office. The latter investigates the matter or completely disregards it because he cannot send the soldier to the prosecutor. Such cases often continue for years. This explains the fact that by the year 2000, some 4000 soldiers were "wanted".

Taking all this into consideration, in December 2000, the Georgian Parliament issued an amnesty for military deserters. The association "Justice and Freedom" met approximately 2 000 soldiers who had received the amnesty. Ac-

---

[11] See Darchiashvili, June 1997, *op. cit.* [Editor's note].

cording to them, some 90 % of soldiers had deserted to escape non-statutory relations. However, by 2004, the amount of deserters had again risen because the underlying reasons for desertion (hazing, etc) had not disappeared.

Approximately 6 000 soldiers a year visit our association's free legal service. All these men have deserted their unit because of non-statutory relations. They come to report violation of rights but will not file complaints with the military management or prosecutor through fear of being labeled "informers" and suffering dire consequences.

3. The underlying causes of non-statutory relations

When discussing non-statutory relations in the Georgian army, the following factors need to be considered: 1) legislative environment; 2) economic environment; 3) social environment.

Legislative environment
According to our investigations, the main reason non-statutory relations develop is the lack of any effective legal mechanism that can oppose it. No legal mechanism currently encourages the revelation of such crimes or provides the framework for effective response and fair punishment of guilty parties. The Georgian army's model is still the soviet one. Such a model simply cannot meet modern requirements. When legislation drastically changed in the country and advanced towards establishing democratic principles, military law lagged far behind.

In current legislation, military commanders are the makers of law. There are no precise mechanisms for protecting servicemen. The statutes allow military commanders to implement whatever punishment they choose. For instance, marching out of time or fighting another soldier can incur exactly the same penalty. Disciplinary measures are ineffective and fail to fit their main purpose, i.e. to prevent further irregularities or misconduct.

Military commanders are divided regarding the current punitive mechanism: one party upholds the notion of maintaining discipline through legislative methods. Such commanders believe in preventing non-statutory relations within their units. They find the situation alarming and feel current legislation substantially hinders good disciplinary management of the army. A second party considers non-statutory methods acceptable. These commanders prefer less restrictive legislation and more mechanisms for individual management. They believe non-statutory methods contribute to maintaining order. In reality, the existing disciplinary legislation and the so-called "unwritten laws" have harmed military management as well as many individuals.

Economic environment
The economic factor vastly influences the development of non-statutory relations. As previously mentioned, the Defense budget was extremely low till 2004. Military units failed to be supplied with adequate stocks, food or uniforms and the living conditions of the soldiers were appalling.

Having conducted research on the matter, the association "Justice and Liberty", reached the conclusion that no military unit whatsoever complied with the standards stipulated by the legislation. In most cases, there was no heating in military units, no correct water supply, barracks were unsuitable for living. As for food and utility objects, the situation was even worse. Soldiers received only 20 % of the legal ration and often verged on starvation. In such conditions, every soldier was fixated on saving himself and finding a way out. The so-called "bosses" tried to relieve their everyday life by overpowering other soldiers: they appropriated men's uniforms and food rations, made them perform tasks to improve personal comfort, etc.

Unable to face such conditions, the psychological condition of most men deteriorated. Nervous illnesses were widespread in the army.

Making matters worse, there was very little military training, again due to lack of funds. Hence, the soldiers were not actively involved in their military service duty and in the context of idleness and bad management, the men had time to "discuss matters" and implement the "unwritten rules". Soldiers who could not cope or who became victims of non-statutory relations deserted.

Conditions were further damaged by the social-economic situation of the officers. Unable to perform their duties because of limited budgets, officers also had too much time on their hands. Their low salaries (approximately $40-100 in local currency) were generally several months late. Consequently, officers either quit service and searched for different jobs or "used their uniform" to run criminal activities. A majority of officers became involved in corruption and committed serious crimes such as selling and smuggling weapons, seizing/selling military stores and supplies, appropriating personal items from military workers to sell them later, etc. All this greatly affected their psyches, which was revealed in their aggressive behavior towards their subordinates.

As mentioned above, officers utilized soldiers as sources of extra income. When officers knew a soldier was in severe difficulty (through hazing, for instance), they would offer to send him on leave in exchange for money or food from the soldier's home. The soldiers had no choice but to accept the deal; they would do anything to escape the conditions in the military units. However, in many cases the men could not gather the money or food demanded. The officers, furious not to receive their backhander, devised more severe punishments.

Officers actively used soldiers' free labor for their own income. Namely, they made a cheap deal with a "client" and obliged the soldiers do perform the job (e.g. repair works on sites, bringing and chopping wood, carrying out agricultural works, etc.).

With the shift to a professional army, it can be hoped that non-statutory relations will cease. Indeed, the economic factor within non-statutory relations was clearly revealed after the introduction of contract-based service in the Georgian army. When the wages of contract-based servicemen increased and their conditions substantially improved, crime practically disappeared from their units. Indeed, professional soldiers have to respect their contract with the Ministry of Defense, and their motivation has altered: to develop their careers and obtain higher wages, they seem less inclined to committing disciplinary irregularities or crimes.

Social environment
The importance of the social environment in respect to non-statutory relations is conditioned by the fact that socially unprotected groups find it even more difficult to assert their rights:
- they have insufficient education about legal matters;

- they are mainly from the regions and have no ability or means to request help from authorities .

Unable to face the problems, they try to ignore irregularities and unfairness. For this reason, non-statutory relations are rarely disclosed to the general public. This leaves added space for irregular activities. The situation is further complicated by the fact that military units are closed sites.

According to current statistics, 90 % of recruits are from unprotected strata of society. For years, aware of the conditions in the army, parents from richer classes delayed their sons' military service by bribing officials. This became so common that in 2002, the Georgian Parliament passed a law allowing men to defer service by 12 months by paying a 200 Laris tax (about 100 USD). This legislation, still in force today, means that only representatives of socially unprotected strata serve[12].

Regarding the education of recruits, a mean 10% had received higher education, 60 % - secondary education, while 30 % had no schooling at all. This was complicated by the fact that a percentage of recruits came from non-Georgian populations and spoke neither Georgian nor Russian. For this reason they were never fully integrated in the army.

The officers also faced similar social problems. Years of hard conditions in the military service had substantially lowered the army's prestige. Extreme conditions led the officers to find additional sources of income through crime. The officers were not authorized to air their problems seeing as the ministry of defense wanted to hide the bad conditions and rampant corruption in the army.

All this created a tense psychological environment for the officers who channeled their frustration through aggressive behavior towards their subordinates. This was exacerbated by the fact that the authorities had grown used to the situation and did nothing to control criminal deeds.

---

[12] Amendments made on 21 July 2002 to the law "On conscription and Military Service" (adopted on 17 September 1997) introduced the notion of a "Military Tax" that came into effect in January 2003: the military tax gives prospective conscripts - unable or unwilling to serve in the army - the option of buying an official 12-month deferral for 200 Laries (about 100 US dollars). According to this law, a significant part of the paid tax is transferred to a special account intended for social and economic repair of the army and reform of the professional army. Theoretically, nothing prevents a recruit from deferring an appeal during several years. This would imply that only those who cannot pay the 200 Laries are called into the army [Editors' note].

The situation changed drastically when contract-service was introduced. Seeing improved economic conditions, the middle class has started to show interest in an army career. This has increased the level of education among servicemen and no doubt contributes to reducing the amount of non-statutory relations.

4. Non-statutory relations after the "Rose Revolution" of 2003

After the "Rose Revolution" of November 2003, society's perception of the army became more positive. Furthermore, at the beginning of 2004, the development of military forces was announced as a top priority: the defense budget was substantially increased. A Partnership Agreement was signed with NATO whose primary aim was not only to bring Georgian military forces into compliance with NATO standards[13] but also to introduce the principles of democracy in the army. This signified increasing the power of civil democratic control over the military forces and protecting human rights. With the budget rise, military barracks were repaired and military personnel were able to work in suitable conditions. The salaries of military servicemen increased, corruption decreased, management posts were filled by officers educated in Western Europe. All these factors further improved society's attitude towards the army and in turn, the authorities' accountability towards society developed. As previously said, cases of non-statutory relations in the army decreased substantially with 50 % of the armed forces becoming contract-based workers.

However, after the "revolution", several cases of non-statutory relations were publicly disclosed.

> Case no. 4
> On December 18, 2004, 65 soldiers wilfully abandoned the Mukhrovani military brigade and walked 20 km in snow to

---

[13] In an attempt to render the Georgian armed forces more effective, in 2002, the United States launched a two-year, $64 million program, "Train and Equip", to create three battalions and one motorized company that would conform to NATO standards (see *RFE/RL Newsline*, 27 February and 3 May 2002). After that program was successfully concluded in 2004, a follow-up program was launched with comparable funding to train a further 4,000 Georgian servicemen (see *RFE/RL Caucasus Report*, vol. 8, no. 24, 22 July 2005) [Editors' note].

reach Tbilisi and inform the Minister of Defense and the President about their "problem" -as they named it. Arriving at the presidential residence, the men declared there was no heating in their military unit and the water system was seriously impaired. They only bathed twice every 2 months and had been oppressed and beaten by officers. They requested transfer to another unit.

The above case received a huge response. The office of the ombudsman interceded and even the President of Georgia commented on the case. The authorities declared the two soldiers should be punished for deserting. But according to public opinion and several NGOs, it was the high-ranking officials of the brigade who were guilty. The soldiers were not punished and the case was handed over to the lawmakers for further investigation.

> Case no. 5
> On April 1, 2005, soldiers from the Saguramo light-infantry battalion protested against the fact the training forced on them by an officer. For disobeying orders, they were forced to run half-naked in freezing cold weather. Several became ill. One of them contracted pneumonia and had to be sent to the military hospital.

Other cases of beating, humiliation and abuse have been reported since the revolution, but overall, non-statutory relations have decreased. However, we are far from erasing non-statutory relations in the army. There are still no effective legislative mechanisms and no management principles to protect human rights and provide fair discipline in the army.

Conclusion

After the collapse of the Soviet Union, the Georgian army adopted several violent practices from the former Soviet army and the Russian post-soviet one. However, it must be noted that the Georgian army did not fully take on the Russian practice of hazing. Many reasons lie behind non-statutory relations in the Georgian army. The fact that the military budget was too limited and there were terrible conditions created or contributed to corruption. In addition, lack of effective legislature and control mechanisms opened the way to "unwritten laws".

The increase of the defense budget, the upgrading of conditions and salaries and the implementation of professional armed forces represent real signs of progress. However, there are still problems, even in the professional army, and further measures must be implemented to achieve a more democratic army where non-statutory relations cannot thrive.

IV *Dedovshchina* and Hazing Abroad

10 Time to Waste. Notes on the Culture of the Enlisted in the Professionalizing Czech Military

Hana CERVINKOVA

This essay draws on interviews with fifty enlisted men with whom I worked during two months in the spring of 2001 on an Air Force Base in the Czech Republic. At the time, I was beginning my sixteen-month employment as a military researcher in the Czech armed forces (CAF), attempting to gain official access to Air Force officers whom I wanted interview about the changing concepts of the military profession in the new political and military system. Gaining access to the military professionals proved to be a formidable task not only because of the aura of secrecy surrounding this professional cast and all things in the post-Soviet military, but also because of the difficulty of explaining the reasons for such an undertaking by a practitioner of cultural anthropology - a field of social science largely unknown in the Czech Republic, let alone in the Czech military. Until my arrival, most Czech military research in the social sciences had been limited to quantitative opinion and satisfaction surveys whose administration was tightly controlled by two other, mutually competing research units within CAF that employed mostly psychologists and sociologists. In order to convince the military leadership of the value of qualitative cultural analysis as I was proposing it, I suggested conducting a pilot study among the enlisted.

Contrary to the case of professional officers, getting the permission for my study among the enlisted was not very difficult. About six weeks after I had submitted my proposal and request, I received the order to carry out my research. Several mornings per week for the duration of two months, the Commander of the Air Base, based on the order of the Chief of the General Staff, sent me two to four enlisted men to be interviewed. In the Czech military institution, the roles of the anthropologist and her subject were defined by the chain of command - my research was an execution of an order from the Chief of the General Staff, who ordered the Commander of the Air Base to order the Captain in charge of the enlisted to order them to come to me for an interview. I could forget about what I had learned in my training about modern anthropological theory and its urge to deconstruct the power relations between the anthropologists and their cultural others[1]. In the relationship between the enlisted as the anthropological subjects and me as the anthropologist, the power was clearly distributed - I was the one ordered to ask questions and they were the ones who were ordered to answer.

My one to two hour interviews followed the same script based on a questionnaire which has been approved by the Chief of the General Staff. The explicitly stated goal of the research for which I had gained the permission was to learn about the views of the enlisted of the military service, their motivation for serving in the military, the comparison between their expectations and the reality of the service, their opinion regarding the contribution of the year in service to their life and career and more general questions targeted at learning about the connection between the motivation of the men to serve in the military and their relationship to the nation state. The findings of this research, which I duly presented to the military leadership as a readable report that included citations and Excel pies based on statistical data and content analysis[2] showed a grim portrait. Except for one interviewee who reported that he had established a nice friendship with another enlisted man, the conscripts felt that military service did not bring them anything. In the words of many interviewees, their service in the CAF was a "waste of time."

The image of time as something being wasted during the military service reappeared throughout the interviews - both in the discourse and the material cultural practices demonstrated to me by my interviewees. In this article,

---

[1] T. Asad, *Anthropology and the Colonial Encounter*, Atlantic Highlands, N.J.: Humanities Press, 1988; Clifford, James, "On Ethnographic Authority", in *The Predicament of Culture: Twentieth-Century Ethnography, Literature, and Art*, Cambridge: Harvard University Press, 1988; G. Marcus and M. Fischer, *Anthropology as a Cultural Critique: An Experimental Moment in the Human Sciences*, Chicago: The University of Chicago Press, 1986; E. Said, *Orientalism*, New York: Vintage Books, 1979.

[2] H. Cervinkova, *Pruzkumna sonda nazoru vojaku zakladni sluzby na pusobeni v ACR* (HF Monitor 80), Prague, July 2001.

I return to the material that I collected during my study among the conscripts. I will argue that "time" serves as a crucial trope for the Czech enlisted men. Through a particular definition of "time," different from that shared by the majority society, the enlisted form a bond as a separate cultural group. The specialized knowledge of "time" of the enlisted is a source of their self-definition as a group - their intimate cultural knowledge. This cultural know-how allows them to assume social agency in a situation when they are turned into liminal personae, placed outside of society by others, temporarily deprived of the individual rights for self-direction, their work alienated. The conscripts' agency, which draws on a unique concept of time, is especially important in the context of the process of military professionalization. This is because professionalization, based as it is on the elimination of general conscription, depreciates the value of the conscripts' work for the military and the nation state. Because of the central role of the soldier in the Czech national imagination, this change in the role and character of the soldier's work and position challenges traditional concepts of national identity. One of the most manifest aspects of this process centers on the symbolic role of the Good Soldier Švejk as the model symbolizing the ideal Czech soldier in the past times, which is currently being deemed unfit for the tasks of the future professionalized military.

1. Professionalization as the decorroding treatment

Military professionalization has been the topic of discussion in the Czech political arena since the end of the socialist times. On the one hand, professionalization was seen as the most efficient way of the depoliticizing and restructuring of the Czech and Slovak military from totalitarian to democratic forces[3]. In addition, professionalization promised to abolish the very unpopular law of general conscription, which has been in existence in the Czech lands since the mid-1900[4]. Despite much political talk, however, it took twelve years for

---

[3] M. Vlachova, "Professionalization of the Army of the Czech Republic." Conference Paper, Transforming Post-Communist Militaries: Professionalisation of the Armed Forces in Central and Eastern Europe. Joint Services Command Staff College, Watchfield, April 2001.
[4] In 1990, the government shortened the two-year period of conscription service to eighteen months and introduced optional civilian service for men who refused to

professionalization to become the official program for the military sector of the state[5].

This slow pace can be explained by the problematic position of the military sector in Czech politics and society. Highly discredited because of its subservience to the Soviet occupying forces since 1968, the Czech military was not perceived by most Czechs as an honorable institution dedicated to the defense of a national territory and Czech citizens, but on the contrary - an ally of the enemy[6]. Moreover, the Czechoslovak People's Army, the pawn of the Soviet colonial empire, has never fought a war in its history - first demobilized under the German and later under the Soviet occupation. Burdened by the history of acquiescence and passivity, the Czech armed forces presented a dilemma for the new leaders of the post-socialist state. This situation began to change when the Czech Republic prepared for its accession to NATO. In 1999, by gaining the NATO membership, ostensibly a political organization which nevertheless relies for its power and influence on military prowess, the Czech state (and the international community) placed an enormous weight of responsibility and importance on the Czech military. After a period of disinterest in military matters following the end of socialism, the military was now endowed with the task of bringing the Czech Republic into the fold of Western democratic states.

In 2001, the new charismatic leader of the military sector, Minister Jaroslav Tvrdik was the first one to realize the upcoming opportunity and to harness the "war machine'" for his party's political agenda. In 2001, replacing his discredited Social Democratic Party colleague, Tvrdik introduced an intensive

---

serve in the army for religious or other reasons. Since 1993, the conscription period has been only one year long, but the number of men entering military service continued to decrease considerably. While in 1993, there were 68 630 enlisted in CAF, their number in 2001 was only 24 955 (Ministry of Defense of the Czech Republic, The Reform of the Armed Forces of the Czech Republic. Prague: AVIS. 2001, p.43). This was both due to the unpopularity of military service and the falling number of male population. The number of 18-year old men in the Czech Republic in 1993 was 94 000, in 2001 only 70 500, with a further decreasing projection for the year 2018 at 46 000 individuals (*Ibid.*).

[5] Vlachova, 2001, *op. cit.*
[6] C. Rice, *The Soviet Union and the Czechoslovak Army, 1948-1983: Uncertain Allegiance*, Princeton: Princeton University Press, 1984; J. Simon, *Warsaw Pact Forces: Problems of Command and Control*, Boulder and London: Westview Press, 1985; M.P. Ulrich, *Democratizing Communist Militaries: The Cases of the Czech and Russian Armed Forces*, Ann Arbor: The University of Michigan Press, 1999.

campaign at military reform. Professionalization appeared as the main reorganizing principle, setting the year 2006 as the last year of general conscription[7]. In Tvrdik's campaign, professionalization is portrayed as the general remedy for the ills of the post-socialist military. One of the most visible forms of the campaign was a series of leaflets distributed with the main Czech daily, *Mlada Fronta Dnes*. The first leaflet, for example, was a large-size photo showing a detail of the Czech insignia on a rusting green metal background of military machinery. The rust was advancing into the center of the ensign and a warning note at the bottom of the page read "Time to do something" ("*Čas něco udělat*"). On the other side of the flyer there were several captions set to the same background of a rusting metal. The first piece of text asked: "What do we feel when hear the name of the Czech armed forces? Self-confidence? Strength? Or even pride?" Clearly the questions were rhetorical, because without providing an answer first, the next note said: "But that is how it should be. But that would mean to have a military always able to protect and to help where help is needed. Professional armed forces - less of a people's military, but a military more humane [*Profesionalni armadu - mene lidovou a vice lidskou*]". The concluding caption provided an explanation and information regarding the authorship of the surprising addition to the daily: "What are we doing to make this happen? Everything. No facials, but a strict diet. A change in thinking, modernization. No ordering around [*Zádná buzerace*], but a lot of work. And the deadline? The year 2006. The Reform of the Armed Forces of the Czech Republic." Signed – "The Ministry of Defense of the Czech Republic, www.army.cz"

In the next flyer that appeared in the paper a few days later, the message was the same, but the photo was different. It showed a military sapper in high-tech protective gear searching for mines on a desolate soccer field located in some remote war-torn place. A large caption at the bottom of the page read: "We are not playing at being soldiers [*Nehrajem si na vojaky*]". The other side contained a "short guide to coping with the military reform," whose goals were: "A healthy, professional military. A military of full readiness, a military able to be in the right place at the right time. A military that is slim, modern and thinking. A military without rust. A military full of good and

---

[7] After Tvrdik's resignation two years later, the new Minister, Miroslav Kostelka, moved the date further up to the year 2004.

competent soldiers." Signed "Jaroslav Tvrdik, the Minister of Defense of the Czech Republic."

These newspaper inserts were accompanied by other propaganda materials such as the small recruitment brochure targeted at youth, Tomorrow Belongs to the Professionals[8]. The campaign, which coincided with the period of my fieldwork on the air force bases of the Czech armed forces (February 2001-June 2002), initiated great upheavals in military matters, which were further intensified by international consequences of the September 11th attacks in the United States and the ensuing war on terrorism. Through it, the Czech state made a serious attempt, for the first time in its post-socialist history, to consolidate its own authority with that of its military institution. It was a peculiar moment in post-socialist modernity, when the strange space of power, which always exists between the state and its institution of legitimate violence, was being filled and organized according to the rules of a new rationality[9]. Professionalization appeared as the technology of this process, through which not only the military, but the larger apparatus of power that Deleuze and Guattari call the war machine began changing its position vis-à-vis the state and society[10].

Allegorically expressed as the decorroding treatment (the warning slogan "Time to Do Something" on a rusting background of military technology or the expressive call "new military without rust"), or as the end of the period of play with respect to things military ("We're Not Playing at Being Soldiers") and summarized eloquently in the prediction "Tomorrow Belongs to the Professionals," the professionalization campaign makes a clear break with the past. The history belongs to the conscription military, to the culture of the enlisted. Professionalization aims at placing the enlisted in the former times, while

---

[8] MOD (Ministry of Defense of the Czech Republic), *Zitrek patri profesionalum* (Tomorrow Belongs to Professionals), Prague: AVIS, 2001, or the more comprehensive handbook, The Reform of the Armed Forces of the Czech Republic: Ministry of Defense of the Czech Republic. *Nehrajem si na vojaky: Strucny navod, jak zvladnout reformu armady*, Prague, 2001.

[9] H. Cervinkova, *We're Not Playing at Being Soldiers: An Ethnographic Study of the Czech Military and its Changing Relationship with the State and Society in the Period of Post-Socialist Transformation*, Dissertation Manuscript, New York: New School for Social Research, 2003.

[10] G. Deleuze and F. Guattari. "1227: Treatise on Nomanology - The War Machine," in *Thousand Plateaus: Capitalism and Schizophrenia*, Minneapolis: University of Minnesota Press, 1987, pp. 351-423.

showing the future as that of the military professionals. As I will try to show and as I argued elsewhere[11], the process of professionalization, based as it is on the elimination of general conscription and technological and organizational modernization, however, involves deep changes both in the culture of the enlisted and the larger field of national cultural imagination and identity politics.

2. Rambos vs. Švejks

In the Czech context, one of the largest tasks for professionalization has been to bring seriousness and importance to the discredited military institution, which has been a target of popular jokes rather than a source of pride and serious respect for the Czechs and Slovaks. The most pervasive symbol of the popular laughter at power has been the Good Soldier Švejk, the internationally famous hero of an antiwar novel by Jaroslav Hasek[12]. Švejk, the literary anti-hero, spends much time professing his patriotism and devotion to the monarchy and its war campaign. Through his behavior, which his superiors name "idiotic" (and Švejk cheerfully endorses this classification), the Good Soldier Švejk literally and perfectly executes orders assigned to him. Nevertheless, he manages to never complete what his superiors want him to do and his actions are unfailingly disastrous for the war effort. Through his actions and stories of quotidian life, grotesque in their mixture of hilarity, cruelty and violence, Švejk disarms his superiors and by never as much as mentioning the war, let alone engaging in it, we are certain in our laughter that he is fully and at every moment victorious over the war machine. Since the interwar period, the Good Soldier Švejk has been a symbol of the common soldier's resistance to war, and by extension - the common citizen's resistance to the absurdities of state bureaucratic power.

For many years, Švejk has functioned as a model for self-identification not only for the involuntary draftees - the enlisted in the Czech military - but

---

[11] Cervinkova, 2003, *op. cit.*; H. Cervinkova, "Military Masculinity in the Czech Military after Socialism", in B. van Hoven (ed.), *Spaces of Masculinity*, London: Routledge, 2004.
[12] J. Hasek, *The Goold Soldier Švejk*, New York: Penguin, 1973.

was frequently extended to include the Czech nation as such: living under foreign military occupation and domestic totalitarianism, the Czechs identified with Švejk's passive resistance to oppression. Most often, Švejk has been evoked through discursive contraptions - "*Švejkárna*", "*Švejkovat*" or "*Švejkoviny*". "*Švejkovat*" (to do things like Švejk), "*Švejkoviny*" (activities reminiscent of those of Švejk) and "*Švejkárna*" (situation evocative of the grotesqueness of Švejk's legendary escapades) are usually spoken to mark situations of absurdity and contradiction. Most obviously, these are situations, in which the common sense of a smaller and less powerful entity confronts the irrational rationality of a larger and more powerful body. But in the resulting effect, the former wins over the latter against all odds by virtue of the comic principle - laughter is what defeats the adversary and brings victory to the powerless. The apparently self-critical identification of the Czechs with Švejk as the anti-hero, has thus always contained a subversive element: through the Good Soldier Švejk who ultimately wins over the war machine by subverting its seriousness through the comic principle, the Czechs have laughed and often won over oppressive power. Consistent with the logic of cultural intimacy[13] Švejk has functioned as the Czechs' self-deprecating label for the outside world, while at the same time performing the role of a social bond among people on the home front.

The professionalization campaign directly challenges this national fantasy. The Czech government officials and the press, concerned with the poor reputation of the Czech military inside and outside of the country have repeatedly evoked the name of the Good Soldier to criticize the institution for its low preparedness and the slow pace of post-Soviet reforms. "Let's Put an End to Švejkism!," screamed a title of a newspaper article published shortly before the Czech Republic joined NATO[14]. The author who subtitled his article, "NATO: We need to convince the public," pleaded with the Czech public, at the time still lukewarm about the upcoming accession to the Alliance, to become serious about military and security affairs and consider all the advantages of NATO membership. According to the author, a major obstacle to

---

[13] M. Herzfeld, *Cultural Intimacy: Social Poetics in the Nation-State*, New York: Routledge, 1997.
[14] P. Kopecky, "Skoncujme se Švejkovstvim", *Lidove Noviny*, 7 March 1997, p. 10.

changing people's attitude toward the role of the military was of course nobody else but Švejk:

> [Š]vejkism, might have helped us survive through the bad times, which we have lived through in this century. But let us face the fact that Švejk is not a hero that should be followed, but a dog thief with the innocent face of a baby, who always took good care - of himself. Today, this kind of thinking will not bring us security.

In a feature article published by a leading Czech weekly shortly after September 11th events in the United States, entitled, "Rambos versus Švejks: Why Do People Laugh at Our Military?", the author describes the Czech military as composed of "handful of elite gunman and thousands of useless men to fill the ranks" - few elite Rambos among many Švejks[15]. In his reckoning, the Rambos are "professionals" in the use of military violence and "to them the future belongs." Their chief attributes are their superior technical and physical skills, which combined with the knowledge of English and personal qualities emphasizing self-confidence and professional detachment make them deployable in international operations, outside of the country borders. The participation of these professionals in international operations brings a good name to the Czech military - a reputation that the country's leaders desperately desire. This is because through the good results of the elite soldiers, not only the Czech military, but the Czech state gain points on the precarious scale measuring the degree of redirected loyalty and Westernization of the Cold War adversary who has only so very recently become an ally. The Švejks are the bored and incapable conscripts who are bringing shame to the military with their negative attitude to service and the military institution in general.

It is understandable that for the achievement of the desired goal - a military full of NATO-compatible Rambos - the Švejks must be eliminated. The current efforts at bringing seriousness to the military through its professionalization, therefore, rely simultaneously on the elimination of the enlisted from the military ranks and on the removal of Švejk from his place of prominence in

---

[15] K. Vrana, "Sedivy kontra Tvrdik: Reform ozbrojenych sil jako stret vojaku a ministerstva", *Tyden*, 14 January 2002, pp. 24-25.

the national imagination. Not surprisingly, therefore, the conscripts' identification with Švejk has been and continues to be strong. During my interviews with them, the conscripts would often interrupt their narrative during interviews with the expression, "That was *Švejkárna*, man!," to comment on a situation when they found themselves on the intersection of two mutually contradictory orders from their superiors. The conscript, by executing these conflicting commands literally, but with disastrous effects for the military institution would then be said to "*Švejkovat*" or to have been engaged in activities summarized under the term of "*Švejkoviny*".

A 22-year-old enlisted man, who had to leave his job as a mason when he was drafted, answered my standard question regarding his opinion of the readiness of the Czech military to engage in combat in the following way:

> This military? This military is that of Švejks and to send us to war would be a sure murder. Look at the equipment and the training we get! I have been here for three months and fired six shots at a training range using a thirty-year old rifle. Instead of teaching us how to fight, they use us to guard the hangars at the airport. But there is nothing inside the buildings that we are supposed to protect! They have no planes there or ammunition, and so we spend the whole draft-year guarding nothing. That's simply a *Švejkárna*! ["*To je normální Švejkárna!*"]

By commenting on their experience from serving in the Czech military as a situation of absurdity reminiscent of Švejk's adventures, the conscripts were reaffirming their connections to the figure of Švejk and his lasting power as an appropriate symbol for describing the Czech military. In stressing the emptiness of the military discipline and lack of the CAF's combat readiness, they were contradicting official efforts at bringing seriousness to the Czech military institution. By reaffirming Švejk's lasting relevance to describing things military and by stressing their connection to the symbol, they were resisting the official efforts at turning the institution into a professional force and making the conscripts irrelevant to the new national military system.

3. Time to waste

In the turning of a negative image into a source of cultural identity and social agency, the Czech enlisted men resemble other disadvantaged cultural groups around the world[16]. The enlisted men in militaries across the globe share the experience of what Erving Goffman has called a "total institution" - a place which imposes a different set of rules, quite separate from those of society. But contrary to the generally assumed image of inmates as passive recipients of orders, inhabitants of total institutions develop various strategies that help them survive the institution in which they have been involuntarily placed[17]. Joris Van Bladel, for example, suggests that Russian *dedovshchina*, "the informal hierarchical structure installed among the group of soldiers that is primarily based on seniority," is such a response of soldiers as active agents to the perverse effects created by total institutions[18]. The application of an anthropological framework, I suggest, can help us further explain the potential of the enlisted to become agents in the conditions of an oppressive total institution that imposes discipline directed at the suppression of their individual and social identity. The enlisted seem to fit particularly well into the anthropological category of liminal beings, a term customarily applied to mark a person or a group in the middle period of the rites-of-passage, such as a neophyte during the puberty initiation rituals that bring him or her into adulthood[19]. Liminal entities are "neither here nor there; they are betwixt and between the positions assigned and arrayed by law"[20]. The enlisted men as liminal entities experience the transitory stage from becoming men from boys, from half to full citizens of their nation states. As Turner reminds us, liminal

---

[16] E. Goffman, *Asylums: Essays on the Social Situation of Mental Patients and Other Inmates*, New York: Anchor Books, 1961; Herzfeld, 1997, *op. cit.*; M. De Certeau, *The Practice of Everyday Life*, Berkeley: University of California Press. 1984; M. Taussig, *Shamanism, Colonialism and the Wild Man*, Chicago: University of Chicago Press, 1984.

[17] Goffman, 1961, *Ibid.*; J. Van Bladel, "Russian Soldiers in the Barracks: A Portrait of a Subculture." in A. Aldis and R. Mc Dermott eds, *Russian Military Reform 1992-2002*, Frank Cass Publishers, 2003.

[18] Van Bladel, 2003, *Ibid.*, p. 64

[19] A. Van Gennep, *The Rites of Passage*, London: Routledge and Kegan Paul, 1909; V. Turner, *The Ritual Process: Structure and Anti-Structure*, Ithaca: Cornell University Press, 1966.

[20] Turner, 1966, *Ibid.*, p. 95.

entities, suspended as they are in a stage of a "post" and a "pre" and excluded from social life, are ambiguous and potentially disruptive, escaping classification and possessing of an openness that challenges harmony, hierarchy and structure. It is in this context that I propose to view the hierarchical system of authority among the Czech enlisted men and its disruptive potential on the formal system of discipline in the Czech military.

Time is a precious commodity in capitalism, which, unlike time in task-oriented societies that follow a nature-bound life rhythm, is strictly measured and can be sold, bought, used well or wasted[21]. As an instrument that measures labor, time in capitalism is also an instrument of control and discipline[22]. In the context of the professionalizing Czech military, which is a part of Czech society experiencing transition into the capitalist system, the liminal period of military service becomes strongly defined by the enlisted as time out of time, as time being lost from their lives. In their interviews with me, the men complained heavily about this aspect of the military service:

> Military service is a total waste of time and money. I think that it is fundamentally useless. Everybody just wants to finish the service and get to the end. [22 years old, high-school graduate]
>
> I thought I would learn something here, but I am just wasting my time. [20-year old, completed vocational training]
>
> While I am here, my colleagues from the university are getting their work experience. They are making money and I am just loosing my time. [23-year old, technical university graduate]
>
> Today, military service is a waste of time. I did not expect it. I thought it would be better. Here, the officers call you during your duty to come and clean their office. That is such a waste of time. I thought I would learn something about combat and things military. But all they do is that they use

---

[21] E. Evans-Pritchard, *The Nuer*, Oxford: Oxford University Press, 1940, pp. 94-138; E.P. Thompson, E.P,"Time, Work-Discipline, and Industrial Capitalism", *Past & Present*, no. 38, 1967, pp. 56-97.

[22] Thompson, 1967, *Ibid.*

us as cheap labor - we are the cheapest cooks and cleaners of trash. [25-year old, completed three years of technical university]

Because of the process of reform, many units in the military had to save money and the most obvious place to do so was the training of the enlisted. Instead of providing military training, the Czech military mostly turned the enlisted into what in their popular jargon the interviewees called UBS, when asked about their function in the unit. UBS stands for *"univerzalni bouchac sluzeb"* (universal duty doer) and consists in standing on guard at the assigned places of the base. Not surprisingly, in their complaints about time wasting, most men were expressing their disappointment when they compared the reality of service with their expectations prior to it. To my surprise, 64 percent of the men responded that they wanted to complete the military service and did not try to avoid it. Importantly, a majority (78%) of this number explained their attitude as: "military service is a part of life and without it, you are not a man". The disenchantment of the enlisted was a result of the discrepancy between their traditional expectations of the military service as a rites-of-passage into manhood. The imagined military service was filled with physical training and hardship as a preparation for defending the nation. The real military service consisted in the passive duty system in an institution that clearly considered the conscripts unfit for any real military tasks. The frustration of the enlisted was further aggravated by the other most frequent activity assigned to them - cleaning and cooking. The traditional "femininity" of these tasks further contributed to the conscripts' feeling of emasculation.

The system of *mazàrna*[23], I suggest, the hierarchical system of authority among the Czech conscripts based as it is on the length time spent in service, is their response to these totalizing effects of the military institution. The year of service is taken out of regular life of the individual and his social time. Life in the system of *mazàrna* starts with the beginning of service and is divided into four principle stages disrespectful of the actual physical age and/or social standing (based on class, profession or education) of the individual

---

[23] Ethymologically, the term *mazàrna* comes from "*mazak*" - colloquial word which stands for an experienced man, a man who is not afraid, knows the world, and from "*mazany*"- an adjective which means "clever", that is someone who knows how to get by and achieve what he needs.

outside of the military. The person's place in the hierarchy is fully determined by the time that he has spent in the military. Each transition to the next stage is marked by the rites-of-passage, which involves psychological and physical violence perpetrated by the senior on the junior conscripts. Importantly, most violence is based on the humiliation of the neophyte by making him do activities traditionally associated with women, such as cleaning or by calling him by derogative names destined for female victims (pussy, whore, etc.).

Because of the dressing code associated with the system of *mazàrna*, the enlisted are easily able to identify the individual's position in the hierarchy. This cultural code works efficiently to determine seniority in social interactions. Because officially forbidden, the breaking of the dress code is also a typical example of "messing up" - a way of showing the senior's conscripts' lack of respect for officers and the military institution[24]. For example, after each stage, the conscript was able to change the system of tying his boots to include more of the so called "bridges." He could also tie his belt lower and loosen the tie on his barrette. A particularly interesting set of hierachical markings included the custom of weaving a special lash, called mazacenka preferably from the boot laces, which the senior enlisted would hang on their key chains. The custom of weaving *mazacenka*, closely resembles another Czech tradition of weaving *pomlazka* - a lash from willow branches made and used by men to lash women on Easter Monday. *Mazacenka* like *pomlazka* are material symbols of men's prowess and dominance over women; in the hierarchical system of *mazàrna*, they can only be woven and worn by *mazaci*, the senior conscripts in the system of *mazàrna*, the only real men among the emasculated and dominated enlisted.

The cultural custom most explicitly connected to time as the basis for the hierarchical system of *mazàrna* and by extension the clearest expression of the reversal of the official military's concept of time, is a system of measurement of days left to the end of service. Once the conscript has 150 days left to the end, he starts counting the dead days, symbolized by a section of the taylor's measuring tape. The measuring tape is placed in an empty plastic container of the Kinder Egg, which is hung on a key chain. Each cut off section of the measuring tape symbolizes a day and is termed "the dead" and

---

[24] Goffman, 1961, *op. cit.*

placed in another Kinder Egg container on the key chain. The connection between two Kinder Eggs on the key chain and men's genitalia (both called *vejce* in Czech) is more than a matter of linguistics. The two "eggs" hanging on the key chain, containing the dead days of completed service are the embodiments of the conscripts' manhood. Moreover, like the Easter eggs that the Czech men get for lashing the women on Easter Monday, the Kinder Eggs on the key chain are earned trophies. Contrary to the passive reality the enlisted's tasks in the professionalizing military, the customs related to the measurement of time which are a part of the hierarchival system of *mazàrna*, mark the time as filled with manhood-building activity.

In a situation which defined them as passive neophytes doomed to wasting one year of their life, the enlisted in the professionalizing Czech military assumed agency in a way typical for their hero - the Good Soldier Svejk. Taken out of society and subjected to the rules of the total institution, they took discipline to the extreme and made time, the military's tool for their oppression, into an instrument of their own, albeit imagined, agency.

4. Postscript

Everyday, as I arrived at work at the Air Force Base, I was welcome at the gate by heavily smoking conscripts. Dressed in green camouflage with blue berets, young and bored beyond belief, their eyes spilling apathy, the involuntary conscripts appeared to me as heralds of earlier times, a dying species in the era of military professionalization. The physical youth of the men contrasted sharply with their occupational obsoleteness as soldiers. They were unwilling laymen in the age that was to belong to enthusiastic professional practitioners of the art of military violence, which made the former appear irrevocably stuck in the past. When I was later traveling through many Czech bases during my research, the enlisted men's boredom, which channelled the general misery of the post-socialist Czech military establishment, projected a distinct aura of intimacy. Because of the initial research, which I was conducting among them, I was able to tell, by the details of their uniforms, the ways that they tied their shoelaces and straps of their beret how many days they had left till the end of his service. This cultural know-how as well as the soldier's distinct unprofessionalism gave me a certain level of self-assurance. As I watched them, filling out my pass, unhurriedly dropping cigarette ashes on my ID, I felt the anthropologist's honor to have been able to witness and record a culture threatened with immediate disappearance.

11 Battling Bullying in the British Army 1987-2004

James K. WITHER

> Bullying has no place in training tough soldiers. –
> House of Commons, 1989

1. Introduction - the UK context

The British Army is renowned as one of the most professional and effective armies in the world. Conditions of service for Britain's volunteer recruits are a far cry from those faced by reluctant conscripts in Russia's under resourced and decaying armed forces. Young British soldiers are not confronted with the phenomenon of *dedovshchina*, the institutionalized mistreatment and misuse of recruits by more senior soldiers and sometimes officers, that remains widespread in the Russian and other conscript armies of the successor states of the former Soviet Union. Nevertheless, there is evidence that the British Army has failed to eliminate incidents of violent and cruel behaviour towards its soldiers despite a longstanding official commitment to tackle the problem. In an internal Army survey in 2003, for example, 43% of a sample of 2,000 soldiers responded that bullying was a problem and 5% claimed to be victims of it[1].

The purpose of this article is to provide insights into the problem of the bullying, particularly of recruits, in the British Army. It will examine the nature and extent of bullying, official policy to combat it, and suggest reasons why the problem persists even in a long established, professional army that is subject to both democratic civilian control and parliamentary and public scrutiny. Although statistics illustrate that bullying takes place in all three British armed services, this study will focus on the Army, which has both the greatest number of recruits and proportionally the largest number of recorded incidents of mistreatment. The choice of 1987 as the starting point for analysis is

---

[1] Interview given by General Anthony Palmer, Deputy Chief of Defence Staff on BBC Newsnight 4 November 2003. Available from: http://news.bbc.co.uk/1/hi/programmes/newsnight (accessed on 6 April 2004)

not arbitrary. It was then that bullying in the Army became a significant matter of public and parliamentary concern, arguably for the first time. Since the late 1980s, it has also became increasingly clear to service chiefs that the ill treatment of soldiers tarnishes the positive public image of the British Army and hampers efforts to recruit and retain personnel with the appropriate aptitudes and skills in the competitive UK employment market.

The UK Ministry of Defence (MOD) defines bullying as: "...the use of physical strength or the abuse of authority to intimidate or victimize others, or to give unlawful punishments,"[2] Official MOD and British Army policy on bullying is "zero tolerance" and specific responsibility is placed on all leaders "to protect others from physical and mental bullying, and to report any incident promptly."[3] The latest Defence White Paper of December 2003 states that: "Our service personnel need to feel confident that they are individually valued and respected, that complaints from them will be dealt with effectively and fairly, and that harassment and bullying have no place in service life and that any perpetrators will be dealt with firmly"[4].

2. MOD attempts to tackle the problem of bullying in the late 1980s

In 1987, about the same time that Gorbachev's glasnost policy drew official and public attention to *dedovschchina* in the Soviet armed forces, a series of revelations about regimental initiation rites in the British Army forced the MOD to place the problem of bullying high on its personnel management agenda. Senior officers and defence officials were shocked by reports of bizarre and vicious initiation ceremonies in the Army involving beatings, humiliation and sexual assaults taking place in prestigious regiments such as The Coldstream Guards and The King's Own Scottish Borderers. Reports of these events

---

[2] UK MOD, The Values and Standards of the British Army - A Guide to Soldiers, March 2000, paragraph 23. Available from: http://www.army.mod.uk/servingsoldier/usefulinfo/valuesgeneral/values/ss_hrpers_values_sldr_w.html (Accessed 24 March 2004).
[3] Ibid.
[4] UK MOD, *Delivering Security in a Changing World*, Defence White Paper, HMSO, 12/03, C16147, Supporting Essays, Essay 5 People, p. 17.

soon reached the press in the UK and abroad[5]. Some of the occurrences appeared uncomfortably similar in brutality to reports of the worst excesses of *dedovshchina* starting to emerge from the Soviet military. One example from a British infantry regiment will suffice to illustrate this point: "a 20 year old private...testified that his initiation consisted of being burned on the genitals, sexually assaulted with a broomstick, forced to march in place with string tied to his genitals and ankles and dropped from a window"[6]. Spokesmen for the MOD and the Army were anxious to stress that bullying was not widespread and claimed that press reports gave a false impression of the extent of the problem. In a statement to Parliament in January 1988, the Under Secretary of State for the Armed Forces, Mr. Roger Freeman, explained that in the previous two years, during which more than 20,000 troops had passed through training, only around 100 allegations of bullying, ill treatment and intimidation had been reported and nearly half of these had not been substantiated[7]. An internal review by the Adjutant General, General Sir David Mostyn, also concluded that bullying and other forms of mistreatment were not prevalent. However, Jack Ashley MP (now Lord Ashley), a leading parliamentary campaigner on behalf of bullied soldiers, expressed the view that the restrictions of The Official Secrets Act, fear of reprisals and an "atmosphere of intimidation" meant that many victims would not come forward to complain or give evidence against their tormentors. He claimed that official figures on bullying were only the "tip of the iceberg" of the problem[8].

The incidents of serious mistreatment of recruits that emerged in 1987 resulted in the sacking of at least one commanding officer, a number of high profile courts martial cases and a vigorous anti-bullying drive by the Adjutant General. The MOD launched a series of measures to tackle bullying, which were reported to Parliament in January 1988[9]. A ban on unauthorized initiation ceremonies was the most significant action. The practice became illegal

---

[5] See for example: D. Hughes, "Army to Fight Bullies", *The Sunday Times*, 29 November 1987, H. Raines, "British Army Stung by Tales of Brutality in the Ranks", *The New York Times*, 6 November 1987, p. 8. and Yvonne Preston, "British Army to Curb Its Bully Boys", *Sydney Morning Herald*, 14 November 1987, p. 23.
[6] Raines, 1987, *Ibid*.
[7] UK Parliament, House of Commons Hansard, HMSO, Col 254, 26 January 1988.
[8] *Ibid.*, Col. 340, 27 October 1987.
[9] *Ibid.*, Cols. 255-256, 26 January 1986.

under military law and the subject was added to the section on discipline in The Queens Regulations for the Army:

> The essential ingredients of discipline and military efficiency owe nothing to any unauthorized initiation or other rites aimed at terrifying or inflicting physical or mental degradation upon any individual. Such conduct would be directly contrary to the requirements of training, morale and good leadership...Allegations of unauthorized activities are to be referred to the Special Investigation Branch for investigation with a view to the taking of disciplinary action under the Army Act 1955 against the instigators and other participants. The contents of this paragraph are to be repeated at least annually in all formation, unit and sub unit orders.[10]

The man management training and selection of Non Commissioned Officer (NCO) and junior officer recruit instructors were also revised, as were screening measures during recruitment to identify individuals who might be particularly vulnerable to bullying. Welfare support for young soldiers was increased with the establishment of 92 additional Women's Royal Volunteer Service (WRVS) posts. These volunteers, quickly dubbed "Agony Aunts" by the press, were intended to provide a source of advice and assistance for junior soldiers who were too nervous to complain about ill treatment through official channels[11]. At the time, complaints under the Army's redress procedure had to be processed through NCOs and officers in the chain of command who might be the source of a grievance in the first place. Extra funding was provided to establish an additional 100 supervisory posts in the Army's training organization, to be implemented by March 1989. However, then as now, the government resisted calls for an independent public enquiry into the bullying of recruits or the appointment of a military ombudsman to provide an element of impartial, external oversight and hear complaints by soldiers unable or unwilling to use the official redress process. The investigation of grievances remained in the hands of commanding officers, who could call on the services of the Special Investigation Branch (SIB) of the Royal Military Police

---

[10] *The Queens Regulations for the Army*, revised edition March 1996, IAC 13206, HMSO, Part 6, paragraph 5.201A.
[11] J. Hay, " Agony Aunts Plan to End Army Bullying", *Sunday Mail*, 31 January, 1988.

when necessary. As such investigations were not independent of the chain of command, this procedure did not satisfy Jack Ashley, who described it as "wholly inadequate", not least because he felt commanders might suppress complaints rather than court bad publicity for their regiments[12]. The MOD also failed to create a centralized database to collate complaints about bullying[13] or monitor the impact of the measures being taken to combat the ill treatment of recruits. A number of the concerns raised in reports and parliamentary debates in the late 1980s have re-occurred periodically in discussions on bullying in the Army up to the present day.

3. MOD policy towards bullying in the post Cold War era

After the furor caused by the graphic press coverage of bullying in the late 1980s died down, there was little sustained public or political interest in the matter. Since conscription ended in 1962, few members of the public in the UK have any direct experience of life in the armed services; subsequently most politicians also take little interest in military matters. Besides, the attention of most defence commentators in the early 1990s was focused on the reduction and restructuring of the armed forces following the end of the Cold War. As a professional military, the British armed forces have traditionally been somewhat separate from the culture and values of wider society. For most senior officers, the Army's relative distance from the public it defends has not been unwelcome as it has helped to safeguard the Service from social trends that could pose a threat to the distinct ethos and discipline necessary to sustain troops in combat. However, in the 1990s the British armed forces faced unprecedented challenges to their assumptions, values and management culture. A growing emphasis on individual rights and a welter of employment regulations and laws, such as the Human Rights Act of 1998, when Britain formally adopted European Union human rights legislation[14] into national law, had a significant impact on the workplace in both the public and

---

12 UK Parliament, House of Commons, Hansard, Col. 341, 28 October, 1987, *op. cit.*
13 Official statistics for incidents of bullying were not kept until December 1997.
14 Unlike those of Spain and France, the British armed forces are not exempt from this legislation.

private sectors. National agencies such as the Equal Opportunities Commission (EOC) and Commission for Racial Equality (CRE) successfully attacked traditional attitudes concerning gender and race, not least in the armed forces. As a result, the Services had made considerable progress towards eliminating racial and gender based discrimination, bullying and harassment by the end of the decade. This was achieved through a package of measures that included a policy of "zero tolerance" of abuse, equal opportunities awareness training programmes and access for soldiers to civilian employment tribunals[15]. The MOD's achievements were even recognized by the CRE, formerly a severe critic of racism in the armed forces[16]. As the MOD's human resource management focus in the 1990s was directed at high profile and legally pressing equal opportunities issues, it is perhaps not surprising that problems associated with the mistreatment of soldiers in basic training were comparatively overlooked. However, some measures introduced to combat racial and sexual abuse and harassment undoubtedly assisted the victims of other forms of bullying. Redress of grievance procedures were revised in 1997, and again in 2002, to enable complaints to be addressed more speedily and efficiently. For the first time, it became possible for individuals to make complaints to officers outside their immediate chain of command[17]. Confidential telephone helplines, manned by welfare support agencies, were introduced in December 1997 to provide information and advice to soldiers who felt unable or unwilling to approach their superiors. Soldiers were also actively encouraged to take problems to medical officers, padres or the WRVS. Official guidance to officers and soldiers, particularly The Values and Standards of the British Army pamphlet of 2000, reinforced the "zero tolerance" of bullying and harassment message. These statements of principle were supported in practice by courts martial, which when appropriate sentenced those convicted of physical violence or degrading and humiliating behaviour towards other soldiers to detention and dismissal from the Army.

---

[15] Military personnel may only apply to Employment Tribunals in cases of alleged sexual or racial discrimination.

[16] See House of Commons Select Committee Appendices to the Minutes of Evidence, Appendix 4, *Racial Equality in the Armed Forces*, HMSO, January 2001.

[17] For details of the British Army's redress procedures see: Army General and Administrative Instructions (AGAI) management and Resolution of Complaints vol. 2 Chapter 70, May 2002. Available from: http://www.army.mod.uk/servingsoldier/termsofserv/discmillaw/ref/index.html (Accessed 8 April 2004)

The MOD has consistently maintained that the bullying of recruits is a minor problem in the Army[18]. Official statistics reported to Parliament have tended to verify this claim[19], although due to the fact that records of complaints about bullying were not introduced until December 1997, it is difficult to make comparisons with data from the 1980s or early 1990s. Even after 1997, significant gaps remained in the collection and collation of data, for example on the potential links between bullying and cases of self-harm[20] or absences without leave (AWOL). There is also evidence, as in the past, that many individuals are reluctant to make formal complaints[21]. A critical Amnesty International Report in 2000 on the UK's recruitment of under 18s, highlighted the particular difficulties faced by young recruits in this respect:

> The MOD's statements of principle do not allay concerns about accessibility to procedures for making a complaint, particularly with regard to children who may be easily intimidated and confused about the right steps to take. Nor do they allay concerns about the popular perception by young recruits that bullying is part of military life and that complaints will not be impartially investigated and acted upon[22].

A number of press reports in the late 1990s, based on soldiers' testimonies and courts martial transcripts, indicated that the official position on the extent of bullying in the Army may have been too sanguine. The results of a Sunday Times newspaper investigation published in October 1997 portrayed an Army in which little had changed since the 1980s, with violent assaults on

---

[18] See for example the comments by the Deputy Chief of Defence Staff in the BBC Newsnight interview of November 2003, *op. cit.*

[19] UK Parliament, House of Lords Hansard text for 20 June 2000, Col. 424 and House of Commons Hansard Written Answers for 5 March 2003, Col. 1028W.

[20] Until as recently as 2002, self-harm was regarded as a disciplinary matter and evidence of "malingering".

[21] Proceedings of the House of Commons Defence Committee Second Report, 14 February 2001, paragraphs 126-127.

[22] Amnesty International Library, "United Kingdom: U-18s: Child soldiers at risk", 7 November 2000, chap. 3.2 Bullying and remedies, pp. 6-8. Available from: http://web.amnesty.org/library/print/ENGEUR450562000 (Accessed 9 April 2004) Uniquely in Europe, the UK's professional armed forces rely on the recruitment of under 18s to meet recruiting targets. This age group represents up to a third of the total intake, particularly in the Army.

recruits and sadistic "initiations" still common[23]. Despite a tendency for the press to sensationalise and exaggerate the extent of mistreatment, a series of reports between 1999 and 2002 of violent assaults on recruits and humiliating initiation rites organized by NCOs and older soldiers suggested that measures introduced to tackle the problem of bullying following earlier scandals were not working[24]. A leading article in The Independent newspaper in 2002 claimed that there was "something deeply wrong" with the way new recruits were treated and described bullying as "routine"[25]. The House of Commons Parliamentary Defence Committee[26] took a somewhat more restrained view in a report of February 2001, which nevertheless concluded that "…regrettable incidents of racial and sexual harassment and other forms of bullying are still occurring and efforts to eradicate these must continue"[27].

4. Isolated incidents or a widespread problem? The impact of recent investigations

During 2002, media and parliamentary attention turned to the issue of suicides of soldiers in training at Army bases in Deepcut and Catterick[28]. Relatives of some of the deceased, unwilling to accept the verdicts of internal Army investigations, lobbied their Members of Parliament (MP) to call for a public enquiry. In a major parliamentary debate in February 2003 on soldiers' deaths in barracks, several MPs expressed alarm about possible links between bullying and suicide and one asserted that: "there is evidence of a cul-

---

[23] J. Carr-Brown and St. McGinty, "Army Recruits Sue MOD over Initiation Beatings", *The Sunday Times*, 19 October 1997.
[24] See for example: "New Recruits were forced to dance Naked Conga", *The Herald* (Glasgow), 4 February 1999, p. 10. and J. Burke, "Bullied army recruits being forced to desert", *The Observer*, 4 June 2000.
[25] Leading Article, "The Army must fight to restore confidence in its training ", *The Independent*, 29 October 2002, p. 16.
[26] The Defence Committee, which has cross party membership, provides parliamentary oversight over all defence policy, administration and expenditure matters. The committee can summon government ministers to give evidence for its enquiries.
[27] House of Commons Defence Committee 14 February 2001, *op. cit.*, paragraph 128.
[28] Ironically, in 2001, Russian officers had asked for help from their British counterparts to combat the high rate of suicide in their armed forces, estimated at around 2,000 per year. See: M. Hall, "Russians call in our Army over suicides", *The Daily Telegraph*, 5 August 2001.

ture of extreme bullying, routine violence and sexual harassment that constitutes torture and inhuman and degrading treatment"[29]. Once again, government ministers sought to illustrate the gap between the rhetoric and reality, pointing out that the number of suicides in the Army was in decline and that statistics generally compared favourably with those for civilians[30]. However, the same statistics revealed that the 16-19 age group was a noticeable exception, with suicide rates in the Army 1.5 times higher[31].

In October 2002, Mr Adam Ingram MP, The Minister of State for the Armed Forces, commissioned a review of the initial training of recruits across all three Armed Services[32]. The timing and focus of the study was primarily motivated by continuing media reports of bullying and harassment and the unexplained suicides of young soldiers in training. The appraisal team's findings were published in February 2003; the MOD was at pains to stress that the consultants involved were both independent of the chain of command and the personnel organization. On the specific issue of bullying, the team found "no evidence of any organized culture of bullying or systematic harassment"[33] and concluded "...our overall judgement is that the situation with regard to bullying has improved in recent years and cases of alleged assault or bodily harm are actually rare in Initial Training establishments"[34]. That said, the appraisal team noted that 7-8% of those interviewed claimed to be the victims of bullying, mainly from their peer group rather than supervisors[35] and concern was expressed about the "widespread reluctance" of recruits to report bullying incidents, which suggested that official statistics of the problem might, in the words of the investigators, be "technically unreliable"[36]. A series of measures

---

[29] UK Parliament, House of Commons Hansard Debates for 4 February 2003 (pt.1), Col. 3WH.
[30] Ibid., Cols. 16WH, 19WH and 20WH.
[31] Dr T. Fear and S. Wiliamson, "Suicide and Open Verdict Deaths among Males in the UK Regular Armed Forces", Defence Analytical Services Agency, 14 July 2003, pp. 2-3. Available from: http://www.dasa.mod.uk/publications/pdfs/suicide/suicide.pdf (Accessed 14 April 2004). The analysis also indicated that the US military had higher rates of suicide than the UK Armed Forces.
[32] Directorate of Operational Capability, MOD, Appraisal of Initial Training, 18 December 2002. Available from: http://www.mod.uk/linked_files/publications/it_appraisal_full.pdf (Accessed 12 April 2004).
[33] Ibid., paragraph 72.
[34] Ibid., paragraph 73.
[35] Ibid., paragraph 71.
[36] Ibid., paragraphs 74-75.

were taken as a result of the report, many of them familiar themes from earlier attempts to eradicate bullying. These included: more rigorous screening of recruits; improved education of instructors; stricter monitoring of training; guaranteed access by recruits to confidential welfare support; opportunities for recruits to provide anonymous feedback to the chain of command and improved ratios of instructors to trainees. A "training covenant" was also introduced to make explicit, and provide a common reference point for, the code of conduct expected of both instructors and recruits[37].

Anxious to be seen to be doing everything possible to improve the care regime for young soldiers, the MOD followed up the earlier report with a reappraisal in July 2003 to assess progress[38]. This second report acknowledged improvements made in many units and praised the ability of training establishments to produce large numbers of high quality, motivated soldiers. But, the team also concluded that the system was "running at risk" and still, "exhibiting the stresses and strains associated with a persistently high throughput of trainees and the effects of under-resourcing, notably in the area of supervisory and instructional manpower"[39]. Lack of investment was also apparent in the shabby accommodation and poor support and recreational facilities found in some Army training units, which combined with an inadequate supervisory regime, created an environment where, "there is continued, high risk of personal and disciplinary problems arising until substantial, decisive corrective action is taken..."[40] The investigators received some reports of "low-level" bullying, again mainly within recruit peer groups, although most training staff interviewed felt confident that they could deter or prevent serious incidents[41]. More disturbingly, investigators found that some instructors in Army training units actively discouraged recruits from seeking help from welfare agencies or those officers specifically charged with recruits' care[42]. Per-

---

[37] MOD Press Notice No: 032/03 Appraisal of Initial Training, 10 February 2003.Available from: http://news.mod.uk/news/press/archive/archive_master.htm (Accessed 14 April 2004).
[38] Directorate of Operational Capability, MOD, "ReAppraisal of Initial Training", 14 July 2003. Available from: http://www.mod.uk/linked_files/publications/it_appraisal_full.pdf (Accessed 16 April 2004).
[39] Ibid., paragraph 56, p.12.
[40] Ibid., paragraph 29, p. 6.
[41] Ibid., paragraph 23, p. 5.
[42] Ibid., paragraph 17, p. 3.

haps, not surprisingly, they encountered evidence of the perennial reluctance of British soldiers to approach officers with their problems[43].

These reports on initial training did little to reassure the growing number of MPs and sections of the media and public that were convinced bullying in the Army was rife[44]. Unfortunately for the MOD, these perceptions were reinforced by the final Surrey Police investigation report, released in March 2004, into the suicide of young recruits at the Royal Logistic Corps (RLC) training establishment at Deepcut in southern England[45]. Bullying, as such, was not the investigators' remit, but their report nevertheless expressed disquiet about wider evidence of mistreatment of soldiers in the Army's training establishments and recommended a broader enquiry into the problem[46]. Whilst acknowledging improvements made in the Army's care regime for young soldiers since 2002, the report was damning on the failings of the preceding 15 years. Among the issues highlighted by the report were the longstanding inadequacy of funding for welfare and supervisory resources in training and the absence of a coordinated, organization-wide response to deficiencies identified by previous investigations. To add weight to those MPs who had been calling for the appointment of a military ombudsman since the late 1980s, the report stressed the need for greater accountability and transparency in the Army's training regime. It recommended a further enquiry to consider the benefits of "a continuous independent oversight mechanism" to enable the Army to strike a balance between the need for tough training and the management of the attendant risks for young soldiers[47].

Following publication of the report, the government agreed that the House of Commons Defence Select Committee would undertake an enquiry

---

[43] Ibid., paragraph 30, p. 6. Researchers have found a greater emphasis on formal military discipline in the British Army, compared with those of other Western European countries. This might be a factor in the reluctance of British soldiers to approach their officers with problems. See: J. Soeters, D. Winslow and A. Weibull, "Military Culture", in G. Caforio (ed.), Handbook of the Sociology of the Military, New York: Kluwer Academic/Plenum Publishers, 2003, p. 243.

[44] See for example: UK Parliament House of Commons Hansard Debates for 12 Jun 2003 (pt. 25) Cols 899 - 900, "Sex fear of Army teens", The Observer, 8 June 2003, and M. Smith, "Secret survey shows Army that bullying is rife", The Daily Telegraph, 3 January 2004.

[45] Surrey Police, Deepcut Investigation Final Report, 4 March 2004. Available from: http://www.surrey.police.uk/Deepcut_final.pdf (Accessed 22 March 2004).

[46] Ibid., paragraphs 1.24 p. 6 and 4.18 p. 23.

[47] Ibid. Executive Summary and paragraph 4.17, p. 23.

to follow-up the concerns and recommendations of the Surrey Police report. To date, details and terms of reference have not been announced, so it remains to be seen how far the committee's deliberations will clarify the extent and nature of bullying in the Army and confirm or allay public fears. Given the historical record, it is probably too much to expect the committee to provide definitive answers.

5. Problems of analysis and the wider societal context

Throughout the period under discussion, the official MOD line has remained consistent that bullying is not a significant or widespread problem in the British Army. There is ample evidence to support these claims, but the MOD has not helped its cause by taking cover behind statistics of questionable value. Spokespersons for the organization have also tended to re-state the mantra of "zero tolerance" rather than responding directly to specific parliamentary and public concerns. For champions of bullied soldiers, the MOD's instinctive culture of secrecy has generated a suspicion of deliberate cover-up, not assisted by continued official reluctance to countenance a full, independent public enquiry into initial training in the Army. As a result, notable efforts made by the armed services to combat bullying since the late 1980s have received scant parliamentary and public attention, whilst media reports that often exaggerate the problem of bullying have gone largely unchallenged. A sober discussion of the issue has undoubtedly been hampered by the relative lack of reliable statistics and the absence of comparative data on bullying from other Western armies. But, it is evident from the MOD's recent reviews that the British Army's training system has suffered from long term under funding. Poor quality facilities and an inadequate level of supervision in some units created an environment that significantly increased the risk of occurrences of bullying. Whilst the MOD identified and introduced appropriate policies to tackle the problem from the late 1980s onwards, it arguably failed to follow through with adequate resources to implement and support them fully, at least prior to 2002. Official complacency, a lack of central policy coordination and direction, as well as the perennial difficulties associated with resource overstretch, all played a role in this failure.

The growing public consciousness of workplace bullying in Britain generally over the last 15 years is another factor that makes it difficult to evaluate the changing nature and extent of bullying in the Army. Because of social and legislative changes, employees are less likely to tolerate what they perceive to be intimidating or offensive behaviour by superiors or colleagues and are more likely to make formal complaints or seek legal redress than in the past. The armed forces are not immune from these changes, nor can they escape the consequences of the resulting trend towards what has been called a "culture of compensation" in which complainants seek to exploit their grievances for personal or financial gain[48]. The Army is by no means the only organization in the UK that is perceived to have a problem with workplace bullying. Other areas of the public sector, including the prison, postal and health services have all suffered their share of damaging disclosures in recent years. The Chartered Institute of Personnel and Development (CIPD) has described bullying in the British workplace as "alarmingly prevalent" and suggested that as many as 10% of British workers may be victims[49]. The CIPD cited heightened awareness of equal opportunities' issues, combined with increased financial and staffing pressures in many organizations as contributing to the increase in incidents of bullying. Findings suggested that bullying was institutionalized in many organisations and complaints' procedures were often inadequate.

More research would be needed before it would be safe to conclude that the Army's record in recent years actually compares favourably with some other public sector organizations, but workplace reports and statistics suggest that bullying in the armed services might reflect a wider societal malaise rather than a peculiarity of the military environment. That said, much civilian workplace bullying involves verbal abuse, harassment or intimidation, rather than the physical threats, humiliation and violence, which have tended to characterize reports of bullying in the British Army. Arguably, the military environment and culture, particularly during recruit training, cause soldiers to be more susceptible to serious bullying than their civilian peers. Recruits are

---

[48] For a disussion of this issue see: J. Lamb, "Bring Your Suit to the Workplace", *People Management: the magazine of the Chartered Institute of Personnel and Development*, 2 March 2000, p. 20.

[49] D. Hammond, "Someone to Lean On", *People Management: the magazine of the Chartered Institute of Personnel and Development*, 6 December 2001, pp. 32-37.

socially and geographically isolated, subject to military discipline and are employed in an organization that values physical toughness and aggression. There is general agreement among sociologists that soldiering is different from other occupations[50]. Soldiers may be required to give their lives for the wider community and their training has to inculcate the necessary physical and mental robustness to accept this. The battlefield is, in the words of Martin van Creveld, "the province of hardship and suffering, of stress, of fear and pain and death"[51].

Essentially, basic training takes the civilian identity of each individual, breaks it down under constant pressure and rebuilds it as a soldier. It is a time of unique psychological vulnerability, especially for adolescent men and women whose personalities are still forming. NCO instructors have a crucial role in this process, reinforcing behaviour that confirms individuals' new identities as soldiers and condemning that which does not. The process is necessarily harsh. Since 1945, there has only been one year in which British soldiers have not been killed in combat. There is, therefore, a fine line between tough training and physical and psychological abuse and it is easily crossed. Vicious, or simply over zealous, instructors are not the only source of potential mistreatment during initial training. Currently, vulnerable recruits in the British Army are more likely to be the victims of peer group bullying. Cruel treatment can never be condoned, but will be hard to eradicate in an organization that values strong group cohesion as essential to success on the battlefield.[52] Such cohesion is particularly important in a small professional army such as Britain's, where even soldiers from specialist and technical corps are expected to fight. It has long been accepted that soldiers are not bound together in battle by ideology or personal values but by the notion of comradeship. Such tightly knit fellowship requires informal group dynamics that reinforce attitudes and behaviours that allow soldiers to overcome and control their fears and emotions. Therefore, a necessary part of basic military training

---

[50] J. Callaghan and F. Kernic, "Social Psychology of the Individual Soldier", in Callaghan and Kernic (eds.), *Armed Forces and International Security: Global Trends and Issues*, Munster: LIT Verlag, 2003, p.21.
[51] M. van Creveld, *Technology and War*, London: Collier Macmillan, 1989, p. 314.
[52] See for example: Lieutenant General J. Kiszley, "What Should We Be Looking For? A Commander's Perspective on Recruits and Recruiting", *RUSI Journal*, vol. 148, Issue 2, April 2003.

is to identify those individuals who cannot be socialized into such informal groups and remove them before they are in a position to undermine unit morale and combat effectiveness. The experience for individuals who fail to conform to the emerging group identity and standards of behaviour during basic training can be traumatic. Again, in such a situation the line between physical and psychological stress and real abuse can be slender.

Given the necessary toughness of military training, the British Army cannot hope to eliminate all forms of behaviour towards its recruits that might be considered bullying in an increasingly sensitive and litigious civilian employment environment. The MOD faces an unenviable predicament. It has to reassure parents that their sons and daughters will not be brutalized during training, whilst at the same time ensuring that soldiers are adequately prepared for the rigours of combat. Outside scrutiny of military training might satisfy some of the MOD's more vociferous critics, but could impose such stringent standards of care for soldiers during training that operational capability is ultimately undermined. Nevertheless, if the British Army is to escape the imposition of external oversight, the MOD's policies to combat bullying must be backed by a real commitment on the part of leaders at all levels to enforce them, as well as continued improvements that build on the training infrastructure and staffing measures launched in 2002. The recruitment process must also identify vulnerable and unsuitable individuals before they enter the military training system. The MOD will have to apply constant vigilance over its training regime if it wishes to retain its independence to train soldiers at the required standard to maintain the British Army's professional competitive edge.

There are many contrasts, not least in culture, traditions and the nature of civilian control and accountability, between the British Army and those of Russia and other post Soviet states. By comparison, British soldiers are well trained, fed and paid; the vast majority of their officers have a strong professional ethos and integrity. The British Army's recruits are volunteers and although they face tough training, it is not a regime of institutionalised cruelty. However, the British Army's efforts to tackle bullying, its successes and failures, can still prove instructive for those militaries currently blighted by *dedovshchina*. British experience suggests that recruits in professional armies can be as vulnerable to mistreatment as those in conscript militaries. Because basic training deliberately isolates soldiers from wider society and necessarily stresses physical toughness, it intrinsically creates an environment in which bullying can occur. Tackling the problem requires, not just the introduction of appropriate corrective measures such as those discussed above, but also a commitment to back them from all levels in the chain of command, especially junior NCOs. Adequate investment in training establishments is essential to ensure that accommodation and supporting facilities are of satisfactory quality, staffing levels are sufficient and instructors are properly selected and trained. These measures are critical to maintain discipline and sustain morale and thus counter the element of bullying behaviour that seems to be present in even the most closely controlled military training establishments. As the British Army has found, greater transparency in the training system may be the price of restoring public confidence in the wake of well-publicized mistreatment scandals. If armies in the successor states of the Soviet Union can overcome the worst excesses of *dedovshchina*, they will, like the British, still face the challenge of striking a balance between tough training for combat and a care regime that prevents the exploitation and abuse of young soldiers by their supervisors or peers.

V *Dedovshchina* and Resistance to Reform

12 The Hazing of Police Recruits: Initiation to Organization and Resistance to Policing Reform in Brazil

Eduardo PAES-MACHADO &
Carlos LINHARES DE ALBUQUERQUE

This chapter examines the hazing ritual within a Brazilian police academy, focusing the initiation of police recruits as part of a political-institutional and cultural resistance to police reform.

The Brazilian police education reform which was initiated at the end of the 1980s, and accelerated in the 1990s, has raised issues that have been studied by researchers in other countries. The studies into the reform of police education show that, despite the fact that certain advances were made, it has had less impact on police practice than was expected[1]. Confirming for-

---

[1] R. Oakley, "Police training in ethnic relations in Britain", *Police Studies*, vol. 13, no. 2, 1990, pp. 47-56; K. Bryett, "Police recruit preparation in Australia", *Canadian Police College Journal*, 1992, vol. 16, no. 3, 1992, pp. 175-183; M. Post-Gary, "Police recruits: Training tomorrow's workforce", *FBI Law Enforcement Bulletin*, vol. 61, no. 3, 1992, pp. 19-24; R. Wortley & J. Homel-Ross, "Police prejudice as function of training and out-group contact: A longitudinal investigation", *Law and Human Behavior*, vol. 19, no. 3, 1995, pp. 305-317; G. Christie, S. Petrie & P. Timmins, "The effect of police education, training and socialisation on conservative attitudes", *Australian and New Zealand Journal of Criminology*, vol. 29, no. 3, 1996, pp. 299-314; N. Marion, "Police academy training: Are we teaching recruits what they need to know?", *Policing*, vol. 21, no. 1, 1998, pp. 54-79; M. Buerger, "Police training as a Pentecost: Using tools singularly ill-suited to the purpose of reform", *Police Quarterly*, vol. 1, no. 1, 1998, pp. 27-63; M. Palmiotto, M. Birzer & U.N. Prabha, "Training in community policing: A suggested curriculum", *Policing: An International Journal of Police Strategies and Management*, vol. 23, no. 1, 2000, pp. 8-21; M. Kempa, "Thinking about political reform through the prism of policing: A review essay of Les Johnston's Policing Britain: Risk, Security and Governance", *Policing and Society*, vol. 10, 2000, pp. 301-316; J. Chan, "Negotiating the field: New observations on the making of police officers", *Australian and New Zealand Journal of Criminology*, vol. 34, no. 2, 2001, pp. 14-133.

mer findings on police socialization[2], these studies showed that the reality principle, represented by the police profession and organization, undermine the idea of instilling the recruits with the principle of minimal force, human rights, tolerance, and social response appropriate to the situations encountered[3].

Amidst the vast literature on the theme[4], we underline the study carried out by Marks[5], on the limitations of the training in promoting change in the post-colonial paramilitary police, aiming at replacing reactive positions based on excessive use of force with preventive and consensual methods. Although the study does not go deeply into the discussion on the complex connections between security policies and educational practices, it was concluded that the failures of training reform were a result of the lack of political will to implement changes in the South African Police Force[6]. Given the overall lack of reliability on the new instructional principles, intermediary leaders, instructors, and police recruits regressed to what felt secure to them, the old lessons of the paramilitary police, placing excessive value on physical and tactical training and rejecting the consequences of this for the intensification of conflict and excessive use of force[7].

Agreeing with the conclusions of Marks, this article discusses rituals of organizational initiation of the Academia da Policia Militar (Military Police Academy - henceforth, MPA), examining its dual role of shaping identity and

---

[2] J. Van Maanen, "Observations on the making of policemen", in: P.K. Manning & J. Van Maanen (eds), *Policing: A View from the Street*, Santa Monica, CA: Goodyear, 1978, pp. 292-308.

[3] M. Marks, "Changing dilemmas and the dilemmas of change: Transforming the public order police unit in Durban", *Policing and Society*, vol. 9, 1999, pp. 157-179; Chan, 2001, *op. cit.*

[4] Oakley, 1990, *op. cit.*; K. Bryett, "Police recruit preparation in Australia", *Canadian Police College Journal*, vol. 16, no. 3, 1992, pp. 175-183; Post-Gary, 1992, *op. cit.*; Wortley and Homel-Ross, 1995, *op. cit.*; Christie et al., 1996, *op. cit.*; Marion, 1998, *op. cit.*; Buerger, 1998, *op. cit.*; Palmiotto et al., 2000, *op. cit.*; Kempa, 2000, *op. cit.*; Chan, 2001, *op. cit.*

[5] 1999, *op. cit.*

[6] Marks, 1999, *op. cit.*

[7] T. Jefferson, *The Case against Paramilitary Policing*, Milton Keynes: Open University Press, 1990; P. Kraska, "Enjoying militarism", *Justice Quarterly*, vol. 13, no. 3, 1999, pp. 405-429; Marks, 1999, *op. cit.*; J. Sheptycki, "Editorial reflections on policing, paramilitarization and scholarship on policing", *Policing and Society*, vol. 9, 1999, pp. 117-123; P. Waddington, "Swatting police paramilitarism: A comment on Kraska and Paulsen", *Policing and Society*, vol. 9, 1999, pp. 125-140.

perpetuating resistance to new police education[8]. In other words, through the description of hazing, our aim is to interpret the relationship between this rite and the socialization process in a context of cultural and practical resistance to the new curriculums and training implemented in the police academies. Marking the transition from ordinary civilians to their new role as officers in the MP[9],[10] hazing reveals the tension in the Bahian police of today, between what is supposed to be, and what is actually applied in the current implementation of a new curriculum created by police reform[11].

Thus, the current study formulates the notion of a counter-curriculum to explain the conjunction between the lack of political will and academic resistance to principles of reformulation of paramilitary police education. This counter-curriculum reveals the fragmented and contradictory characteristics of the new curriculum, filling it educational vacuums and asserting the "last word" of the police organization with regard to the proposed reforms.

---

[8] C. Shearing & R. Ericson, "Culture as figurative action", *British Journal of Sociology*, vol. 42, no. 4, 1984, pp. 481-506.

[9] The Military Police, which is responsible for regular and preventive police work, is the largest police force in Brazil, employing 350,000 officers throughout the country. It has an ambiguous legal status, and is coordinated by state governments and the federal government through the Army, of which is it an auxiliary branch. Closely identified with the Army in its history, legislation, organization, accountability and repressive attitude towards social movements, the Military Police is well known for gross human rights violations like summary executions and torture (P. Chevigny, *The Edge of the Knife: Police Violence in the Americas*, New York: New York Press, 1995; A.T. Lemos-Nelson, *Judiciary police accountability for gross human rights violations: The case of Bahia, Brazil*. Doctoral dissertation, University of Notre Dame, 2001; J.P. Bisol, "Foraclusao institucional" in: B. Mariano & I. Freitas (eds) *Policia: desafios da democracia brasileira*, Porto Alegre: Corag, 2002, pp.11-20; E. Paes-Machado, C. Noronha & F. Cardoso, "No olho do furacao: brutalidade policial, preconceito racial e controle da violencia em Salvador", *Afro-Asia*, vol. 19/20, 1997, pp. 201-226; M. Huggins, "Urban violence and police privatization in Brazil: Blended invisibility", *Social Justice*, vol. 2, no. 2, 2000, pp. 113-134; L.E. Soares, *Meu casaco de general: 500 dias no front da seguranca publica do Rio de Janeiro*, Companhia das Letras, Sao Paulo, 2000; E. Paes-Machado & C.V. Noronha, "Padroes de trabalho e tendencias do uso da forc‚a policial no Brasil", in: R. Pinto Lyra, (ed) *Direitos humanos: os desafios do seculo XXI—uma abordagem interdisciplinar*, Brasilia: Brasilia Juridica, 2002, pp. 225-240; E. Paes-Machado & C. Levenstein, "'I'm sorry everybody, but this is Brazil': Armed robbery in Brazilian cities", *British Journal of Criminology*, no. 44, 2004, pp. 15-33.

[10] V. Turner, *The Ritual Process*, Chicago, IL: Aldine, 1969; C. Riviere, *Os ritos profanos*, Petropolis: Vozes, 1996.

[11] C.F.L. Albuquerque, *Escola de bravos: cotidiano e curri´culo em uma Academia de Policia Militar*, Master's thesis, Universidade Federal da Bahia, Brazil.

1. Hazing script

By the time the school year begins at the Academy[12], the senior cadets have already planned their reception of the new recruits, who are also called *calouros* ("freshmen"), *bichas* ("queers"), *novinhas* ("new girls") and *lesos* ("spastics")[13]. This takes place during the special week when the Academy officially welcomes freshmen with tributes, parties, lectures, tournaments and, in parallel, hazing. The freshmen are aware that the playful character and aggressive humour of the ritual can easily be taken too far.

Hazing at the BMPA begins with the noisy predawn awakening of the freshman class in their dorms. The senior cadets swarm into the dormitory and drag the freshmen from their bunks, while strongly impressing them with the penitential nature of hazing. Amid the confusion, the senior cadets fire blanks in the dorm and blow strident whistles in the ears of their sleepy victims, roughly shaking their hands and feet, screaming like maniacs and sending out dozens of contradictory expletive-laden messages about making and unmaking their beds, standing up and crawling at the same time and other orders that make the new recruits' heads swim.

The hazing lasts six days, during which time the seniors (the only legitimate wielders of the power to conduct the process) are the agents of a number of ambivalent practices such as painful pranks that exhaust the

---

[12] This ethnographic study is based on research into the daily lives of players at the Bahia Military Police Academy (BMPA) conducted through participant observation, semi-structured interviews and field notes. The information came from the recruits themselves, and the fact that one of the researchers was hired to teach at that institution as a faculty member facilitated this. Given their weekly contact, as well as growing bonds of friendship and trust, the recruits decided to discuss the subject as part of classroom projects. These activities produced materials that sparked the researchers' curiosity and guided the formulation of their first interpretations of the ritual. Later, classroom debates on this subject supplemented the written information, bringing to light disagreements about the validity of the ritual for entering the police academy. Although many written answers were contaminated by the prototypical censorship of the military police's world, cathartic and heated discussions enabled further revelations and interpretations of hazing to surface. Of the statements obtained from the 67 recruits in two second-year classes at the BMPA, we only made use of those of 31 recruits because they were the most detailed, clear and complete. We also interviewed four officers who graduated over 10 years previously and had different opinions about hazing.

[13] T. Leemon, *The Rites of Passage in a Student Culture: A Study of the Dynamics of Transition*, New York/London: Teachers College Press, 1972.

freshmen and sometimes leave them in need of a doctor; and humorous activities where freshmen humiliate themselves and get involved in embarrassing situations that leave them feeling deeply shamed. Paradoxically, however, as we will see further on in this article, these sadistic activities serve to strengthen the bonds between freshmen and seniors[14].

The freshmen undergo the exhausting hazing period while enduring jokes, pranks, skits and embarrassment. This may include activities like: a car race where the real engines are turned off and the freshmen are used instead, pushing vehicles crammed with seniors and racing against other freshmen; having to "pay" several times a day, for no apparent reason, for something they did or did not do with hundreds of sit-ups and push-ups; eating manioc flour with their mouths open, spitting when they talk to other freshmen and getting spat upon; having to shout their own names and meaningless phrases; and crawling several times a day—all without getting enough food or sleep. Also regarding food, the newcomers must eat their meals backwards, starting with dessert (*guava paste*) and then going on to the main course of manioc flour, rice and beans, while eating with their mouths open and showing everyone what they are chewing.

Within the pedagogy of extremes[15], the seniors overturn order and sense by dressing up and militantly imposing disorder, pranks, psychological pressure and brutality amid howls of laughter and the violent expression of basic impulses[16]. The clearest image of this game of inversions is the rookie who is forced to display sexism at one point and later dress and act like a woman, dancing with gyrating hips. In the macho world of the BMPA, this form of playacting broadens the transgressive significance of these acts in an extraordinary fashion[17].

Although most known forms of hazing use playful means of ridiculing sexuality, hazing at the BMPA cannot include overt references to it. This is a taboo at this institution, which has not yet managed to deal with the presence

---

[14] C. Castro, *O espirito militar: um estudo antropologico na Academia Militar das Agulhas Negras*, Rio de Janeiro: Zahar Editor,1990.
[15] Castro, 1990, *op. cit.*
[16] G. Mattoso, *O calvario dos carecas: historia do trote estudantil*, Sao Paulo: EMW, 1985.
[17] P. Kraska, "Enjoying militarism", *Justice Quarterly*, vol. 13, no. 3, 1996, pp. 405-429.

of young men and women naturally, although it has been co-educational for the past ten years following over 150 years as an all-male academy. This may be why the ritual does not involve different practices for men and women[18]. One of the most symbolic and challenging points in the rite is when freshmen are ordered to hold a live cockroach in their hands for hours on end without releasing or killing it. The culmination of the ritual takes place at the end of the first week, at the integration of new members when the seniors put their responsibility into perspective, depersonalizing and reinforcing the role of hazing in the socialization of older and new generations of recruits[19].

2. The Brazilian police forces

Police force goes back to Brazil as a colony and during the period of slavery where, apart from existing private policing carried out in the sugar plantations by overseers or country captains, there was public policing to assist the troops responsible for territorial defense. Such a type of policing persisted until the first decade of the 19th century, when the first specialized police force was created: The General Superintendency of the Police and The Royal Guards of the Police, the former having been inspired in the French institution Lieutenant General de Police[20].

By means of these two police forces, the state began to provide instruments of control, which before this were entrusted only to the land-owners and their private agents, in order to repress and exclude the segments which received little or nothing of the benefits guaranteed for the ruling minority[21]. This system began to fulfill new functions in a changing socioeconomic context, maintaining, however, a reasonable continuity regarding structure and procedure[22].

---

[18] Turner, 1969, *op. cit.*
[19] Castro, 1990, *op. cit.*
[20] J.V. Tavares dos Santos, "A arma e a flor: formacao da organizacao policial, consenso e violencia", *Tempo Social*, vol. 9, no.1, 1997, pp. 155-167.
[21] T.H. Holloway, *Polícia no Rio de Janeiro: Repressão e resistência numa cidade do século XIX*, Rio de Janeiro: Fundação Getúlio Vargas, 1997.
[22] *Ibid.*

Created for the purpose of patrolling the streets, the Royal Guard was substituted, in 1831, by the Military Police, conceived as the Armed Forces of the Police of Rio de Janeiro, then capital of the Empire, and model for similar organizations in the rest of the country[23]. From its beginning, the Military Police applied punishment and employed policing techniques, such as humiliations, threats, and physical aggressions, which reinforced public hostility against it[24].

The Republic, proclaimed in 1889, contributed to the improvement of qualification and in making the police a little less subject to the game of political influence[25]. Amid these advances, the police reaffirmed clientelistic relationships with the elite in power, who tolerated the police violence and corruption as long as they were only being directed towards the popular classes. The expectation of the elite was that public order be maintained, no matter what methods were used by the policemen, reputed, by them, as being uncontrollable and inferior[26].

With the Revolution of 1930 the power of the local private authorities was reduced, and the first police academies were founded. The Civil (or Judiciary) Police, in turn, was refashioned to act as a secret political police force against political adversaries of the dictatorial regime Getulio Vargas. This legacy prevailed in the following decades, when new authoritarian impulses, such as the 1964 coup d'état, prioritized the ideology of the cold war and the fight against the domestic allies of international socialism and communism. For this reason, the policemen began to be trained in antiguerrilla techniques by qualified instructors from North American military academies. The police forces were armed with machine guns, developing coordinated actions among themselves and with the armed forces, to watch, arrest, extract information, and to eliminate members of political organizations considered subversive.

It was also a time in which the death squads, which initially arose in Sao Paulo, in the Civil Police Force, at the end of the 1950s, in order to execute

---

[23] K. Mattoso, *Bahia, século XIX: Uma província do império*, Rio de Janeiro: Nova Fronteira, 1992; Holloway, 1997, *op. cit.*
[24] Mattoso, 1992, *op. cit.*; Holloway, 1997, *op. cit.*
[25] M.L. Bretas, *Ordem na cidade: O exercício cotidiano da autoridade policial no Rio de Janeiro*, 1907-1930, Rio de Janeiro: Rocco, 1997.
[26] *Ibid.*

delinquents, began to integrate the repression of political opponents of the government, intensifying the elimination of suspects and eventually becoming an important link to organized crime in the 1980s[27].

During the transition from a military to a civilian regime, from 1979 to 1985, the congressional lobby of the military police obstructed (as it continues to obstruct) reforms by members of parliament who feared being accused of retaliation against the authoritarian regime, and thus kept the old police model intact.

The Military and Civil Police Forces (from now on referred to as CP), act within the limits and under the administration of the 26 states of the Union. The MP (with 345,487 officers) and the CP (67,525 officers) have differentiated responsibilities of preventive and investigative policing, which, in the majority of modern police forces, are gathered into a single organization. The consequences of this fragmentation of activities, called police dualism[28], go beyond the traditional rivalry among police departments, increasing the competition for scarce resources, limited communication, and impeding joint decision-making.

Both police forces nominally are accountable to the stage governments, under specific secretariats. However, only the CP is effectively subordinate to the state governments, given that the MP is under their administration and at the same time under the control and coordination of the federal government, and, in particular, the armed forces[29]. Though a subversion of federative principle[30], the juridical statute of the MP, as an auxiliary force to the Army, guarantees the power of the latter over the civilian political institutions, restricting the authority of the states and reducing accountability[31].

In copying the military model of organization, the MP characterizes itself by the concentration of decisions, inflexibility of communication, and stan-

---

[27] G. Mingardi, *Tiras, gansos e trutas; Cotidiano e reforma na Polícia Civil*, São Paulo: Scritta, 1991; C. Barcelos, *Rota 66: A história da polícia que mata*, São Paulo: Ed. Globo, 2001.
[28] Soares, 2000, *op.cit.*
[29] D.H. Bayley, *Patterns of policing: A comparative international analysis*, New Brunswick, N.J.: Rutgers University Press, 1985; J.P. Brodeur, *Violence and Racial Prejudice in the Context of Peacekeeping: A Study Prepared for the Commission of Inquiry into the Deployment of Canadian Forces to Somalia*, Ottawa: Canadian Government Publishing, 1997.
[30] Soares, 2000, *op. cit.*
[31] Lemos-Nelson, 2001, *op. cit.*

dardization of procedures, giving more value to internal discipline than to end product of the policing[32]. Although the police reform in the 1990s has reduced the number of ranks, the MP maintains a super-centralized standard which conditions the base of the pyramid to adopt passive behavior[33]. Among the models of conduct, that of the police hero or super-hero, embodied in courageous men, capable of committing aggressive and violent acts against delinquents (and suspects), is mostly valued[34]. That dominant model, prevalent across Brazilian society, prioritizes emotions, producing amateur and harmful actions, with unexpected results and unnecessary consequences, for policeman as well as for other involved persons[35]. The power of this conception also permeates the performance evaluations and the results of inquiries, resulting the tolerance and approval of misconduct, among which executions stand out[36].

The MP own academies and training programs, which work on the circumstances in which the policemen can use force or firearms, but the lack of standardized procedures on the subject, favors a variety of interpretations, many times guided by individual values or standing corporatives. The influence of militarism warrior mentality[37] is expressed in what little importance is given to the transmission of negotiation (disescalation) techniques of conflicts, and moderate use of the so-called intermediary resources of force. In addition to this, silhouette models for shooting are used in training, give priority to the lethal parts of the human body, not emphasizing the importance of preserving lives. The almost complete lack of weapons and ammunition constitutes a serious obstacle for the shooting training, causing the policemen not

---

[32] L.A.B. Guimaraes, "Valores institucionais: a pratica policial militar e a cidadania", *Policing & Society*, 191 Unidade-Revista de Assuntos Tecnicos da Policia Militar, Ano XVIII, vol. 4, January/ March 2000, pp. 45-85; L.E. Soares, 2000, *op. cit.*
[33] *Ibid.*
[34] *Ibid.*
[35] *Ibid.*
[36] Chevigny, 1995, *op. cit.*; I. Cano, *The use of lethal force by police in Rio de Janeiro*, Rio de Janeiro: Instituto de Estudos da Religião (ISER), 1997; Centro de Estudos de Cultura Contemporânea (Cedec), *Mapa de risco da violência de Salvador, São Paulo: Cedec*, 1997; Huggins, 2000, *op. cit.*; Lemos-Nelson, 2001, *op. cit.*; Paes-Machado and Noronha, 2002, *op. cit.*
[37] P. Kraska, 1996, *op. cit.*; V.C. Franke, "Duty, honor, country: The social identity of West Point Cadets", *Armed Forces & Society*, no. 26(2), 2000, p. 175.

to acquire proficiency[38], and making them a threat to public safety when obliged to shoot.

3. The Police Academy

The education of Bahia Military Police recruits takes place within the walls of the Villa Militar (military base) in Salvador at the BMPA. It is a complex covering large area that has been in existence for over a century, and is steeped in history and tradition. Like other police academies, before a student enrolls and obtains a four-year scholarship, he or she must take a competitive admissions test. Approximately 280 cadets attend the Academy every year. These young men and women (aged 18 to 24, with the exception of some older recruits) are taught by about 40 teachers and instructors, including civilians and military police officers.

The BMPA's new official curriculum was developed between 1992 and 1994 as part of the police reforms, and was first implemented in 1996. This programme arose from a situation marked by the growth of fear of crime and criticism of the effectiveness of the police policies implemented to date. This led the Bahia Military Police to introduce police training reform that had been in existence since the second half of the 1980s in the more politically advanced Brazilian states[39].

Compared to reforms undertaken in democratic countries, which aim at increasing police legitimacy, the Brazilian reforms are intended to democratize, without rupture, a militaristic model that had historically been outdated in the process of institutionalizing citizens' rights and the construction of hegemony in west Northern hemisphere countries[40]. The aim when developing this democracy-oriented curriculum was to overcome distortions in prior police training that resulted from an aversion to civilian teachers, little room for

---

[38] Alburquerque, 1999, *op. cit.*
[39] The breadth and depth of police reform depended on its scope, whether extensive or sectoral, and the relationship between the political forces in Brazilian states. It has had a greater impact in the state of Rio Grande do Sul, where it was part of a broader democratic reform aimed at de-privatization, or placing the state machine in the service of the public interest (Paes-Machado & Noronha, 2002, *op. cit.*).
[40] Tavares dos Santos, 1997, *op. cit.*; Jefferson, 1990, *op. cit.*; Sheptycki, 1999, *op. cit.*; Brodeur, 1994, *op. cit.*; Waddington, 1999, *op. cit.*

the humanities and an excessive number of hours devoted to physical education[41]. Following the introduction of this curriculum, the period of instruction of future officers grew from three to four consecutive school years. For the sake of comparison, the schooling of future non-commissioned officers and soldiers takes six months under far inferior conditions.

Recruit education is divided into five main pillars of learning: administration and organizations; legal; physical education and sports; specific police studies; and humanities and Portuguese language studies. In addition to these subjects, there is also a highly prized centre for extracurricular activities, including participation in military Olympics, sports competitions and rehearsals for official celebrations. Alongside this, there are professional internships at Military Police units and experience outside the physical space of the academy, such as the Military Training Camp[42].

During the first three years, the recruits are half-boarders: they stay at the Academy from Monday morning to after lunch (2 pm) on Friday, and spend the weekends with their families if they have earned a pass and are not being punished with an excruciating weekend stay at the Academy. The recruits are mainly from lower middle-class backgrounds, and the low-income districts near the BMPA, which is located in a run-down part of Salvador. For example, over 85 per cent of the recruits who enrolled in 1994 came from families where neither parent had a college education. It is very unusual for recruits to come from a white middle-class family with two college-educated parents. Poor white candidates from the interior of the state are in the same boat as Afro-Brazilian candidates from Salvador: vulnerable to harsh treatment to succumb to the socialization process and becoming excessively authoritarian police officers[43].

---

[41] Albuquerque, 1999, op. cit.; V. Federico, Um caso de policia. Reorganizacao, capacitacao profissional e policia Comunitária na PMBA, Escola de Administracao da UFBA, Salvador; L.F. Sapori, A parceria policia-universidades-ongs: sinais promissores de mudanca na sociedade brasileira. Manuscript, (forthcoming).

[42] E. Paes-Machado & C.F.L. Albuquerque, "Jungle ID: Educational reform inside the Brazilian paramilitary police", Policing and Society, vol. 13, no. 1, 2002, pp. 59-78.

[43] L. May, "Socialization and institutional evil", in: L. May & J. Kohn, (eds) Hannah Arendt: Twenty Years Later, Cambridge, MA: MIT Press, 1997, pp. 83-105; M. Brogden & C. Shearing, Policing for a New South Africa, London: Routledge, 1993. A small but significant number of recruits are the children of military police officers. These recruits are bearers of subtle information about the ethos of the organiza-

4. Power delegation

Hazing works in two ways: it celebrates the inclusion of newcomers, playfully exorcising their civilian identities, as well as benefiting the seniors[44], the operators on the scene, who take the lead in a decisive initiatory rite and milestone (see Figure 1). The ultimate responsibility for hazing lies with the academic institution, which delegates it to the official members of its supervisory staff. These supervisors authorize seniors to perform the hazing rite as tradition dictates. As one instructor describes:

> The seniors are the ones who give orders and decide just about everything in hazing. We trust them and delegate this task [to them]. After all, they are the result of over 3 years of our work at the Academy. [Captain Claudio, age 38]

The seniors view this delegation of responsibility as a sign of trust. It is not surprising that they supervise the ritual with a certain amount of pride and arrogance, as they have been waiting for this moment for years. In light of these observations, it could be argued that these seniors are part of an initiatory context that involves a change in status. They, too, are in transition from a life of subjugation and academic theory to a practical world in which they will become Military Police leaders responsible for making decisions as officers. As Captain David, 37, the course director, observes:

> We value hazing because it prepares recruits for the many things that await them. The students who are here at the academy this year will be making decisions next year as part of an operational unit, acting as officers, giving orders, deciding, taking the initiative.

Therefore, the subject who takes the lead in hazing is the fourth-year student (senior) who is about to become an officer, and not the freshman, who is the subjected one. Hazing viscerally rehearses the military police offi-

---

[44] tional culture and *protégés* of "godparents" or *peixes* (literally "fish"), who are important for negotiating the best training conditions and jobs in the Military Police. Mattoso, *op. cit.*, 1985.

cer's style of leadership, and none of the pale organizational management subjects in the official curriculum can match its subtle complexity. As Captain David attests:

> As coordinators we have to keep a close eye on seniors when we delegate activities to them. We observe them during hazing as well as during extracurricular activities, such as their competitions, freshman week, fund-raising parties and tournaments. We believe they can always be observed and assessed better in these situations than through tests and written exams, for example, because then we can see the individual as a whole.

The task assigned to the seniors affirms and tests their capabilities in terms of the transmission of professional identity, temporarily mediating between directors and trainees[45]. Before they have even graduated, these young people are already qualified to reproduce the contents of police education[46].

As we can discern in their enthusiastic behaviour, hazing gives seniors that pleasure: being addressed as a superior, even when playacting, as the holder of a powerful rank, an authority—in short, an officer. Furthermore, this ritual offers seniors catharsis, and they can use this opportunity to vent the grudges, anger and resentment built up during the previous four years.

Hazing, as other rituals in other different contexts[47], generates a certain mistrust in the leadership team[48] that is implementing the educational modernization programme. The team doubts the validity of the rite because, after all, since 1996 the BMPA has adopted a new curriculum of over 4,000 class hours that theoretically promotes values that are very different from those inherent in the hazing.

On many occasions, we saw senior recruits receive warnings from the Commander to be careful with hazing excesses. As one instructor observed:

---

[45] P. Willis, *Learning to Labor: How Working-class Kids get Working-class Jobs*, New York: Columbia University Press, 1977.
[46] P. Bourdieu, P. & J.A.Passeron, *A reproducao: elementos para uma teoria do sistema de ensino*, Rio de Janeiro: Francisco Alves,1992.
[47] Turner, 1969, *op. cit.*
[48] I. Goffman, *Manicomios, prisoes e conventos*, Sao Paulo : Perspectiva, 1996.

> Hazing is one of those occasions [that] deserve monitoring because the seniors feel that they are the masters of the situation, but they must not go too far ...We keep a close eye on them, spying on them, because problems can occur. Some people always go too far, and of course those who do are punished. That is why one of us [instructors] is always close at hand. [Captain Claúdio, age 38]

Aware that seniors are still not mature enough to control their aggressiveness and that hazing can go to undesirable extremes, the Military Police Commander assigns a group of officers to co-direct hazing to set limits and apply brakes. In the words of Cristiana (age 21), a second-year student, it is clear that: "the fourth-year recruits control the hazing but only under the supervision of officers who are aware of the scheduling of events involving freshmen. Recruits from other years don't have the right to haze [newcomers]."

The right of seniors to haze freshmen is based on the justification that the younger recruits are not as psychologically developed as the older ones, always supposing that the more immature ones might distort the ritual with extreme exercises, losing control emotionally and compromising its effectiveness. It is also illustrative that while the hazing is going on, no contact is permitted between second-year (sophomore) and first-year (freshman) cadets. That way, according to Leila (age 21): "No contact with the newcomers is allowed and no one can even talk to the freshmen. You're not supposed to talk to the queers."

Younger recruits are excluded from the agency of hazing because they are supposedly incompetent and inept transmitters of the rite: they would lack the maturity of the Military Police spirit. They are not authorized to engage in hazing because they have not yet processed their entire immersion in the organizational logic or completed their metamorphosis. However, not all fourth-year recruits want to take part in hazing. Although being the agent of hazing is optional, being the "patient" is not. Leading the rite also involves sacrifices, such as sleepless nights, extra work and numerous advance-planning meetings to thoroughly discuss the process[49]. Team members must submit de-

---

[49] Leemon, 1972, *op. cit.*

tailed advance reports to the officers who will present them to the Commander. According to Iracema (age 20):

> [The] activities are listed in the report. The BMPA's commanding officer is informed about everything, the senior recruits devise them and present them to the Commander, and they may or may not be censured.

Rather than being a secret rite, hazing can be regarded as a mixed-agency venture, and the seniors who conduct it can already feel their authority and inclusion in the lineage of officers. Therefore, hazing simulates the art of leadership; seniors work side-by-side with officers, confirming that their learning cycle is coming to an end. It seems that the leadership team trusts in the capacity of senior recruits to repeat the model of stress training, based on punishments they experienced in the course of their BMPA instruction[50]. Confirming the redundancy of the BMPA pedagogy, freshmen expose the component of stress and psychological manipulation in the ritual, as we can see in this statement by Joao (age 23):

> The aim of hazing at the [B]MPA is to affect people's minds. We are led to take part in situations that we think are absurd, such as telling jokes to statues, saying something funny when our name is called, etc. They also affect people's minds through pressure and stress such as waking at 3 am to run until 6, getting different orders at the same time, following one and still being in the wrong. ... Ideas are fostered that can crop up in the [hazing] exercises, there's a secret and oppressive power, hazing is an in-depth experience of the best military style of pure pressure.

The Commander knows that he will not be able to say everything he needs to say in the official language. There is a certain faith in the simulation of reality found in hazing. The leadership team unconsciously recognizes that the "newbies" will have to undergo a dense and punishing processing rite that

---

[50] Palmiotto et al., 2000, *op. cit.*; Post-Gary, 1992, *op. cit.*; Paes-Machado & Albuquerque, 2002, *op. cit.*

sums up the signification the organizational culture utilizes to assert its power. It is better to put up with hazing in practice, even when taken to excess, because it also has advantageous qualities, including that of perpetuating the organization[51]. According to another instructor:

> On the whole, this is a good and natural practice. Every college has a hazing week for freshmen, right? All of us officers went through it. What's more, it's a very important experience for seniors because it increases the group's unity and *esprit de corps*. [Captain Orlando, instructor, age 38]

It seems that the ritual is seen as a necessary evil that contributes to reinforce the *esprit de corps* and brings a certain real-life realism to training, transmitting knowledge about the practice of policing to recruits that may not be taught in context of a classroom. It might bear mentioning that this is in keeping with conceptions of policing as a "craft" rather than a profession, in the sense that much of its art is learned through the mysteries of apprenticeship rather than instruction[52]. Hazing is seen as a programme for initiation into power, filling the vacuum of an explicit stage of initiation into the tactics of coordination and leadership.

Because this initiation takes place in an academic setting, we should ask whether it does not cancel out a good part of the new curricular ideology. After all, where do such practices fit in, in the modernizing philosophy of the official curriculum? Why is the tone not set by integration and leadership attitudes? Our answer is that the preservation of this and other traditional practices that permeate the daily life of the BMPA[53] form part of a dualistic rationale that drives the BMPA command to renovate discourses while activating strategies against them.

---

[51] P.W. Leon, *Bullies and Cowards: The West Point Hazing Scandal*, 1898-1901, Westport, CT/London: Greenwood Press, 2000.
[52] R. Reiner, *The Politics of the Police*, 3rd edn., New York: Oxford University Press, 2000.
[53] Paes-Machado & Albuquerque, 2002, *op. cit.*

5. Baptism like humiliation

As many other rites of status elevation[54], BMPA hazing marks the boundary people cross when going from one realm to another, from the civilian/no status world to the world of the military police. This procedure is similar to those carried out by other civilian and military organizations where it is important to mark a person's passage, his or her transition from one culture to another[55]. The idea, following the ritual process, is that if freshmen want to enter that world, they cannot simply walk in: their passage must be marked[56]. To do so, they must be emptied and stripped of their previous identity[57].

In general, candidates join the academy as if they were entering a new world, feeling deep anxiety characteristic of the second phase of police socialization or encounter with the police academy[58]. Overall, the encounter phase involves separation, liminarity and integration of freshmen (see Figure 1). Their former repertoires—personal and parental—are useless to them at this stage. Except for former recruits of the Military Police College at the Villa Militar and children of military police officers, who already know some of the *macetes* (insights), newcomers enter that territory gravely without any idea of what lies ahead of them. The loss of familiar points of reference plunges them into a unique crisis that is a watershed in the lives of many. This crisis is frequently expressed through complaints and nostalgic comments that accentuate the contrasts between their former and present lives. We can see this in a statement by Antonio (age 22), a third-year student:

> Yes, I miss a lot of things from when I was a civilian. When people at home cared for me and I had my own space...My parents had their rules, they made demands, sure, but nothing like this place, where I have to do what I'm told 24 hours a day, and focus on discipline all the time, facing up to some insanely tough regulations, and what's worse—you know what really makes me homesick? When I remember

---

[54] Turner, 1969, *op. cit.*
[55] Turner, 1969, *op. cit.*; Riviere, 1996, *op. cit.*
[56] Leemon, 1972, *op. cit.*; Turner, 1969, *op. cit.*
[57] S. Dornbusch, "The military academy as an assimilating institution", *Social Forces*, vol. 33, 1955, pp. 316-321.
[58] Van Maanen, 1978, *op. cit.*, pp. 292-308.

that [when I lived at home] I didn't have these sick bastards giving me orders and screwing me around all the time.

Lucia, a 21-year-old recruit, illustrates the crisis from a woman's perspective, mentioning her difficulty in adapting to the shaping of body and identity:

> For me wearing a uniform is a difficult experience. This uniform isn't me; I don't like the rough, harsh cloth, or the color or the tailoring. I think it's too heavy and hot. Suddenly I started despising my uniform and really rebelling against these clothes, because at first you wear them on the outside and later you feel that it's too late. The uniform gets to you and you start wearing it on the inside too.

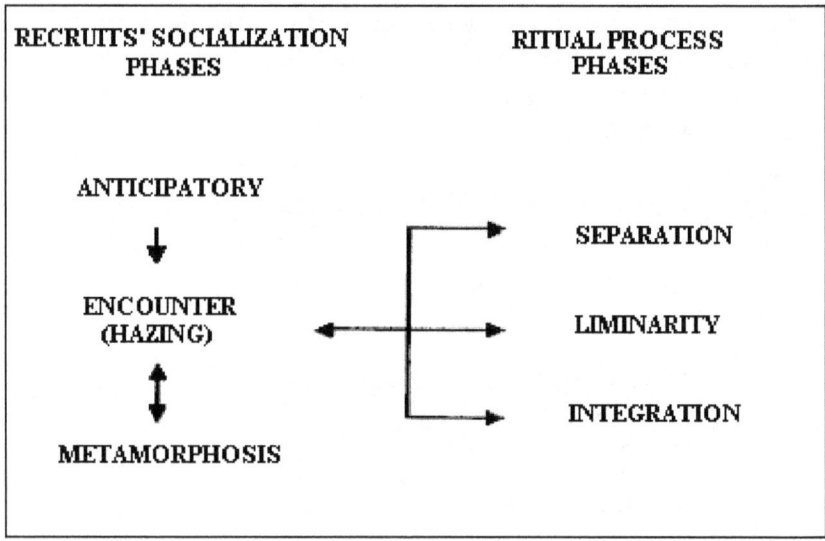

Figure 1: Police recruits' socialization[59] and ritual process phases[60].

During hazing, these recruits in crisis, who already live in a total institution[61], receive an extra load of mixed expressions from seniors who are near-

---
[59] Van Maanen, 1978, op. cit.
[60] Van Gennep, 1960, op. cit.; Turner, 1969, op. cit.

ing the end of the cycle of academic socialization or completing their metamorphosis into military police officers[62].

The fact that recruits are separated from their social networks and placed at the institution's disposal makes the work of the seniors in charge of hazing much easier, reducing the possibility of resistance from the freshmen and enabling seniors to focus exclusively on stripping newcomers of their identity in the liminarity phase[63]. Disfigured and covered in a mixture of urine, talcum powder, mud and paint; cross dressing; becoming cockroaches in the hands of their masters, the newcomers will only regain their dignity if they comply with the demands of the new situation of the life to which they aspire. In this sense, the ritual can be interpreted as part of a pedagogy of affirmation rather than dialogue in which initiates must keep silent, consenting to everything that will make them full members of the community[64].

The hazing ritual includes a vocabulary of verbs, founded in the senior and new recruits' discourse, that are perfectly understood by the leadership team. So, for example, one will hear expressions like *"amassar o otário"* ("crush the moron"), *"modelar os viadinhos"* ("shape up the little queers"), *"apagar o civil"* ("wipe out the civilian"), *"arrancar o burguesinho"* ("tear out the little bourgeois") and others. As we can see in the sexist, homophobic terminology ("queers", "new girls", etc.) and the ridiculing of freshmen forced to cross-dress by the seniors, some forms of humiliation that hazing inflicts attest to the association between masculinity (viewed as stoicism) and submission to the group code. Refusing to cry, withstanding pain and worshiping strength are the virtues of a valiant warrior, a champion sportsman and a new member of the Military Police brotherhood.

The tone is set when all participants are humbled—all of them must be humbled and softened by the act of crawling. Why is there so much crawling/horizontality in a culture where the hierarchy aspires to the utmost verticality—where the erect, trained body embodies readiness to attack? Crawling is inherent to invertebrates, imposing on the body a return to the base, the

---

[61] Goffman, 1996, *op. cit.*
[62] Van Maanen, 1978, *op. cit.*
[63] Van Gennep, 1960, *op. cit.*; Turner, 1969, *op. cit.*; Riviere, 1996; Leemon, 1972, *op. cit.*
[64] Turner, 1969, *op. cit.*; P. Clastres, *A sociedade contra o Estado*, Rio de Janeiro: Francisco Alves, 1990.

ground, like the cockroach held in their hands, initiating the apprentice from a common starting point where colour, class, gender and other marks of status are irrelevant[65]. This was clearly expressed by Alcides (age 23):

> It's no use, there was a rookie who acted like a *"patricinha"* [middle-class young woman], who lives in Pituba [a middle-class neighbourhood], studied at a Catholic school and so on, and during the hazing she had to *"traquejar"* [undergo a grueling effort] just like everybody else, she had to crawl around like everybody else. It's all the same, there she was covered in flour, mud, clay, right next to other guys from poor neighbourhoods on the wrong side of the tracks. There are no whites or major's kids. Everybody's crawling with a cockroach in their hand.

Clearly hazing does not humiliate people aspiring to superior status. Instead, it teaches that before they can rise, they must become just like everyone else[66]. Therefore, senior recruits, the agents of the rite, do not recognize important surnames, money or social prestige. The freshman's previous life is dead and it is unwise to demand special treatment due to their prior status.

The "holding a live cockroach" prank is shocking, and many descriptions of hazing mention it. The violence inflicted on the cockroaches seems to be analogous to the violence the freshmen fear themselves. Some sort of identification with the image is repeated in the new recruits' accounts of hazing: both, the cockroach and the newcomer could be crushed at any time, but this is not part of the game, nor its logic or ethics. The merit of the violent game is to keep the other alive, but as an insect, even if this makes the student quoted above indignant: "What fun is there in being forced to walk hand-in-hand with a cockroach and then have to turn it in alive at the end of the day?" Culturally, extreme revulsion towards that insect is more explicit among women. During hazing, the young women who undergo this punishment face a much greater challenge than the men, who have been trained to repress their fears during the extensive shaping period[67] of masculinity. However, to

---

[65] Leemon, 1972, *op. cit.*; Brodeur, 1997, *op. cit.*
[66] Turner, 1969, *op. cit.*; Clastres, 1990, *op. cit.*
[67] N. Elias, *Os alemaes: a luta pelo poder e a evolucao do habitus nos seculos XIX e XX*, Rio de Janeiro: Jorge Zahar, 1997.

become warriors, the young women must overcome their disgust and any form of frailty that might make them seem unsuited to a career in the military police.

The cockroach metaphor dramatizes the power relationships inherent to the ritual by exposing the freshmen's vulnerability and possibly, later on, the fragility of civilians. This analogy unfolds into multiple pedagogical possibilities proclaiming the academy's institutional ambivalence as it welcomes freshmen while being able to crush them at any time. It also reinforces the dogma of hierarchy by establishing the superiority of those who can embody the strong hand of the law over those who play the vulnerable role of an invertebrate—in other words, people of colour, the poor and the unemployed[68].

Some forms of address also indicate the institution of these relationships of power and place throughout the rite. Newcomers are obliged to call seniors "*senhor*" ("sir") and "*senhora*" ("ma'am")[69]. It might be ridiculous but they treat them with respect, remembering that the rite establishes a reverential atmosphere, even when the drama is apparently commonplace. As the senior Rodrigo (age 23), complaining about this abuse of power, said:

> At the BMPA, hazing is rite of initiation into the concept of hierarchy, obedience, accepting each person's place and position in the ranks at a point in time, where the older recruits have the power and the newcomers are like pariahs.

In short, hazing "wipes out" the civilian's status as a "*burguesinho*", "*patricinha*" or "*mauricinho*" ("middle-class young man") and prepares newcomers for inclusion in an "us"—members of the police academy who are preparing to become creatures dedicated and sacrificed to police work—rather than and unlike "them"—the "snooty civilians" who have not gone through the cycle of police socialization and make use of police work without giving it its due.

---

[68] E. Paes-Machado & C.V.Noronha, "Policing the Brazilian poor: Resistance to and acceptance of police brutality in urban popular classes (Salvador, Brazil)", *International Criminal Justice Review*, vol. 12, 2002, pp. 53-76.

[69] Leemon, 1972, *op. cit.*

6. Body inscriptions

In the dynamics of the initiation ritual, the recruits' own bodies become the prime surface for institutional inscriptions. Having become a useful text, the body documents the knowledge and powers of the organizational culture through marks cut into the freshmen's flesh. Many of the marks will serve as reminders of those days of transposition and qualitative leaps where they left behind their civilian identities and embraced their condition as disciplined recruits[70].

Like Kafka's (1995) penal colony where the agents of the penal system inscribed the rules directly into the skin of those who had broken them so they could learn from their own wounds, in the BMPA's rite, young people's bodies are treated like blank sheets of paper on which the organization's code can be written. The law is viscerally inscribed on the body, on both sides of the page, affecting muscles, clothing and accessories, eating habits and table manners.

Many of the hazing challenges are tests of physical endurance. How could it be otherwise in an institution like the BMPA, which is largely masculine and sexist? As a result, a number of arduous exercises, scares, simulated combat, prostrations and crawling help give a foretaste of future academic tests awaiting the recruits, emphasizing the need for them to adopt a physical posture compatible with their new identity[71].

Clothing, which is targeted by all hazing activities in different organizations, is also a way of initiating people into a new identity. The idea is to defile the recruits' social image by stripping them of their usual clothing and preparing them to wear the mythical uniform of the Military Police. That is why, during the most intense parts of the hazing rituals, freshmen are obliged to dress outlandishly with their clothing turned inside out and looking ridiculous or wearing garbage bags as t-shirts and men's briefs as caps, their faces smeared with paint, egg yolks, mud, mayonnaise, flour or yogurt. Their clothing defiled, the recruits appear with a new body, a foreign appearance where

---

[70] Foucault, 1984, *op. cit.*; Riviere, 1996, *op. cit.*; R. Teather, *Mountie Makers: Putting the "Canadian" in RCMP*, Surrey: Heritage House, 1997.
[71] Turner, 1969, *op. cit.*; Clastres, 1990, *op. cit.*; Riviere, 1996, *Ibid.*

their dirty clothing can be considered the best translation of an unmade identity, or one that is about to be re-made.

The defiling use of food is not limited to the pollution of clothing. It also includes eating habits and the rules of the mess. By forcing recruits to challenge their eating habits, as we have seen in the initial scenes of hazing, inverting the order of consumption of different kinds of foods in the backwards meal (e.g., savories/sweets) introduces a ritual food, a sacrificial meal that, although made up of familiar ingredients rather than foreign and culturally censured elements[72] unites the participants in a transgressive experience. Also as part of this kind of meal, the rules of the mess acquired during the civilizing process are broken—eating with your mouth closed, not spitting food on the table[73]. This disorients the recruits, shaking their self-image, forcing them to regress to the primary stages of their personal development. Having become children again, the recruits re-travel their paths as socialized beings, becoming predisposed to take on a new socio-professional and personal identity.

Hazing ritualizes the initiation of bodies into the military police spirit, taming them and transforming them into machines that are suited to the institution's needs[74]—they will soon be promising recruits at an academy that demands that they fully internalize its code. In a word, the law, as the substance inherent to the group, becomes the substance and personal desire of the individual[75]. As we have seen, the legislators are the seniors who have already internalized the house rules and become machines that inscribe the institution's code on others. In the course of this inscription, the seniors make the freshmen their accomplices in the disturbing belief that hazing is necessary in order to achieve laudable identity transformations.

---

[72] Leemon, 1972, *op. cit.*
[73] N. Elias, *O processo civilizador*, Rio de Janeiro: Jorge Zahar, 1993.
[74] Foucault, 1984, *op. cit.*
[75] Clastres, 1990, *op. cit.*

7. Hazing keepers

In contrast to members of old military academies who view hazing as a positive thing[76], the BMPA's recruits are a little bit more critical vis-à-vis the ritual. Thus, when taking a stance on the validity of hazing in the process of academic socialization, the new recruits pointed to the positive as well as negative sides of the practice. Hazing, for them, is more useless (irrational and lacking in educational purpose) than useful (rational and a valid part of the educational process). Hazing that gives lessons in life, provides the discipline needed for life in the barracks, brings new and older recruits closer together and encourages attitudes such as courage, selflessness, resistance to pain and exposure to extreme situations, which are important to the occupation of the police officer. Useful hazing includes exploiting the recruits' labour to look after uniforms, shine boots, polish belt buckles and clean the seniors' weapons. Yet tests of physical endurance are also meaningful because, according to the recruits interviewed, there is a correspondence between being a police officer and being an athlete, even if these tests are administered in embarrassing situations. In any case, the recruits' reports provide an enormous list of irrational tests that are incoherent and of no value that characterize hazing as, in their view, sessions of disguised vengeance, arbitrarity, sarcasm and humiliation without any sense of confraternity.

Some informants can discern the relationships of power imbedded in this sense of hierarchy, through which the older recruits must confirm that they have learned their lessons and teach the rules of the game to the newcomers[77]. In addition, some informants, like Aline (age 22), point out some ritual learning implications:

> I'll never forget [it], and that was where I learned, at the beginning of the course, that this here [the Academy] strips me of my dignity all the time, just see how the officers treat us, they are rude to the recruits. For them, the only people who aren't worthless are the officers. Society is running a big risk with the beasts the BMPA produces.

---

[76] Leon, 2000, *op. cit.*
[77] Mattoso, 1985, *op. cit.*; Leemon, 1972, *op. cit.*; Leon, 2000, *op. cit.*

The interviewee shows that she has not accepted the rules of the game, and is warning against the impacts for society of this practice within the BMPA. She also discerns the relations of power, but does not seem to have internalized the rules or accepted her responsibility to transmit them to subsequent cohorts of new recruits. However, when presented with the hypothetical possibility of choosing to eliminate or maintain the BMPA's hazing rite, 29 of the 31 subjects interviewed were in favour of maintaining it, albeit with some changes. Thus, even the recruits who object to it the most are not inclined to eliminate the practice altogether, but to redesign it with a view to avoiding physical scarring and extreme humiliation.

The most pragmatic respondents like Pedro (age 21) proposed "replace hazing with a week of socializing including lectures and explanations about how the BMPA operates: it would lessen those guys' shock when going from the civilian world to the military one. It should be more instructive and not based on "*besteirol*" [rubbish]." Those who believe hazing should continue agree with Roberto (age 21), who told us that this ritual contains strength and wisdom in the tradition that serves to test the new recruits' psychological capacity. Many also mention the importance of learning the insights ("*macetes*") of life at the academy during the hazing period. The good or positive part about hazing, according to the freshmen, is that despite its discrepancies, it can produce a relaxed atmosphere and closer relations between freshman and senior recruits.

Hazing must be viewed as an artificial crisis when confronted with the real, subjective crisis of recruits who are having their first experience of police instruction. Although the rite creates a tremendous amount of stress, this is trivial in light of the other emotional overcharge the newcomers are carrying in their bodies and minds. The freshmen are challenged to face their fears, and placed in tense, painful situations to make them shed other tensions, strip their old ties of their meaning and make them cast off their former civilian group. From now on, their new family is right there; they are meant to feel heartily welcomed and sheltered by their classmates and instructors at the police academy. With the blessing of the leadership team and the participation of the seniors, the newcomers walk in through the front door of the academy, where, when their time comes, they will have to carry out the same experience with freshmen, dazed by their encounter with police instruction.

It is ironic to find that recruits' criticism and resistance to hazing, as we have seen, are not enough to put an end to this Darwinist educational practice[78], and they have not prevented successive generations of freshmen from going from victims to victimizers, giving in to the tactics of socialization and ensuring the ideological reproduction of militaristic police instruction. The cathartic nature of hazing could explain the "amnesia" and loss of critical thinking among the seniors, who once complained bitterly about the hardships of their years at the academy, but suddenly begin not only to idealize the supposed effectiveness of their education, but to respect the traditional scheme of things.

Conclusion

Hazing is one of a range of psycho-social experiences conducted by the MPA, which promotes *esprit de corps* through the mortification of personal identity. It is developed, as we have seen, within a zone of space and time marked by the density of signifiers and the intensity of contents, as well as by a phenomenology of violence inflicted and inscribed on the bodies of the officer-candidates.

If police socialization implies profound identity change among recruits, the hazing ritual dramatizes and anticipates this identity change[79]. Like the stress training methods characteristic of traditional police training, hazing instills in recruits a militaristic sense of what it is to be a police officer, including abuse of rank, breaking and silencing others that have predictable negative consequences for police work and democracy. It has therefore been difficult to establish a new learning environment and invest in practices whose tone is conducive to reflection, situation analysis, the study of decision-making strategies and other skills that could improve the performance expected of new police officers[80].

---

[78] Leon, 2000, *op. cit.*
[79] Although this practice does not exist in many police academies, its principles (e.g., eliminating differences and disregard for the individual rights of the recruits) are still found in the day-to-day activities of those academies.
[80] Guimaraes, 2000, *op. cit.*; Palmiotto et al., 2000, *op. cit.*; Post-Gary, 1992, *op. cit.*

Furthermore, hazing is in keeping with concepts of policing as a "craft" rather than a "profession", in the sense that much of its art is learned through the mysteries of apprenticeship rather than instruction. This is valid to freshmen as well to seniors, for whom the ritual is a crucial moment to make decisions and exercise leadership.

The Police Academy adopt a twisted logic which is surmount to perversion. They teach the knowledge of the reformed curriculum, which guarantees a good contemporary image of the moderate policeman, while conserving roots in the mythical landscape, where the police continues its cruel stereotype, of exaggerated use of force, certain of exercising a paternal function in society[81].

The agendas encountered in the hazing can be opposed to the proposals in the new official curriculum, just as, in some cases, they may complement them. They are opposed because the police corporation itself refuses to believe in the capacity of a new curriculum to form officials in its own likeness. They can complement the new proposals because they qualify and deepens notions of this image, reinforcing militarist aspects which the formal curriculum do not foster. In any case, hazing is part of a counter-curriculum that is as (or more) efficient than other teaching methods in transmitting the values and attitudes of the paramilitary police, filling gaps and putting the police organization's stamp on training, old and new[82].

If hegemonic states can set limits to these negatives effects, the same is not true for authoritarian, weak (and also permissive) post-colonial states such as Brazil, where this kind of habitus predisposes police officers to amplify violence against working poor and black-mestizo youngsters[83].

Given this, any criticism could promote a new sense of memory, and warn the police that their fathers' era has changed, that the social network

---

[81] L.G. Gabaldon, C. Birkbeck & D. Bettiol, *La policia en el vecindario*, Merida: Gobernacion del Estado de Merida/Universidad de los Andes, 1990; A. Lévy, *Ciências clínicas e organizações sociais: Sentido e crise de sentido*, Belo Horizonte: Autêntica Forense, 2001; P. Stenning, "Regulación del uso policial de la fuerza en Canadá", in L.G. Gabaldón and C. Birkbeck, *Policía y fuerza física en perspectiva intercultural*, Caracas: Nueva Sociedad, 2003, pp. 53-67.
[82] Paes-Machado & Albuquerque, 2002, *op. cit.*
[83] Jefferson, 1990, *op. cit.*; Huggins, 2000, *op. cit.*; Paes-Machado & Noronha, 2002, *op. cit.*; A. Goldsmith, "Policing weak states: Citizen safety and state responsibility", *Policing and Society*, vol. 13, no. 1, 2003, pp. 3-21.

operates better as a fraternal function[84] and cause the Corporation to question what type of father figure can exist in a democracy. It's important to remember that a democracy is the dynamics of a social situation moved by the unfamiliarity of still having a father, a father who is so omnipresent and controlling. The criticism will be able to stimulate the operators of public security to conceive another model of paternal authority, and become a partner in taking over this imaginary fortress.

With the current circumstances of external and internal pressures for the reform of police forces, it is necessary that they not only reformulate their instructional programs, as has already been done in Bahia and other Brazilian states, but, also change their deeper institutional and cultural values. The organizations will therefore have to overcome internal resistance which, using the pretext that there is a risk of discharacterization, sabotage the democratization agenda.

The overcoming of this resistance, however, is beyond the scope of the reform of the police education implemented to this date, depending on broader changes to guarantee the consolidation of citizenship and democratization of policing.

---

[84] Lévy, 2001, *op. cit.*

VI *Dedovshchina* and the All-Volunteer Force

13 Is the all-Volunteer Force a Solution for Draft Problems?

Joris VAN BLADEL

In the discussions about how to eradicate *dedovshchina* in the Russian armed forces, it is often stated that professionalization of the armed forces is the ultimate solution. The reasoning behind this statement is that if you bring soldiers voluntarily together and you pay them a reasonable salary, the nasty effects of *dedovshchina* would disappear. The studies about professional armed forces, as they appear in Western industrial societies in the second half of the twentieth century, may give reason to this reasoning. This is not to say that there are no abuses in the Western armed forces, but the systematic abuse of soldiers does certainly not exist and, if there are abuses, these cases are politically so sensitive that there are for each of them political and military logical repercussions. But even if the basic reasoning behind professionalization as a solution to *dedovshchina* seems to be correct, we have to be careful with our conclusions. Therefore this chapter will study carefully the basic characteristics of the western professional armed forces, which are called post-modern armed forces in the sociologic literature. If we compare, in a second step, the Russian idea of professionalization, we may, perhaps, come to other conclusions. The basic question is thus: are there different ideas of professional armed forces, or, are there different types of professional armed forces?

1. Change in military organizations

Clark Kerr's convergence theory postulates that industrial societies become increasingly alike and evolve as a whole because the character of the dominant technology enforces specific forms of social organization, political life, cultural patterns, every day conduct and even beliefs and attitudes[1]. This idea can be used to show that military organizations are in the long run a reflection of state and society. Furthermore, the open organization hypothesis underscores the co-evolution between the military organization and society. These insights lay at the basis of military sociology as an applied field of sociology. The idea of organizational evolution presented here fits the approach outlined during the 1960s by Morris Janowitz (who is regarded as the founder of this applied field of military sociology). Janowitz hypothesized that there was a resemblance between the evolution of civilian organizations and military organizations. This is the so-called "civilianization hypothesis" which James Burk describes as follows[2]:

> The central argument was that the boundaries separating the military from civilian society had progressively weakened since the turn of the century. It described a military organization that was forced to participate more actively in the life of the larger society and yet maintain its relative autonomy, competence, and group cohesion.[3]

In addition Jacques Van Doorn noticed a qualitative mutation in the character of military organizations. In a seminal article on "the decline of the mass army", Van Doorn argued that military organizations evolved from a modern mass-army to a professional army[4]. Janowitz's and Van Doorn's ideas were

---

[1] Mentionned in P. Sztompka, *The Sociology of Social Change*, Oxford: Blackwell, 1993, pp.133-135.

[2] M. Janowitz, *The Professional Soldier, A Social and Political Portrait*, New York: Free Press, 1971 (second edition), pp. xii-xv.

[3] J. Burk, "Morris Janowitz and the Origins of Sociological Research on Armed Forces and Society", *Armed Forces and Society*, Vol. 19, no. 2, Winter 1993, p. 179.

[4] J. Van Doorn, "The Decline of the Mass Army in the West: General Reflections", *Armed Forces and Society*, vol. 1, no. 2, February 1975, pp. 147-157. Although Van Doorn spoke instead of an all-volunteer force (AVF) and never used the terminology

visionary at that time. When many of their postulated ideas were realized, other military sociologists expanded and refined the idea of the professional armed forces and they subsequently created the model of the post-modern army. Thus the evolving theoretical discourse on organizational change in business and government and the narrow discussion on military change are now comparable. In fact, the similarities between business and military organizations were not accidental: they are both affected by profound changes in the external environment.

In order to outline the ideal models of the modern and post-modern variants of military organizations, the environmental changes that precipitated the mass army and the post-modern All-Volunteer Force (AVF) will be reviewed. Structural variables are employed to examine what the logic or the pattern of military organizational change is and from this discussion typical characteristics of different military organizations types will be outlined.

2. Changing environments

Environmental aspects of the mass army
The "mass army" is a type of military organization that developed during the French and American revolutions and this form of military organization prevailed until the end of the Second World War. The armies that fought in the First World War can be considered as archetypical mass army types. Mass armies were closely related to the development of the industrial society and as well to the notion of nationalism[5]. The growth of the industrial sector which was based on the production and use of sources of energy such as coal, steel and steam made mass production possible. Mass production in the weapons industry made it feasible to procure weapons for large armies. The development of a factory system and a refined division of labor in the textile industry, enabled the state to produce uniforms on a massive scale for the army. Finally, the development of the railway system, telecommunications

---

[5] of post-modernity. However, the context, referents and form of argumentation used in the article render the interpretation possible.
For a good overview see for instance: A. Vagts, *A History of Militarism: Civilian and Military*, New York: The Free Press, 1959; and Ch. Tilly, *Coercion, Capital and European States*, AD 990-1990, Cambridge: Basil Blackwell, 1990, pp. 96-126.

and food industry allowed states to mobilize, transport and feed huge armies in a relatively efficient way.

The emerging nation state - "the political consequence of modernity"[6] - was an essential element in the socio-cultural environment of mass armies. The nation-state was able to mobilize the whole community under the banner of nationalism. The state intervened directly and bluntly in the life of the individual citizen. Charles Tilly called this the imposition of the state's "direct rule"[7]. In exchange for protection and increasing education the citizen had to be willing to perform military service. State nationalism was the myth that justified the practices of modern society:

> The essence of the mass army is only partly its size, although it is a great deal larger than most of its predecessors. The essence of the mass army is its ability to maintain its size in the face of the rigors of war: the attrition exacted by the unhealthy conditions of the campaign, the temptation of individuals to desert, and the firepower of the enemy.[...] Thus the recruits must arrive with a certain willingness to become soldiers, a certain educability [sic], and a certain commitment to the outcome of the battle. This makes political motivation, and ultimately literacy, key elements of the mass army. [...] The problem becomes how to keep these dispersed, scared, and lonely men risking their own lives, and cooperating to take the live of others.[8]

Conscription was seen as an accomplishment of the French Revolution. Universal compulsory military service contributed to the democratization of society on three levels[9]. The duty and the right to bear weapons was a totally new idea. It was perceived as a compulsory contribution of civil rights by the citizen. Moreover, the fact that conscription was supposed to be distributed equally over the male population meant that the introduction of compulsory

---

[6] C. Offe, *Modernity and the State*, Cambridge: Polity Press, 1996, p. 61.
[7] Tilly, 1990, *op. cit.*, pp. 103-117.
[8] B. R. Posen, "Nationalism, Mass Army, and Military Power", *International Security*, vol. 18, no. 2, Fall 1993, pp. 83-84.
[9] See for instance: Tilly, 1990, *op. cit.*, pp. 122-126 and J. Burk, "Citizenship Status and Military Service: The Quest for Inclusion by Minorities and Conscientious Objectors", *Armed Forces and Society*, vol. 21, no. 4, Summer 1995, pp. 503-529.

conscription, a core characteristic of the mass army, can be seen as a contribution to the democratization of society. Finally, citizenship and military service were two narrowly related ideas. Military service made the individual take part in society. Rejection of military service excluded him from society. Janowitz remarked in this context that military service was the hallmark of citizenship as citizenship was the hallmark of political democracy[10] and Tilly summarized it in another one-liner, "Militarization = civilianization"[11].

Frontiers and territory were important elements of the state during the Nineteenth Century and the threat of invasion was a primary concern of the state and its military organization(s). In addition, this period was characterized by the concept of total war in which the mobilisation of the whole society was necessary to wage war. The concept of total war is embodied in Posen's comment, "economy, education, culture... all this stood in the function of the preparation and waging of the next war."[12] The military institution was consequently regarded as the most important institution in society, the primus inter pares, of the state's agencies. Military organizations enjoyed a high level of esteem and resources were made readily available to them. The army was therefore an integral part of state nationalism. In contrast to the Nineteenth Century environmental characteristics, the world changed dramatically in the second half of the twentieth century.

Environmental aspects of the post-modern military

The first contours of the postmodern military appeared in the 1960's, but it was during the Gulf War of 1991 and different peacekeeping and peacemaking actions in the 1990's which can be seen as prototypical for this army type[13]. The post-modern variant of the military organization must be seen in

---

[10] M. Janowitz, *On Social Organization and Social Control*, Chicago: University of Chicago Press, 1991, pp. 226-227.
[11] Tilly, 1990, *op. cit.*, p. 122.
[12] Posen, 1993, *op. cit.*, p. 87.
[13] It is important to remark that the transition from the "mass army" to the "postmodern" army type took considerable time and in fact passed over a third, specific (transitory) type army. This transitory type of army is called in the literature of military sociology the "force-in-being" and was related with the idea that armies evolved to a "constabulary force" rather than the traditional fighting force (See: M.Janowitz, *op. cit.*, 1971, p. ii and pp. 417-442) Also K. Haltiner stressed the transitory character in the evolution between the two extreme army types. Based on the quantitative variable "Conscript Ratio", he stated that: "the transition between the different types

the context of a fundamental change in the geopolitical situation in the world, rapid economic and technological changes, and changes in the world's populations' attitudes to war. This ever growing rapidity of change has made the organizational environment profoundly unstable. Instability and unpredictability are key characteristics to which the military organizations have had to find organizational answers.

The fall of the Berlin Wall and the ultimate collapse of the Soviet Union led to the break-up of the certainty and predictability of a bipolar international system. The new security era could be characterized as one of risk, complexity and uncertainty in comparison with the relative certainty of the preceding four decades. The outbreak of total war, already in doubt by the introduction of nuclear weapons during the Cold War, changed fundamentally[14].

Whereas deterrence was the core of the mission of the military organization during the Cold War, the collapse of the Soviet Union produced a completely different scale and set of threats and missions. The missions were called "missions other than war" or "low intensity conflicts" and were against such threats as terrorism, organized crime, and local nationalism. Humanitar-

---

of force format is rather gradual, and the mass army format of the armed forces apparently rises relatively continuously in the transition from type 0 (all-volunteer systems) to type III (hard-core conscript systems [with a conscript ratio above 66%])." See: K. Haltiner, "The Definite End of the Mass Army in Western Europe", *Armed Forces and Society*, vol. 25, no. 1, Fall 1988, pp. 7-36. Ch. Moskos made room for three periods in his famous post-modern typology, namely Early-Modern, Late-Modern and Postmodern periods. It implies also the "force-in-being" idea. (See: Ch. C. Moskos and J. Burk, "The Postmodern Military", in: J. Burk (ed.), *The Military in New Times, Adapting Armed Forces to a Turbulent World*, Boulder: Westview press, 1994, p. 147 and Ch. Moskos, J. Williams and D. Segal (eds), *The Postmodern Military, Armed Forces after the Cold War*, Oxford: Oxford University Press, 2000, pp. 1-2) In the less accurate, but more generally used notion -especially in Russia- of the "mixed army" type, the idea of a transitory army type is also suggested. The mixed army type refers to the fact that recruitment is based on both, compulsory conscription and contract basis. Conventionally and for matters of analytical explicitness, this study limits itself to the dichotomy between the mass army and the post-modern army type. It is important to bear in mind that this is a simplification of historical and social reality, but nevertheless applicable to Russia.

[14] See for instance: M. Shaw, *Post-Military Society, Militarism, Demilitarization and War at the End of the Twentieth Century*, Cambridge: Polity Press, 1991, pp. 19-23 and pp. 64-105; J. van der Meulen, "Civiel-militaire betrekkingen in verandering: wisselwerking tussen maatschappij en krijgsmacht", in: H. Born, R. Moelker and J. Soeters (eds.), *Krijgsmacht en samenleving: klassieke en eigentijdse inzichten*,Tilburg: Tilburg University Press, 1999, pp. 54-66.

ian aid, refugee support and aid in areas of natural disasters became part of military missions.

The rapid changes in the nature of the threats facing Western militaries, when deployed on a particular mission, were also a notable characteristic of the new geo-political environment. A good example is provided by British forces deployed in Macedonia during May-June 1999. During the NATO air campaign over Kosovo they prepared and trained initially for a full-scale ground war. But after Kosovar refugees flooded Macedonia and Albania they changed their mission and became a humanitarian force. Finally, after a peace agreement, they entered Kosovo with a peacekeeping mandate. Thus, in a time frame of two months, the missions of these elite troops changed fundamentally. The tempo and the nature of the changes possible in the post-modern military environment have urged the British forces to become both more flexible and better trained.

Economically in the world today there is a trend towards globalization. Predominantly national markets have evolved into global markets. This increased competition combined with technological and information revolutions have made organizations less labor-intensive and more capital-intensive. As a result of globalization there has been a change from extensive to intensive growth, and the famous quantity-quality innovation has taken place. Firms have become smaller but their capacity and their ability to provide services have increased in inverse proportion.

These factors have also affected military organizations. The third industrial revolution, with computer technology as a key factor, allows armies to work with technological advanced weapons. This context has led to the so-called "revolution in military affairs" with significant consequences, such as military organizations requiring on the one hand more and more highly trained personnel with higher educational qualifications; and on the other hand the least specialized military functions have begun to disappear because they can be automated or out-sourced; and the training of these military specialists takes too long and is expensive[15].

---

[15] D. Snow, *The Shape of the Future: the Post-Cold War World*, New York: M.E. Sharpe, 1991; Alvin and Toffler, 1993, *op. cit.*

The ideas of materialism and individualism have also grown to extreme levels in post-modern society[16]. Consequently, values and attitudes have evolved in the direction of "self realization", consumerism and hedonism. The "Welfare State" mechanism supports this situation as a safety net for those who cannot compete in this type of society. Within the overall societal dynamic people are no longer prepared to give up their privileges for reasons of state security. Carroll J. Glynn and others noted this in their paraphrase of Inglehart's ideas:

> In the United States and Western Europe, the general increase of prosperity over most of the twentieth century had profoundly altered the balance between materialist and postmaterialist values. Each new generation tended to be less concerned about materialistic values such as prosperity and security. Postmaterialist values-such as more say in government, a less impersonal society, and freedom of speech-gradually rose in importance.[17]

In its attempt to cope with highly complex social problems, the state appears to be in crisis. It finds itself in a contradictory (post-modern) state of being too small and too big at the same time. On the one hand, states seem to be too large to cope with the individual problems of the increasingly demanding citizenry. On the other hand, given the growing trend of giving more authority to international institutions such as the United Nations and the European Union, states are too small to handle classical state matters; and this perception is taking the efforts to create common defense (although political obstacles related to individual states' perceptions of their role in the world create stumbling blocks).

---

[16] See for example: R. Inglehart, *Culture Shift in Advanced Industrial Society*, Princeton: Princeton University Press, 1990; R. Inglehart, *The Silent Revolution, Changing Values and Political Styles Among Western Publics*, Princeton, Princeton University Press, 1977; and R. Inglehart, *Modernization and Postmodernization*, Princeton: Princeton University Press, 1999. For an application of this idea on the military organization see F. Battistelli, "Peacekeeping and the Postmodern Soldier", *Armed Forces and Society*, vol. 23, no. 3, Spring 1997, pp. 467-484.

[17] C. Glynn, S. Herbst, G. O'Keefe, and R. Shapiro, *Public Opinion*, Boulder: Westview Press, 1999, p. 269.

In this situation, the narrow relationship of citizenship and military services dominant in the modern era no longer exist. The status of the army changed dramatically. The allocated state resources for defense shrank proportionally and were re-allocated to what can be broadly called "welfare matters". The fall of the army's status, as an international phenomenon, can be explained by several interacting processes: the fundamental shift in state priorities in the "post-nationalistic era"; the indifference and even hostility of the population toward military missions (except for peacekeeping and other humanitarian missions); and the cost-intensity of the technological revolution in military affairs meaning that maintaining a broad suite of capabilities is untenable for any single nation[18]. Bernard Boëne calls this last element "structural disarmament"[19].

To conclude this description of the changed (and changing) logic of military organizations in similarly changing societies, the previous tabulation can now be completed:

	Closed System	Open System
Period	1890-1950	1960 onward
Organizational type	Bureaucratic-traditional, hierarchic corporation	Post-Bureaucratic- Virtual and Matrix corporation
Management Philosophy	Taylorism	Human Resource Management
Organizational environment	Modern society	Post-Modern society
Military organizational type	Mass Army	All Volunteer Force

Table 2: Organizations as Closed versus Open Systems (complement 2).

---

[18] See for instance: Ph. Manigart and E. Marlier, "New Roles and Missions, Army Image and Recruitment Prospects: the case of Belgium", in: Ph. Manigart (ed.), *Future Roles, Missions and Structure of Armed Forces In The New World Order: The Public View*, New York: The Nova Science Publishers, 1996, pp. 8-12; L. Mandeville, P. Combelles and D. Rich, "French Public opinion and new missions of the armed forces", in Ph. Manigart (ed.), 1996, *Ibid.*, pp. 55-59.

[19] B. Boëne, "A tribe among tribes...post-modern militaries and civil-military relations?" paper presented at the interim Meeting of the International Sociological Association's Research Committee 01 (Armed Forces and Conflict Resolution), Modena, Italy, January 20-22, 1997.

3. Changing military organizations

The mass army

The mass army organization type can be described in two different ways: as "minimalist" (in quantitative terms) and "maximalist" (qualitative). The maximalist description allows more aspects of the mass army to be taken into account. However, both approaches are complementary.

The Swiss military sociologist, Karl Haltiner, presented a working definition of a mass army in order to describe "the end of the mass army in Western Europe". His approach stressed quantitative variables related to the structure of the organization, namely "size", "social mobilisation" and "homogenization"[20]. The definition contained the following elements[21]:

1. The recruitment system is based on universal or selective conscription.

2. The effective strength of regulars and reserves in the armed forces comprises a relatively high share of the national population. This strength can be measured in the so-called Military Participation Rate (MPR)[22].

3. Specific-age cohorts of the male population are liable for military service, and the majority of these military-age cohorts are also drafted.

4. The conscripts make up more than 50 percent of the total strength of the national armed forces. This percentage is called the Conscript Ratio (CR). Accordingly, the share of volunteers, especially women, is relatively low.

5. The level of military technology is relatively low. This allows the air force and the navy to rely primarily on conscripts who serve for short time periods.

---

[20] "Size", "level of mobilisation" and "homogeneity" are the three basic meanings of the adjective "mass" in the sociological interpretation of Jacques van Doorn on this subject. Jacques Van Doorn who wrote in the founding years of military sociology a classic article on the mass army. J. Van Doorn, "The Decline of the Mass Army in the West: general reflections", *Armed Forces and Society*, vol. 1, no. 2, February 1975, pp. 147-157.

[21] Haltiner, 1988, *op. cit.*, p. 10.

[22] MPR is a concept that was first proposed by S. Andreski and defined as "the proportion of militarily utilized individuals in the total population". See: S. Andreski, *Military Organisation and Society*, London: Routledge and Kegan Paul, 1968 (Second Edition), pp. 33-34.

6. The armed forces are army-dominated, that is, the share of the navy and air force is relatively small compared with the ground forces.

Although Haltiner's working definition is useful, it does not contain all aspects of a mass army. Therefore a more complete and more qualitative ideal type is presented as well. In the qualitative interpretation, the following features of a mass army are identified:

1. It is a huge army ("quantity" and "extensive growth" are basic features).
2. There is a high degree of societal participation in the army through the practice of conscription in peacetime, and through the practice of mobilisation of reserves in wartime.
3. There is a high degree of homogeneity. The social differentiation is relatively small. Practically all soldiers have combat functions. The infantry soldier is prototypical for the military.
4. There is a small nucleus of professional soldiers around which a mass of mobilized civilians is enrolled.
5. The functions executed by the military are less differentiated and specifically military (combat functions). As a result, the military is a very different organization from the civilian society.
6. Authority is based on domination. An explicit order, without any explanation, directs the conduct of the subordinate. Threatening and negative sanctions are used in this kind of authority (see also the management principles of Taylor, and the remarks on the problem of control in the mass army treated below).
7. An institutional understanding of the military profession. This is a traditional view of the military profession characterized by vocation, patriotism, dedication and sacrifice. The military feel themselves different from the civilian. There is even a feeling of supremacy over the civilian world. General interests prevail over individual interest. The military are generalists, who feel themselves to be a "twenty-four hour" military. They are always available. Being a military man is a way of life.
8. Politically, the army has a great deal of internal autonomy. There is practically no control from outside.

"The army of the Nineteenth Century" thus had a classic bureaucratic outlook and was governed by Taylorian management principles. The high status and the closedness of the organization (aptly termed "walled-in organizations" by Erving Goffman) assured the traditional autonomy of the institution[23].

The closedness of the military organization which made the military so different from civil society also influenced the internal culture in the organization. They are related with achieving control and the resulting "soldiers' culture" in the mass army. Several aspects related with the culture of the inmates of closed organizations might be helpful to highlight the problem[24]. During the 1950s-1960s, Goffman, Cressey and Krassowski researched behavior among and between inmates in closed (but public) institutions as mental hospitals, prisons, and concentration camps that contain people against their own free will.

Their ideas to the same extent can be applied to life in the military barracks throughout the period of the mass army because soldiers during this era served compulsorily. This specific element of holding people against their will, combined with the specific tasks of training soldiers for a job which was life threatening, resulted in major problems for the officer corps. The core problem was how to control soldiers in this situation. The officer corps was admonished to train soldiers, but its over-all success as a corps was measured mainly both by the degree to which 'trouble' was absent during peace time and missions were accomplished in war time. Thus success was measured by the effective installation of obedience[25]. "Control" and "obedience"

---

[23] E. Goffman, "The Underlife of a Public Institution: A Study of Ways of Making Out in a Mental Hospital", in: O. Grusky and G. Miller (eds), *The Sociology of Organizations, Basic Studies*, New York: The Free Press, 1981 (Second Edition), p. 302.

[24] D. Cressey and W. Krassowski, "Inmate Organizations and Anomie in American Prisons and Soviet Labor Camps", *Social Problems*, vol. 5, no. 4, 1958-59, pp. 217-230.

[25] A typical practice in mass armies was the tradition of collective punishment, in which the group was punished for a mistake or infraction of the individual. Nowadays, this practice is unacceptable in the post-modern army. Another extreme example of installing obedience on the soldiers in war time was the execution of deserters and of people who committed less important infraction on military law to set an example for the others. This practice was more or less common in the mass armies on the Western Front during the First World War. The fact that this issue is even in the year 2000 a taboo for Western governments underlines that this practice is an anachronism in postmodern times which damages the image of the armed

are obtained at a (high) price. The roots of this high price may be seen through the sociological work of Cressey and Krassowski who describe the effect in American prisons and Soviet Labor camps. Due to the closed character of the military organization their conclusions may also be applied to the study of armed forces. Cressey and Krassowski observed the following aspects in the problem of controlling inmates[26]. Firstly, they stated that the way control was exercised in barracks depended on the values of the society, especially on the values of persons and groups which had special interests in the army. The officer corps' idea about how a soldier should do his job and behave heavily influenced the way control was exercised. This view was also influenced by how war was perceived by the officer corps. Secondly, two kinds of (contradictory) relationships among soldiers could be discerned. On the one hand, soldiers lived in isolation and conditions of anomie[27]. On the other hand, there was a strong tendency toward self-organization and interdependence among soldiers which is a result of emerging informal groups in which leaders of various types dominated and enforced their own code of behavior. These codes had several core elements as basic rules: do what is asked from you; maintain social distance from the officers; and honor soldiers' solidarity. This code was based on one golden rule, namely the "law of silence". Whoever broke the "law of silence" could expect (cruel) punishment from the informal leaders. Thirdly, both the state of anomie and informal organization among the soldiers were of functional utility for the officer corps. The state of anomie in which soldiers were kept psychologically isolated and unorganized minimized the danger for revolt, riot, or other collective action. Furthermore, allowing informal organization among soldiers made control complete. It complemented the effect of anomie upon the soldiers. These features colored the relationship between officers and other cadres. When a par-

---

[26] forces. Moreover, it demonstrates that "functional violence" outside its historical and societal context may seem for the "distant" observer absurd and inexplicable.

D. Cressey and W. Krassowski, "Inmate organizations and anomie in American prisons and Soviet labor camps", *Social Problems*, Vol. 5, no.4 , 1958-59, pp. 217-220.

[27] The concept of anomie is a typical sociological concept introduced by Emile Durkheim and further used by Robert Merton and Talcott Parsons. It equates "extreme instability" with "demoralization" and "de-institutionalization" caused by a lack or break down of guiding norms, which consequently leaves individuals with neither restraints nor guidance.

ticular group of soldiers was allowed to control the rest of the soldiers, a kind of non-written contract was signed in which a certain liberty of action was permitted by the informal leaders (in which formal institutional rules could be broken) in exchange for control over the rest of the soldiers. In other words, if the informal leaders allowed military training and maintained order among the soldiers, they had freedom of action in the informal power structure of soldiers.

Finally, both the conditions of alienation and of self-organization existed under conditions of systematic deprivation, usually taking either physical or psychological forms. Scarcity created jealousy, suspiciousness, mistrust, and other indices of anomie among soldiers. The officer corps manipulated this situation in order to reward the informal leaders with symbols of power and status. Therefore the officer corps selectively distributed scare goods, as food, cigarettes, alcohol, or immaterial goods such as free time.

To conclude: in order to install control, a relationship of interdependence among soldiers and officers or "a system of reciprocal adjustment" existed[28]. This was probably not an explicit administrative policy, but it was certainly a principal technique for controlling men in the barracks. Moreover, besides installing control, it also made the process of socializing the new inmates "easier". The price for this practice was a tolerance for deviant behavior as beating, physical and psychological torture. However, the specificity of the soldiers' job could in a certain way justify these practices: it created hard-nosed soldiers ready for battle.

Officers saw "toughness" which was obtained by conditions of anomie, deprivation and the reign of informal leaders as a necessary military characteristic which was determined by the harshness of the system of control. The idea of interdependence without much external control, embedded in a specific military mentality, resulted in a soldiers' culture which was difficult to change[29]. Indeed, as long as "the military mentality", "the interdependence

---

[28] *Ibid.*, p. 219.
[29] The "military mentality" can be compared with what Huntington wrote about the "military mind" and the "military ethic". The first, he described as "conservative realist" and the latter as "pessimistic, collectivist, historically inclined, power-oriented, nationalistic, pacifist, and instrumentalist in its view of the military profession". See S. Huntington, *The Soldier and the State, The Theory and Politics of Civil-Military Relations*, New York: Vintage Books, 1957, p. 79. Concerning "the military mind"

between the leading inmates and staff" and "the closedness of the organization" were unchanged, this vicious circle could not be broken; and the resulting perverse consequences could not be avoided.

The post-modern military organization

Parallel with the evolution of the bureaucratic organization to the post-bureaucratic organization, the military organization in the West underwent a similar evolution. The modern organization type (or the mass army) evolved over time to the post-modern military organization. Dandeker has outlined the following features of the post-modern military organization as distinct from its modern antecedent[30]:

1- Responsibility shifts to lower levels. Even the individual soldier at the lowest level has to take decisions autonomously, even ones with important political consequences.

2- The military job is intensive and very demanding, but also very rewarding, with increased responsibility for equipment, people and the success of the operation.

3- Flexibility means an emphasis on the multi-rolling of equipment and a consequent desire to recruit and retain personnel able to take on multiple roles, creating and necessitating a more flexible work force at all levels of the hierarchy and in all specialties.

4- The "mixing and matching" of components from different services and countries pose problems of establishing effective command and control links of a lateral as well as vertical kind.

---

[30] see also Feld who stated that "…the emotional and intellectual positions under considerations are the models guiding the modes of organization and employment of military forces…". M. Feld, *The Structure of Violence, Armed Forces as Social Systems*, Beverly Hills: Sage Publications, 1977, pp. 33-34.
C. Dandeker, "Flexible forces for a post cold war world: a view from the United Kingdom", *La revue Tocqueville/ The Tocqueville Review*, vol. 17, no. 1, 1995, pp. 23-38 and C. Dandeker, "New Times for the Military: Some Sociological Remarks on the Changing Role and Structure of the Armed Forces of the Advanced Societies", *British Journal of Sociology*, vol. 45, no. 4, 1994, pp. 637-654. See also: D. Segal, *Organizational Designs for the Future Army*, Alexandria: U.S. Army Research Institute for the Behavioral and Social Sciences, Special Report no. 20, 1993 and Ch. Moskos, J. Williams and D. Segal (eds), *The Postmodern Military, Armed Forces after the Cold War*, 2000, *op. cit.*, pp. 1-11 and 265-275.

The following features can be added to this conceptual interpretation[31]:

1. To work effectively, this system requires fundamental changes in the relationship between the military/political center and the force commanders. Here a new and contradictory situation is faced: the political control involves a shift away from detailed control to acceptance of discretion within the constraints of the overall strategic objective. The omnipotence of the media leads to an overall and detailed control of the fourth force in modern society. Besides the media, the non-governmental organizations control the military and even become concurrent in humanitarian operations. The autonomy of the military is fundamentally affected. The force commander thus receives on the one hand more autonomy but on the other is more controlled and constrained than ever by the media and non-governmental organizations.

2. Authority is based on manipulation[32]. This type of authority is based on explanation, competence of the leader and consensus in the group. Instead of negative sanctions, the leader uses positive stimuli. The military leader has to take into account the motivation and morale of the individual. The most brutal procedures for schooling and training are not tolerated anymore. Primary groups and leadership are key elements in manipulation type of authority.

3. There is an occupational perception of the military profession.[33] The military profession is a job like any other. The military personnel serve for economic reasons, not for patriotic reasons. The military profession is not a way of life anymore, it is a way of obtaining extrinsic rewards. Professional organizations as well as unions defend the collective interests of the members of the military organization.

---

[31] These features are borrowed from the literature and completed with some personnel insights. Janowitz, 1974, *op. cit.*; Ch. Moskos, "From Institution to Occupation: Trends in Military Organizations", *Armed Forces and Society*, vol. 4, no. 1, November 1977, pp. 41-50; Ch. Moskos, "Institutional/ Occupational Trends in Armed Forces: An Update", *Armed Forces and Society*, vol. 12, no. 3, Spring 1986, pp. 377-382; Ch. Moskos and J. Burk, "The Postmodern Military", in: J. Burk (ed.), 1994, *op. cit.*, pp. 141-162. P. Vennesson, "Le triomphe du métier des armes: dynamique professionnelle et la societé militaire en France", *La Revue Tocqueville/The Tocqueville Review*, vol. 17, no. 1, 1996, pp. 135-157.

[32] Janowitz, 1971, *op. cit.*, pp. xvii-xxiv.

[33] Moskos, 1977, *op. cit.*, pp. 41-50; and Moskos, 1986, *op. cit.*, pp. 377-382.

4. Diversity, rather than homogeneity is the central characteristic of the AVF[34]. The introduction of women and ethnic minorities in the military is an example of this trend. In addition to tolerance, flexibility is rewarded in this kind of organization.

Charles Moskos summarized his view on the how military organizations are changing in a typology. This typology is based on the distinction between the institutional and the occupational interpretation of the military profession. The original idea was proposed in 1977 and it has been expanded upon and refreshed over the years[35]. Moskos' typology, represented in the following table, is a good summary of the change that is taking place in military organizations.

---

[34] J. Soeters and J. van der Meulen (eds), *Managing Diversity in the Armed Forces, Experiences From Nine Countries*, Tilburg: Tilburg University Press, 1999, especially pp. 211-221.

[35] Moskos, 1977, *op. cit.*, pp. 41-50; Moskos, 1986, *op. cit.*, pp. 377-382; Ch. Moskos and F. R. Wood (Editors) *The Military: More than Just a Job?*, Washington D.C.: Pergamon-Brassey's, 1988. Ch. Moskos and J. Burk, "The Postmodern Military" in: J. Burk (ed.), 1994, *op. cit.*, pp. 141-162.

Variable	Institutional	Occupational
Legitimacy	Normative values	Marketplace economy
Role Commitments	Diffuse	Specific
Basis of Compensation	Rank and seniority	Skill level and manpower
Mode of Compensation	Much in non-cash form or deferred	Salary and bonus
Level of Compensation	Decompressed; low recruit pay	Compressed; high recruit pay
Residence	Adjacency of work and residence locales	Separation of work and residence locales
Societal Regard	Esteem based on notion of service	Prestige based on level of compensation
Performance Evaluation	Holistic and qualitative	Segmented and quantitative
Legal System	Military justice	Civilian jurisprudence
Reference Groups	"vertical"-within the organization	"horizontal"-external to organization

Table 3: Military Organizations: Institutional versus Occupational. Source: adapted from Ch. Moskos, "Institutional/Occupational trends in Armed Forces: An Update", *Armed Forces and Society*, vol. 12, no. 3 Spring 1986, p. 378 and Ch. Moskos, "Toward a Postmodern Military: The United States as a Paradigm", in: Ch. Moskos, J. Williams and D. Segal (eds), *The Postmodern Military, armed Forces after the Cold War*, Oxford: Oxford University Press, 2000, p. 15.

As a final, but important remark, on the post-modern military organization, it is necessary to stress the difference between the concept of an all-volunteer force and the idea of a post-modern All-Volunteer Force. An all-volunteer force is just a way of manning a military organization. It basically expresses a recruitment policy. There are many examples of this recruitment system all over the world. In Africa, Asia, etc., there are many (regular or irregular, state controlled or mercenary) military organizations who recruit their soldiers on a voluntary basis. In this case, soldiers are just paid for their military services. The post-modern All-Volunteer Force, however, is a specific type of military organization, which is found in Western post-industrial societies. In what follows, whenever the all-volunteer force concept is mentioned, it is meant the post-modern variant of this idea. Consequently, the exercise is to found out whether the Russian State can reform towards a post-modern All-Volunteer Force. Differently put, the assumption is that the Russian armed forces can not become a post-modern All-Volunteer Force, which does not necessarily mean that it can not adopt an all-volunteer force recruitment policy.

The Soviet type mass army
The reliance on some form of conscription is one of the strongest military traditions in Russia. This tradition goes back to the very beginning of the Russian Imperialist period. Conscription definitely predates the French Revolution's *"levée en masse"*, which is often seen as the first example of the mass army. Russia has forced young men into the Imperial army as early as the eighteenth century, when men were recruited as a result of the Petrine reforms.[36] Although the conscription system itself has changed considerably in Russia and the Soviet Union, specific Russian-Soviet traits of the 300-year conscription system can still be identified. This is illustrated by an evocative picture of a conscript soldiers' life in the early 19th century.

"Economic instability and the struggle to survive in the most basic physical sense were constant features of military life...The character and the abilities of individual officers had a decisive effect on the social and economic conditions of the lower ranks. The state either chose or was forced, because of inadequate economic, and administrative resources, to rely extensively on ad hoc measures taken by individual officers and to tolerate flagrant violations of the law- all of which eroded bureaucratic rationality and professional effi-

---

[36] About the Russian imperial tradition see for instance E. Wirtschafter, *From Serf to Russian Soldier*, Princeton: Princeton University Press, 1990, pp. 3-25; John L. H. Keep, *Soldiers of the Tsar: Army and Society in Russia, 1482-1874*, New York: Oxford University Press, 1985; J. Bushnell, "Peasants in Uniform: the Tsarist Army as a Peasant Society", *Journal of Social History*, vol. 13, no. 4, Summer 1980, pp. 753-780; D. Beyrau, *Militär und Gesellschaft im Vorrevolutionären Russland*, Cologne: Bohlau Verlag, 1984; J. Shelton Curtiss, *The Russian Army under Nicholas I, 1825-1855*, Durham: Duke University Press, 1965; A. Wildman, *The End of the Russian Imperial Army*, Princeton: Princeton University Press, 1980. L. Beskrovnyi, *Russkaia armiia I flot v XVIII veke*, Moskva, 1958; L. Beskrovnyi, *Russkaia armiia I flot v XIX veke*, Moskva, 1973; P. Zaionchkovskii, *Voennye reformy 1860-1870 goduv v Rossii*, Moskva, 1952.

ciency...The army was then left with the unenviable task of trying to transform an obligation that...society regarded as an unmitigated disaster into a glorious and heroic deed."[37]

Today's Russian army shares many similarities with its Tsarist and Soviet past. The Soviet army relied heavily on recruiting a large number of soldiers as the Soviets especially emphasized "size" in their concept of a mass army[38]. "More is better" was their motto. The Soviet Union had a standing army of about 4.5 to 5 million soldiers and a reserve force which stood at an estimated number of about 50 million men and women. Soviet strategists believed the USSR was prepared for waging total war and a mass attack which would be decisive in future conflicts. These numbers also prepared the USSR for a protracted conflict. Mobilisation and recruitment were considered the key aspects of Soviet manpower policy and it was practiced to the point of obsession[39]. Reliance on the concept of mobilisation capacity, and the Soviet interpretation of combat readiness, originated in the traumatic experience of the Second World War, as the "Barbarossa Syndrome". Historically, invasion by foreign powers had been a reality, but it had become a nightmare in the minds of Soviet military planners. This paranoid fear of external invasion together with the practice of total warfare, led to the conviction that society as a whole, and not just the armed forces, had to prepare for war. Besides this purely military understanding of the armed forces, the Soviet military organization fulfilled a considerable economic function as well. The military was used as a "flexible labor force" for different societal needs, such as agricultural and construction projects. The Soviet military-industrial complex, which represented the majority of Soviet industrial capacity, supported the armed forces. Moreover, the Soviet military were seen as an important educational agent in Soviet society. It was regarded as the school of the nation in which

---

[37] Wirtschafter, 1990, *op. cit.*, pp. 149-150.
[38] Lenin's comment "quantity is quality" may have been inspired by military issues.
[39] See for instance E. Jones, *Red Army and Society, a Sociology of the Soviet Military*, Boston : Allen and Unwin, 1985, *op. cit.*, p. 38-41 and Ch. Donnelly, *Red Banner, the Soviet Military System in Peace and War*, Coulsdon: Jane's information group, 1988, pp. 153-161. In a paper presented by Dr. Charles Dick, Director of the Conflict Studies Research Centre at Sandhurst, the author emphasized the importance of Russian invasion history in order to understand Russian military policy in the 1990s (presentation of Dr Ch. Dick on Friday 2 June 2000 at the seminar "Rebuilding Cooperation", UK-Russian Security Support Seminar, organized by Air Vice-Marshal Professor T. Mason, Birmingham University, 1-4 June 2000.)

multi-cultural attitudes could be installed and basic education could be provided. Ellen Jones, for instance, emphasized the socializing role of the Soviet army, which was in essence aimed at producing the notorious "Soviet Man". In short, the army fulfilled an all-embracing political role in the Soviet polity and society.

All these military, economic, educational and political arguments resulted in an even higher incentive to call up as many as possible of the young men in the Soviet Union. Ellen Jones estimates that between 65-70% of the 18-year old pool were drafted in the 1970's, and up to 75-80% in the beginning of the 1980's[40]. Once they were enlisted, Army and Air Force conscripts served for two years, and three years when they were assigned to the Navy. Prior to the 1967 conscription law the service terms were even longer and the generals were only open for a reduction of training-time when this loss was compensated for by the revival of a program of initial or basic military schools, the so-called *nachalnaia voyennaia podgotovka*, or NVP. The intention was to give students of secondary schools "an introduction to military skills at an early age in order to instill enough military-technological knowledge to facilitate the absorption of a military specialty once the conscript was drafted"[41]. The NVP also increased the mobilisation readiness of Soviet society.

Christopher Donnelly has observed that the Soviet conscription practices had an important impact on the technological level of weaponry. He noted that there were strong pressures on the Soviet weapons procurement system to produce equipment which was simple to operate, highly robust, and on which it was relatively simple to do battlefield maintenance and repair[42]. Soviet manpower philosophy thus influenced the technological innovation (or the lack of it) in the Soviet Union. As a result of all these considerations, the Soviet Union lived under a very high MPR and CR. Jones estimated that in

---

[40] H. Goldhamer estimated that in 1967, the moment when a new Law of Universal Military Service replaced the 1939 Law, about 50% of the 18-year cohort was conscripted. H. Goldhamer, *The Soviet Soldier, Soviet Military Management at the Troop Level*, New York: Crane, Russak & Company, 1975, p. 7. The way deferments based on health, education and family situation were interpreted as well as demographic considerations influenced how "universally" conscription laws were implemented in the Soviet Union. The estimates of Jones and Goldhamer demonstrate that it changed considerably over time.

[41] Jones, 1985, *op. cit.*, p. 69.

[42] Donnelly, 1988, *op. cit.*, p. 180.

total the Soviet armed forces professional-conscript ratio was 30:70. This rate corresponds with the figures of The Military Balance that noted that all branches in the Soviet forces used between 70% and 75% conscripts to fill the ranks[43]. Based on Haltiner's typology, a CR of 70% means that the Soviet army can be labeled as a "hard-core mass army", like countries such as Turkey, Greece, Finland and Switzerland[44].

Finally, the Soviet armed forces were intended to be a homogeneous organization. This was emphasized by the fact that the Soviet Union strove to develop one specific type of man who had well defined characteristics that were embedded in an ideological framework. The nature of Soviet ideology thus only strengthened the phenomenon of homogenization. However, social, educational and ethnic realities proved to be more difficult to cope with as the evolution from 1988 onwards demonstrated.

Two specific Soviet characteristics installed control in the conscript army. First, the Soviet Union did not have a non-commissioned officer corps such as Western armies did. Small Unit command was given to the corps of *serzhanty*, which actually were fellow conscripts who had received additional specialized training of only six months[45]. At the beginning of the 1970s a corps of so-called *praporshchiki* and *michmany* (warrant officers in the Army and Navy) were installed to cope with small unit command. However, this experiment to professionalize small unit command may not be seen as an overall success and this will be explained in the third part of this study. Secondly, besides the company commander, every company had a political officer (*zampolit*) who was formally responsible for the discipline and welfare of the soldiers. This difficult situation of dual command greatly lacked legitimacy at the troop level and was one of the reasons that an informal system of control came into existence. This system was the notorious *dedovshchina* system that Jones described as follows:

---

[43] Jones made room for some nuance on this issue when she observed that technology and the rapid expansion in both general and technical education of the Soviet youth influenced enlistment rates in the different forces. (Jones, 1985, *op. cit.*, pp. 70-73.)
[44] Haltiner, 1988, *op. cit.*, p. 18.
[45] Donnelly, 1988, *op. cit.*, pp.180-182. A. Lieven saw the continuation of this tradition at first hand in the first Chechen war.

> Control is also maintained through an informal and [officially] unauthorized seniority or 'caste' system among conscripts. Because soldiers are drafted at six-month intervals, a typical ground force unit will have four classes of conscripts: new soldiers [freshly arrived conscripts], soldiers with six or twelve months' previous service, those with twelve to eighteen months' service, and senior conscripts with less than six months' service remaining before demobilisation. While informal customs regarding responsibilities and privileges of each 'class' vary from unit to unit, the senior soldiers enjoy a far higher status than their newly arrived counterparts, who must endure a six-month period of hazing by conscripts with longer time in service. The system is widely accepted by both conscripts and the career force. Conscripts accept the hazing they receive in the first six months in return for the privileges they receive upon achieving 'senior' status. The career force accepts the system because it simplifies the problems of maintaining control of large groups of post-adolescent males.[46]

This system of informal control corresponds with the idea of the closed organization system. This system was shrouded in secrecy and mythology, just as the Soviet military actually was within Soviet society.

Samuel Huntington has noted that in traditional military thought, the state is considered to the most important political institution. In the Soviet context, the officer corps was encouraged to develop statist attitudes. This meant that the state always came first, even before personal liberty, personal freedom, individuality and human rights. In the Russian language it was said that officers were "*derzhavniki*" or (extreme) state servants. The idea of *derzhava* was also related with the idea of *gosudarstvo* which means "state" with the attributes of greatness and/or superiority as well as firmness towards the people. Such an understanding of the idea of *derzhava* had the implication that the officer corps was in principle not against values such as personal liberty, personal freedom, individuality and human rights as long as they were compatible with the idea of the state. Clearly, such an attitude goes together with a higher tolerance of losses in combat and casualties even in peace

---

[46] Jones, 1985, *op. cit.*, p. 130.

time. This attitude was reflected in the high casualty and death rates seen during the different wars that the Soviet Union fought[47].

In conclusion, the formation of the Soviet armed forces is based on developing a mass army which has specific Soviet features. The Soviet type mass army was a military force in which direct rule of the western type was replaced by totalitarian rule that was embedded in a particular ideological context. The Soviet-type mass army must be understood in the particular political context of the Soviet Union and its traumatic combat experiences. In the 1970-1980's, the Soviet military was still experiencing the consequences of supporting a mass army, while in the West the first contours of decline in Western military organizations were being observed in the scientific literature. Thus it is due to its extreme appearance and its persistence, that the Soviet mass army was considered to be different than armies in the West. The assertion that "the Soviet Union had no army, but was an army" illustrates the Soviet militarization rate.

4. An analysis of a manpower crisis: towards an hybrid army type

The main characteristics of the present Russian military manpower policy and its relationship with the ideal types of the mass and post-modern military organization will now be assessed[48]. Parallel with the presentation on the case of the Belgian, French and Dutch experience, the structural variables of "size", "mobilisation level" and "homogeneity" of the Russian armed forces will be reviewed. This point of comparison will provide a summary of what the Russian crisis in manpower exactly meant and it will indicate what the main causes of the crisis were.

---

[47] See for instance: A. Sella, *The Value of Human Life in Soviet Warfare*, London: Routledge, 1992. This observation completely contradicts the body bag hypothesis in the West.

[48] Data are again retrieved from The Military Balance (edition 1986/87-1997/98). Russian sources generally affirm the IISS data. See for instance: A. Arbatov, "Military Reform in Russia, Dilemmas, Obstacles, and Prospects", *International Security*, vol. 22, no. 4, Spring 1998, pp. 83-134; and G. Ziuganov, *Voennaia reforma: otsenka ugroz natsional'noi bezopasnosti Rossii*, Moskva: Obozrevatel', 1997, pp. 79-80.

Size

The personnel levels of the Soviet-Russian armed forces have been reduced over time as anywhere else in the world[49]. The Soviet armed forces shrank by 33% during the last four years of its existence (1988-1992). In the post-Soviet Russian Federation, the armed forces' have declined by 65%. In absolute figures this meant that the Soviet armed forces stood at 5,096,000 soldiers in 1988, 3,400,000 in 1992 and 1,159,000 in 1998. This is illustrated in Graph 6 where the decline is represented during the period from 1970 to 1998. This thirty year overview gives the reader a better understanding of the scope and velocity with which the decline of the armed forces occurred in Russia. Moreover, it can also be read as an extension and prolongation of Ellen Jones' overview of the trends between 1970 and 1985.

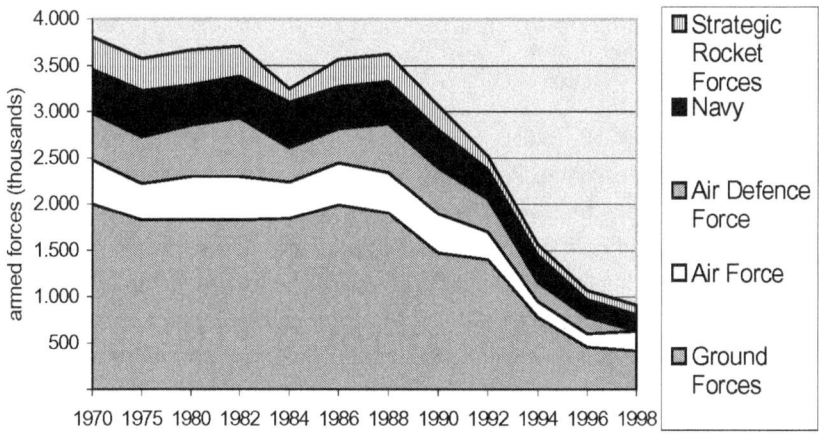

Graph 1: Estimates of Active Duty Armed Forces Personnel (Thousands)

---

[49] Manpower reduction went along with a severe reduction of the military arsenal. Andrew Duncan wrote a good overview of this issue on the basis of the latest CFE data: see A. Duncan, "Russian Forces in decline-Part I", *Jane's Intelligence Review*, September 1996, pp. 404-408; A. Duncan, "Russian Forces in Decline-Part II", *Jane's Intelligence Review*, October 1996, pp. 442-447; St. Goldman did the same exercise for the Library of Congress. See: St. D. Goldman, *Russian Conventional Armed Forces: On the Verge of Collapse*, Washington: Congressional Research Service-The Library of Congress, 4 September 1997, pp. 4-9.

The scale and the velocity of decline were therefore so great as to render it incomparable with the gradual, evolutionary process observed in France, Belgium and The Netherlands. The use of the words "devolution" or "collapse" used by Meyer or Goldman are therefore appropriate.[50]

	Soviet Union (1988-1992)	Russian Federation (1992-1998)
Army	-26%	-70%
Navy	-30%	-43%
Air Force	-32%	-56%
Air Defense Force	-12%	-62%
Nuclear Rocket Forces	-51%	-30%

Table 4: Manpower Development in the Armed Forces in the Soviet and Russian Experience (1988-1998)

The decline of personnel in the forces was a dramatic phenomenon in the Russian Federation between 1992 and 1998. The army especially underwent a "decline beyond control", while the Nuclear Rocket Force was - in the context of the wider implosion - the least affected. The impression that the figures for the 1988-1992 period give us, is that during this period there is greater control of the policy intentions by the parties involved than there was during the 1992-1998 period in which there appears to have been not only a lack of control over military reform policy but the policy itself was unclear. Indeed, Gorbachev's nuclear disarmament initiatives are shown in Table 5 in which the Nuclear Rocket Force was reduced by 51%, while the other forces underwent a steadier decline. The fact that reduction of the armed forces in the Russian period was apparently out of control, is therefore an important characteristic of a military crisis. It appears that decision-makers in the Russian government were powerless to these influence events.

---

[50] S. Meyer, *The Devolution of Russian Military Power*, Defense and Arms Control Studies Working Paper, Cambridge: MIT, November 1995; Goldman, 1997, *op. cit.*

If one was to compare the relative importance of each separate force with the total armed forces the following findings can be noted:

	1988	1991	1998
Army	52,4%	55,5%	46,1%
Navy	12,6%	12,6%	19,7%
Air Force	12,2%	11,9%	23%
Air Defense Force	14,3%	14,1%	Merged with Air Force
Strategic Rocket Force	8,2%	5,7%	10,9%

Table 5: Relative Decline of the Forces in the Soviet and Russian Manpower Development (1988-1998)

What is remarkable is that the relative importance of the forces in the Soviet-Russian military organization was more or less stable or in other words, the basic nature of the forces stayed the same. There was - again in the context of the personnel implosion - no real sign of a qualitative change. Table 5 shows that there is an increase in the importance of the Air Force in 1998 compared with 1988, which is due to the merging of the Air Force with the Air Defense Force in 1998. This merger was an important decision from a structural point of view. Apparently, the Navy was the only force that survived the turbulent times of the 1990's relatively well, however this observation must interpreted with caution. Indeed, when the CR of the forces is examined a different aspect of this evolution becomes clear.

Graph 2: Conscription Rate over the Forces in the Soviet Union and Russia (1988-1998)

The conscription rate (CR) of the forces illuminated an atypical characteristic. In the second half of the 1990's the CR of the Navy was the highest of all the forces, followed by the CR of the Strategic Rocket Forces while the CR of the Army was comparable to that of the Air Force. These data contradicted the idea of using conscripts in the least technically sophisticated forces, while- inversely- there were more conscripts in the more technical forces. When in the former paragraph the relative importance of the Navy in the armed forces was noted, it must be said that this force was filled with an "undereducated workforce" to a large extent. This can be perceived as a remnant of the Soviet tradition, but certainly it did not conform with the idea of professionalizing the armed forces. It is also an atypical result when it is compared with the evolution of events in the West. Another point that may be made about this table is that these data reflect the chaotic, unstable and incoherent developments in the Soviet-Russian military organization. It was as if the developments that took place in the armed forces were beyond the control of the decision-makers. This idea of an "out of control" evolution is further reflected upon and will be discussed in the following paragraph.

Militarization and Mobilisation

While overall manpower levels collapsed between 1988 and 1998, the Russian Military Participation Rate (MPR) was still remarkably high. Russia's MPR (MPR 1998 = 2.4) decreased by 1.5 points during the last decade. But this was still more than twice as high as France (MPR 1998= 1.1), The Netherlands (MPR 1998= 0.8), and Belgium (MPR1998= 1.1). If the MPR was one variable that expressed Russia's mobilisation capacity, it also showed that this key aspect of the mass army was still present in the Russian army. Moreover, if the MPR is considered to be a reflection of the relative militarization of a society, then Russia, although significantly demilitarizing during the 1990's, was still more militarized than countries with a post-modern military organization[51].

---

[51] J. Schmidt-Skipiol came to the same conclusion as he published the following data concerning the number of military personnel per thousand citizens in 1998: USA: 5,2; France 6,1; Great Britain: 3,6; Germany: 4,1; and Russia: 8,2 (even 13,5 if all military personnel in other ministries besides the MoD is counted). See: J. Schmidt-Skipiol, "Die Militärreform in Rußland Teil II: Aktueller Stand und Zukunft", *Berichte des Bundesinstituts für Ostwissenschaftliche und Internationale Studien*, no 54, 1998, Köln: Bundesinstituts für Ostwissenschaftliche und Internationale Studien, 1998, p. 22.

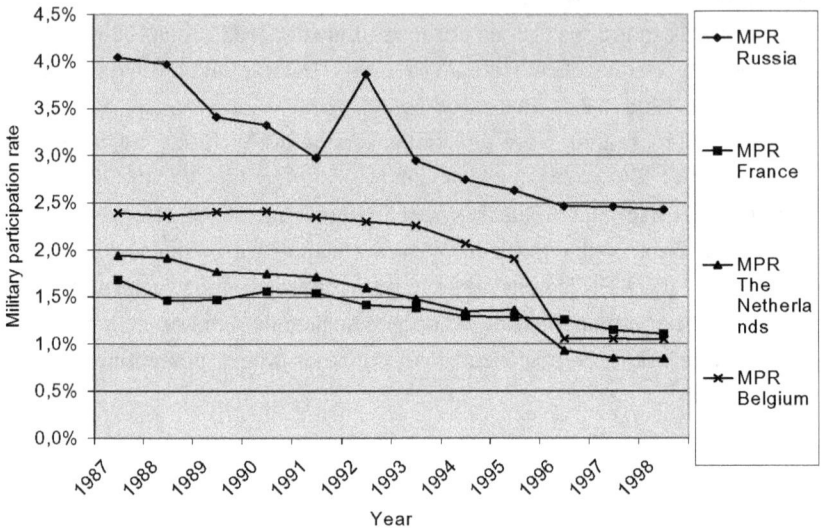

Graph 3: Military Participation Rate Russia-France-the Netherlands-Belgium (1988-1998)

Another variable that reveals what type of military organization a nation has is the Conscription Rate. Based on the general CR in 1998, the Russian armed forces was not a typical mass army. But, although the CR definitely fell below 50% after 1994, the decline was incoherent. It therefore probably had more to do with societal and organizational chaos rather than a deliberate choice. Hence, the collapse of the CR in 1994 (without special policy changes in that year) subsequently had more to do with the inability of the Russian state to implement conscription effectively rather than with implementation of a policy on this issue. Moreover, the Russian CR slightly increased after 1996 while the CR in Belgium, France and The Netherlands constantly declined. Instability and incoherence are the persistent characteristics of a crisis situation that can be noted here.

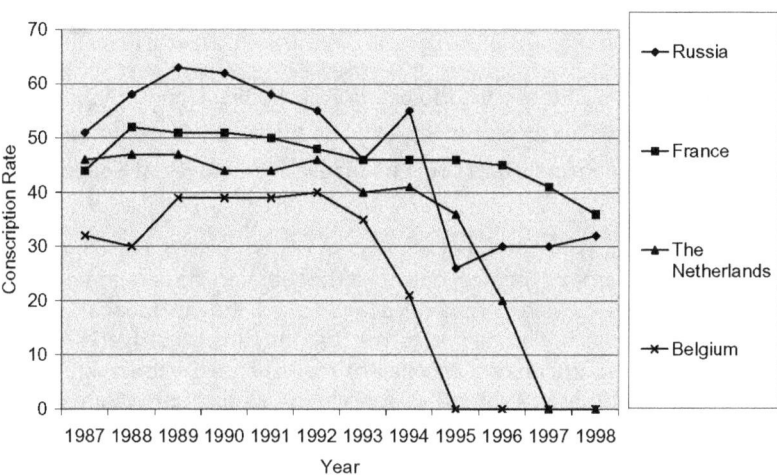

Graph 4: Conscription Rate Russia-France-the Netherlands-Belgium (1988-1998)

5. Reform failure synthesized

The crisis the Russian armed forces experienced had several important characteristics. They are synthesized below with reference to the structural variables that have already been presented.

Between 1988 and 1998, there was a chaotic evolution. This chaos resulted in a hybrid type of army that contained Soviet, "Western" and atypical characteristics. Some demobilisation (and demilitarization) of Russian society undoubtedly took place, but comparatively speaking, the level of mobilisation remained higher in Russia than in France, Belgium and The Netherlands.

From 1994 onwards the CR collapsed, but this did not demonstrate a constant downward trend. The use of conscripts in the forces, expressed in the Conscription Rate in the forces, show two things. Firstly, compared with the West, the Russian armed forces' crisis was and is a crisis of the army. The army suffered the most and seemed to be the least resistant to instability. This is consistent with the Western evolution. Secondly, the Navy resisted the turbulent times the best: but their intensive use of conscripts reflects a Soviet tradition. The use of conscripts was not decisively influenced by the technological demands of respective forces. Ideological, cultural, political, and economic factors all made conscript labor a tradition that is embedded in the Russian armed forces.

The evolution of the armed forces in Russia developed in tandem with another domain of Russia's post Soviet period. Richard Erickson suggested that Russia's economic system could be labelled as "Industrial Feudalism" [52]. He observed that:

> The transformations to date clearly seem to have eliminated the Soviet 'command economy' as the operational system, but it also seems to me that they have not [yet?] succeeded in creating a coherent market-based economic system. What is evolving appears to be neither a modern market economy, of whatever variant, nor a continuation of its modern challenger, the bureaucratically managed Soviet-type economy. Indeed, in many of its structural and operational characteristics it seems to be recreating the economic system of an earlier, pre-industrial, era-medieval feudalism.[53]

In other words, Erickson observed the emergence of a hybrid economic system in which achievements of the industrial era were combined with structures and operations of the past. Given the structural analysis of military manpower policy, Erickson's argument is interesting because it shows that

---

[52] See R. Erickson, "The Post-Soviet Russian Economic System: An Industrial Feudalism?" at http://www.columbia.edu/-ree3/ January 1999 and G. Breslauer, J. Brada, C. Gaddy, R. Erickson, C. Saivetz, and V. Winston, "Russia at the End of Yeltsin's Presidency", *Post-Soviet Affairs*, vol. 16, no. 1, 2000, pp. 1-32. (especially, p. 18-31). Also V. Shlapentokh used the "anarchic quasi-feudalism" idea in his thinking. (See: V. Shlapentokh, "Russia as a medieval State", *Washington Quarterly*, vol. 19, no. 1, 1996, pp. 395-412, and V. Shlapentokh, "Early Feudalism-The Best Parallel for Contemporary Russia", *Europe-Asia Studies*, vol. 48, no. 3, May 1996, pp. 393-411). A. Lieven opted for the "cacique" system analogy in his writing to characterize the hybrid political system in Russia. (See A. Lieven, *Chechnya, Tombstone of Russian Power*, New Haven: Yale University Press, 1998, pp.151-152). Many others commented the hybrid system as for instance M. McFaul who called Russia quite optimistically an "unconsolidated democracy or illiberal democracy" (See M. McFaul, "Russian Democracy: Still Not a Lost Case", *The Washington Quarterly*, vol. 23, no. 1, Winter 2000, p. 163.)

[53] Erickson, 1999, *op. cit.*

the military system co-evolved in parallel with the structure of the economy and society in general. At the same time it gives us grounds to adopt the open-organization paradigm in order to study the Russian military organization. Finally, it can be argued that Russian military organizational evolution is not "exceptional".

Not only is the evolution of the Russian military not exceptional, but it may be argued that: the deterministic evolution from a command economy towards a market economic system and the evolution from a mass army towards a post-modern All-Volunteer Force is a complex phenomenon and therefore a difficult objective to achieve. Cultural and political decision-making in Russia have had a major impact on society; but organizational change is apparently not determined to evolve along Western lines, despite all hope and efforts embodied in the "Washington Consensus" and European euphoria concerning Russia's political, economic, and military development in the 1990's. [54]

6. An ignored socio-cultural argument

In a certain way, it is understandable that studying the socio-cultural environment of an organization in order to evaluate the Russian military forces is a perspective that has often been neglected[55]. By using the socio-cultural argument, Russia is confronted with its contemporary self, its history and society. At the base of the socio-cultural variable lies a daring question: is the idea of the All-Volunteer Force suitable for Russian society at present? Are the "normative" socio-cultural conditions present in Russia for this transformation to an All-Volunteer Force to take place?

These conditions are situated in the mentality of the individual, in Russian society in general, and in the Russian military organization itself. The fact that the whole of society itself is intimately related to the idea of having professional armed forces is not only an academic issue. It also locates the re-

---

[54] The "Washington consensus" was the US administration's definition of reform in Russia, which contained the idea of installing "democracy" and a "free marked economy". Especially President Clinton, Vice President Al Gore, Strobe Talbott and Lawrence Summers were important authors of this policy.
[55] An exception is Lieven, 1998, *op. cit.*, especially pp. 186-219.

sponsibility for either success or failure of the project in Russian society as a whole and not solely with one actor, be it either the military or the state apparatus.

For instance, violence in the ranks, and the responsibility for it, is not only a problem of the military organization, but is also a crime committed by a "civilian" youth against one of his peers. Besides individual malpractice in the army, there is also a revealing parallel between the army's conditions and the conditions in prisons and even in orphanages in Russia.

The following questions are a result of this observation. Firstly, is it possible to speak about a particular Russian condition, perhaps steered by necessity and scarcity rather than by choice and abundance? If this is the case, is it not an absolute contradiction to introduce an ultra- modern idea into a "retarded" social environment? This unevenness, or this "cultural lag", lies at the core of this survey and it is not a new idea in Russian studies. Students of Russian history are familiar with this topic. Alex Simirenko noted "one of the striking features of Soviet society as it emerged from its world isolation during the post-Stalin era was its superior technological and industrial position coupled with predominantly nineteenth-century Russian and European culture."[56] Significantly, Orlando Figes concluded in his study of the Russian revolution that: "Russia's prospects as a democratic nation depend to a large extent on how far the Russians are able to confront their own recent history; and this must entail the recognition that, however much the people were oppressed by it, the Soviet system grew up on Russian soil."[57]

Conclusion

If we speak about the professional armed forces we have to be careful what we exactly mean. If we mean that it is a way of recruiting soldiers, without qualitative changes in the armed forces, with its closedness as the most important feature, *dedovshchina* will not disappear. The same malfunctions and

---

[56] A. Simirenko, *Soviet Sociology, Historical Antecedents and Current Appraisals*, Chicago: Quadrangle Books, 1966, p. 328.
[57] O. Figes, *A People's Tragedy, The Revolution 1891-1924*, London: PIMLICO 1996, p. 808.

abuses will be continue in the then new Russian professional armed forces. If we mean with the professional armed forces, the adaptation of the postmodern military organization type, the chance exist that *dedovshchina* will progressively disappear. But therefore the focus has to be put on the sociocultural aspects of the Russian armed forces and its environment rather then the purely economic conditions of the Russian armed forces. Based on our analysis of the reform endeavor during the 1990's in the Russian armed forces, I stay rather pessimistic about the conditions in which the paid and the unpaid soldier, the voluntary and the involuntary soldier have to serve in the Russian army.

Dr. Andreas Umland (Ed.)

SOVIET AND POST-SOVIET POLITICS AND SOCIETY

ISSN 1614-3515

This book series makes available, to the academic community and general public, affordable English-, German- and Russian-language scholarly studies of various *empirical* aspects of the recent history and current affairs of the former Soviet bloc. The series features narrowly focused research on a variety of phenomena in Central and Eastern Europe as well as Central Asia and the Caucasus. It highlights, in particular, so far understudied aspects of late Tsarist, Soviet, and post-Soviet political, social, economic and cultural history from 1905 until today. Topics covered within this focus are, among others, political extremism, the history of ideas, religious affairs, higher education, and human rights protection. In addition, the series covers selected aspects of post-Soviet transitions such as economic crisis, civil society formation, and constitutional reform.

SOVIET AND POST-SOVIET POLITICS AND SOCIETY

Edited by Dr. Andreas Umland

ISSN 1614-3515

1   *Андреас Умланд (ред.)*
    Воплощение Европейской конвенции по правам человека в России
    Философские, юридические и эмпирические исследования
    ISBN 3-89821-387-0

2   *Christian Wipperfürth*
    Russland – ein vertrauenswürdiger Partner?
    Grundlagen, Hintergründe und Praxis gegenwärtiger russischer Außenpolitik
    Mit einem Vorwort von Heinz Timmermann
    ISBN 3-89821-401-X

3   *Manja Hussner*
    Die Übernahme internationalen Rechts in die russische und deutsche Rechtsordnung
    Eine vergleichende Analyse zur Völkerrechtsfreundlichkeit der Verfassungen der Russländischen Föderation
    und der Bundesrepublik Deutschland
    Mit einem Vorwort von Rainer Arnold
    ISBN 3-89821-438-9

4   *Matthew Tejada*
    Bulgaria's Democratic Consolidation and the Kozloduy Nuclear Power Plant (KNPP)
    The Unattainability of Closure
    With a foreword by Richard J. Crampton
    ISBN 3-89821-439-7

5   *Марк Григорьевич Меерович*
    Квадратные метры, определяющие сознание
    Государственная жилищная политика в СССР. 1921 – 1941 гг.
    ISBN 3-89821-474-5

6   *Andrei P. Tsygankov, Pavel A. Tsygankov (Eds.)*
    New Directions in Russian International Studies
    ISBN 3-89821-422-2

7   *Марк Григорьевич Меерович*
    Как власть народ к труду приучала
    Жилище в СССР – средство управления людьми. 1917 – 1941 гг.
    С предисловием Елены Осокиной
    ISBN 3-89821-495-8

8   *David J. Galbreath*
    Nation-Building and Minority Politics in Post-Socialist States
    Interests, Influence and Identities in Estonia and Latvia
    With a foreword by David J. Smith
    ISBN 3-89821-467-2

9 Алексей Юрьевич Безугольный
   Народы Кавказа в Вооруженных силах СССР в годы Великой Отечественной войны 1941-1945 гг.
   С предисловием Николая Бугая
   ISBN 3-89821-475-3

10 Вячеслав Лихачев и Владимир Прибыловский (ред.)
   Русское Национальное Единство, 1990-2000. В 2-х томах
   ISBN 3-89821-523-7

11 Николай Бугай (ред.)
   Народы стран Балтии в условиях сталинизма (1940-е – 1950-е годы)
   Документированная история
   ISBN 3-89821-525-3

12 Ingmar Bredies (Hrsg.)
   Zur Anatomie der Orange Revolution in der Ukraine
   Wechsel des Elitenregimes oder Triumph des Parlamentarismus?
   ISBN 3-89821-524-5

13 Anastasia V. Mitrofanova
   The Politicization of Russian Orthodoxy
   Actors and Ideas
   With a foreword by William C. Gay
   ISBN 3-89821-481-8

14 Nathan D. Larson
   Alexander Solzhenitsyn and the Russo-Jewish Question
   ISBN 3-89821-483-4

15 Guido Houben
   Kulturpolitik und Ethnizität
   Staatliche Kunstförderung im Russland der neunziger Jahre
   Mit einem Vorwort von Gert Weisskirchen
   ISBN 3-89821-542-3

16 Leonid Luks
   Der russische „Sonderweg"?
   Aufsätze zur neuesten Geschichte Russlands im europäischen Kontext
   ISBN 3-89821-496-6

17 Евгений Мороз
   История «Мёртвой воды» – от страшной сказки к большой политике
   Политическое неоязычество в постсоветской России
   ISBN 3-89821-551-2

18 Александр Верховский и Галина Кожевникова (ред.)
   Этническая и религиозная интолерантность в российских СМИ
   Результаты мониторинга 2001-2004 гг.
   ISBN 3-89821-569-5

19 Christian Ganzer
   Sowjetisches Erbe und ukrainische Nation
   Das Museum der Geschichte des Zaporoger Kosakentums auf der Insel Chortycja
   Mit einem Vorwort von Frank Golczewski
   ISBN 3-89821-504-0

20   Эльза-Баир Гучинова
      Помнить нельзя забыть
      Антропология депортационной травмы калмыков
      С предисловием Кэролайн Хамфри
      ISBN 3-89821-506-7

21   Юлия Лидерман
      Мотивы «проверки» и «испытания» в постсоветской культуре
      Советское прошлое в российском кинематографе 1990-х годов
      С предисловием Евгения Марголита
      ISBN 3-89821-511-3

22   *Tanya Lokshina, Ray Thomas, Mary Mayer (Eds.)*
      The Imposition of a Fake Political Settlement in the Northern Caucasus
      The 2003 Chechen Presidential Election
      ISBN 3-89821-436-2

23   *Timothy McCajor Hall, Rosie Read (Eds.)*
      Changes in the Heart of Europe
      Recent Ethnographies of Czechs, Slovaks, Roma, and Sorbs
      With an afterword by Zdeněk Salzmann
      ISBN 3-89821-606-3

24   *Christian Autengruber*
      Die politischen Parteien in Bulgarien und Rumänien
      Eine vergleichende Analyse seit Beginn der 90er Jahre
      Mit einem Vorwort von Dorothée de Nève
      ISBN 3-89821-476-1

25   *Annette Freyberg-Inan with Radu Cristescu*
      The Ghosts in Our Classrooms, or: John Dewey Meets Ceauşescu
      The Promise and the Failures of Civic Education in Romania
      ISBN 3-89821-416-8

26   *John B. Dunlop*
      The 2002 Dubrovka and 2004 Beslan Hostage Crises
      A Critique of Russian Counter-Terrorism
      With a foreword by Donald N. Jensen
      ISBN 3-89821-608-X

27   *Peter Koller*
      Das touristische Potenzial von Kamj''anec'–Podil'sk'yj
      Eine fremdenverkehrsgeographische Untersuchung der Zukunftsperspektiven und Maßnahmenplanung zur Destinationsentwicklung des „ukrainischen Rothenburg"
      Mit einem Vorwort von Kristiane Klemm
      ISBN 3-89821-640-3

28   *Françoise Daucé, Elisabeth Sieca-Kozlowski, (Eds.)*
      ***Dedovshchina* in the Post-Soviet Military**
      Hazing of Russian Army Conscripts in a Comparative Perspective
      With a foreword by Dale Herspring
      ISBN 3-89821-616-0

29 *Florian Strasser*
Zivilgesellschaftliche Einflüsse auf die Orange Revolution 2004
Die gewaltlose Massenbewegung und die ukrainische Wahlkrise 2004
Mit einem Vorwort von Egbert Jahn
ISBN 3-89821-648-9

FORTHCOMING (MANUSCRIPT WORKING TITLES)

Nicola Melloni
The Russian 1998 Financial Crisis and Its Aftermath
An Etherodox Perspective
ISBN 3-89821-407-9

Rebbecca Katz
The Republic of Georgia
Post-Soviet Media Representations of Politics and Corruption
ISBN 3-89821-413-3

Laura Victoir
The Russian Land Estate Today
ISBN 3-89821-426-5

Stephanie Solowyda
Biography of Semen Frank
ISBN 3-89821-457-5

Margaret Dikovitskaya
Arguing with the Photographs
Russian Imperial Colonial Attitudes in Visual Culture
ISBN 3-89821-462-1

Stefan Ihrig
Welche Nation in welcher Geschichte?
Eigen- und Fremdbilder der nationalen Diskurse in der Historiographie und den Geschichtsbüchern in der Republik Moldova, 1991-2003
ISBN 3-89821-466-4

Sergei M. Plekhanov
Russian Nationalism in the Age of Globalization
ISBN 3-89821-484-2

Михаил Лукянов
Российский консерватизм и реформа, 1905-1917
ISBN 3-89821-503-2

Robert Pyrah
Cultural Memory and Identity
Literature, Criticism and the Theatre in Lviv - Lwow - Lemberg, 1918-1939 and in post-Soviet Ukraine
ISBN 3-89821-505-9

Dmitrij Chmelnizki
Die Architektur Stalins
Ideologie und Stil 1929-1960
ISBN 3-89821-515-6

Andrei Rogatchevski
The National-Bolshevik Party
ISBN 3-89821-532-6

Zenon Victor Wasyliw
Soviet Culture in the Ukrainian Village
The Transformation of Everyday Life and Values, 1921-1928
ISBN 3-89821-536-9

Nele Sass
Das gegenkulturelle Milieu im postsowjetischen Russland
ISBN 3-89821-543-1

Josette Baer
Preparing Modernity in Central Europe
Political Thought and the Independent Nation State
ISBN 3-89821-546-6

Ivan Katchanovski
Cleft Countries
Regional Political Divisions and Cultures in Post-Soviet Ukraine and Moldova
ISBN 3-89821-558-X

Julie Elkner
Maternalism versus Militarism
The Russian Soldiers' Mothers Committee
ISBN 3-89821-575-X

Maryna Romanets
Displaced Subjects, Anamorphosic Texts, Reconfigured Visions
Improvised Traditions in Contemporary Ukrainian and Irish Literature
ISBN 3-89821-576-8

Alexandra Kamarowsky
Russia's Post-crisis Growth
ISBN 3-89821-580-6

Martin Friessnegg
Das Problem der Medienfreiheit in Russland seit dem Ende der Sowjetunion
ISBN 3-89821-588-1

Vladimir Kantor
Willkür oder Freiheit?
Beiträge zur russischen Geschichtsphilosophie
ISBN 3-89821-589-X

Florian Mühlfried
Postsowjetische Feiern
Das Georgische Bankett im Wandel
ISBN 3-89821-601-2

Series Subscription

Please enter my subscription to the series *Soviet and Post-Soviet Politics and Society*, ISSN 1614-3515, as follows:

❐ complete series   OR   ❐ English-language titles
                                        ❐ German-language titles
                                        ❐ Russian-language titles

starting with
❐ volume # 1
❐ volume # ___
   ❐ please also include the following volumes: #___, ___, ___, ___, ___, ___, ___
❐ the next volume being published
   ❐ please also include the following volumes: #___, ___, ___, ___, ___, ___, ___

❐ 1 copy per volume   OR   ❐ ___ copies per volume

Subscription within Germany:

You will receive every volume at 1st publication at the regular bookseller's price – incl. s & h and VAT.
Payment:
❐ Please bill me for every volume.
❐ Lastschriftverfahren: Ich/wir ermächtige(n) Sie hiermit widerruflich, den Rechnungsbetrag je Band von meinem/unserem folgendem Konto einzuziehen.

Kontoinhaber: _____ Kreditinstitut: _____
Kontonummer: _____ Bankleitzahl: _____

International Subscription:

Payment (incl. s & h and VAT) in advance for
❐ 10 volumes/copies (€ 319,80)   ❐ 20 volumes/copies (€ 599,80)
❐ 40 volumes/copies (€ 1.099,80)
Please send my books to:

NAME_____ DEPARTMENT_____
ADDRESS _____
POST/ZIP CODE_____ COUNTRY _____
TELEPHONE _____ EMAIL_____

date/signature_____

A hint for librarians in the former Soviet Union: Your academic library might be eligible to receive free-of-cost scholarly literature from Germany via the German Research Foundation. For Russian-language information on this program, see
     http://www.dfg.de/forschungsfoerderung/formulare/download/12_54.pdf.

Please fax to: **0511 / 262 2201 (+49 511 262 2201)**
or mail to: *ibidem*-Verlag, Julius-Leber-Weg 11, D-30457 Hannover, Germany
or send an e-mail: ibidem@ibidem-verlag.de

ibidem-Verlag
Melchiorstr. 15
D-70439 Stuttgart

info@ibidem-verlag.de

www.ibidem-verlag.de
www.edition-noema.de
www.autorenbetreuung.de

www.ingramcontent.com/pod-product-compliance
Lightning Source LLC
Chambersburg PA
CBHW051804230426
43672CB00012B/2631